A Brief History of the

Royal Navy
Its People, Places and Pets!

Michael W. Williams

First published by The London Press, UK 2006

ISBN: 978-1-905006-23-6

A C.I.P. reference is available from the British Library.

Printed and bound in Great Britain

Contents:

Dedication

To PJP

Acknowledgements

Many people have been most helpful in compiling this book; the staff at the following establishments in particular:- the Public Records Office, The Greenwich Museum and Library, The Imperial War Museum and Libraries, Portsmouth and Chatham Royal Historic Dockyard Museums and The Ganges Museum.

The family of PJP have been very supportive and very patient, their assistance was most helpful and is appreciated. There have been many readers who have advised and criticised the drafts along the way; their interest in this project has been really sustaining.

I am also grateful to the many authors whose works I have referred to. Their labours have inspired me to set my own thoughts into the printed word and whenever possible permission has been sought to use their material. Where this has not been possible full acknowledgement is given in the notes and bibliography and their contribution is hereby acknowledged.

Introduction

The inspiration for this book comes from the discovery of a 'Certificate of Service' and the accompanying medals. These were not for meritorious or gallant deeds but for good conduct in the service of the Royal Navy in a variety of theatres of war. The owner of these artefacts was the late Peter James Powell, who served in the Royal Navy, man and boy, for 29 years. He walked into *H.M.S. Ganges* on 10th September 1925 and finally went ashore, from *H.M.S. Excellent*, for the last time with the rank Chief Petty Officer (Gunnery Instructor) on 26th October 1949. His base was Portsmouth and his service was primarily in big ships, battleships and cruisers. This provided an ideal starting point for exploring the origins of the Royal Navy and its primary weapon, the battleship, in its various forms, the galley, square-rigger and dreadnought.

There are a great many books about the Royal Navy, as the short bibliography in this one hints at, but each of these books is rather specialist in nature, about ships, about people, about armament and so forth. This book aims to give the layman an overview — without offending those authors who have created substantial and scholarly works, more comprehensive and meticulous than this book intends to be.

A précis will necessarily lose a great many details but this should not be at the expense of accuracy, wherever possible reference sources are given so the reader can pursue points of interest at their leisure. There are some deliberate inaccuracies, for the sake of brevity. One such 'error' is in the use of the term 'Britain'. Clearly, when the story of the Royal Navy began some thousand years ago Britain was not Great, indeed 'England' was not itself a united land. However, for the sake of brevity and style the term Britain is used unless the context requires a clearer explanation as to which of the countries, England, Scotland, Ireland or Wales, is referred to.

There will be those readers who have an opinion about references to ships' names; in particular the use of the definite article *'the'* to precede a ship's name. The author has sought to maintain tradition; ships will either be H.M.S. *Malaya*' or 'the *Malaya*'. The rational for this is that a reference to the ship's name is a reference to the Captain and not the ship itself — unless prefixed with the definite article. Sailors should be *in*, not *on*, the ship in the same way people live *in* houses not *on* them. Lloyds Register (the insurance people) announced in 2004 that they would no longer refer to ships as "she", the author has therefore decided to discontinue that particular tradition in most instances.

Despite this nod towards gender equality, the Navy was for many centuries run by men and for clarity the male form 'he' is used to avoid complicated his/her references. This is not intended to ignore the contribution of women and a whole chapter provides some interesting details of their part in the making of the Royal Navy.

Geographical locations in this book are within Great Britain, and not infrequently Southern England, unless otherwise specified. Imperial units of measurement, feet, inches, miles, fathoms, cables, knots, and nautical miles will be used throughout. Dates are given without precise reference to the Julian or Gregorian Calendars, so dates earlier than 1752 are likely to be 11 days adrift of the modern Gregorian dating system.

Michael W. Williams

Chapter 1: Origins
The navy royal
~~~~~~~~~~~

Many sailors can't swim – if you're in the Royal Navy the idea is to keep your ship afloat and stay out of the water. This anecdote and a few more in this book may well be apocryphal. It is sometimes hard to discern fact from fiction and the Royal Navy certainly has its share of myths. This book is a landlubber's view of the Royal Navy's history and many details purporting to be facts may be no such thing. Drake is credited with defeating the Spanish Armada in 1588. In reality Lord Howard of Effingham commanded the English fleet but, like Nelson and Beatty, they were more effective self-publicists than their commanders in chief, Parker and Jellicoe respectively, and so they ensured their own immortality.

This short work pieces together some fascinating details about the Royal Navy from a wide variety of sources, some serious others more light-hearted but still educational, even so there will be many gaps and many points that may be disputed. This book is intended to give a brief overview of the Royal Navy's development, it will be wide ranging but without an excess of detail.

Portsmouth's City crest

There are three elements to the Navy; its sailors, its ships and its shore-bases. This book is primarily about the first two but Portsmouth, the home of the Navy for hundreds of years, will feature from time to time, not least because more than 370 warships have been built there since the 15th Century and it was already a busy dockyard in the reign of King John – who, in 1212, gathered at Portsmouth a fleet of no less than 500 ships for an expedition to France and so Pompey was already by that time regarded as England's principle naval port. As the First Sea Lord said during the 200-year celebrations of Trafalgar, if Britannia ruled the waves then Portsmouth was her throne.

Portsmouth has never been the greatest trading port; Bristol and the London Docks were much bigger. Its ships have never carried more sea-going passengers than the docks in Southampton or Liverpool and Portsmouth was never a seat of government unlike the nearby town of Winchester but its location has made it the centre of the Royal Navy's universe. This is reflected in the City's crest, a crescent moon and star and in its motto "Heavens Light Our Guide", signifying the importance of navigation by starlight for the many sailors to leave its shores.

Amongst the many sailors whose names and reputations have passed down in history we may discover the father of the navy. Inevitably, with the passage of time, it is the Kings and Queens of England whose contributions are best documented, King Alfred the Great and the wicked King John for example, but there are many commoners who contributed to the navy's development. Samuel Pepys used his diary to catalogue his efforts to bring order to the chaos of naval administration in the 17th century. Pepys, by the way, had a very poor opinion of Portsmouth, he thought it full of the most 'debauched, damming and swearing rogues...'. Given his own debauchery that was a rather unkind observation but Nelson agreed; he too thought it a 'horrid place'. Nevertheless it was an important naval base and has at least one sea battle after its name and several of her Majesty's ships were named Portsmouth. The Battle of Portsmouth was against the Dutch Navy in 1653. As this was an early conflict between the English and the Dutch they probably won that little local difficulty they had at that time a more advanced and experienced naval force than England.

The Battleship *Michael*, circa 1512

As for the ships of the Navy, the main ship in any sea battle is, or, to be more accurate, *was* the battleship. Battleships took many forms, galley, cog, carrack and so on, reaching its zenith as the steel-hulled, oil-fuelled, turbine-driven, all-big-gun dreadnought of the early 20th century.

A naval fighting force is an exceedingly expensive thing, even for a wealthy nation. Unlike a land-based army, which could be brought together at times of conflict, a battle fleet has to be built and maintained in readiness for war. Given the expense, was a navy force really needed? The role of such a force remains the same in that a large and powerful navy (as well army and air-force) serve a number of purposes. It is a deterrent. Even the most foolhardy and belligerent of rulers will be very cautious about attacking another nation with greater military forces. Military strength is therefore a deterrent against full-frontal assault – but of course it is no deterrent against terrorist style warfare.

If war is declared the relative strength of the opposing forces will determine tactics. Sabotage and covert operations by "Special Forces" will be favoured above massive confrontation unless the opposing sides are roughly equal in strength. Germany recognised that the British Grand Fleet was at least equal if not superior to their own High Seas Fleet and so sensibly if somewhat callously used covert submarine operations in preferences to full scale sea battles — with the exception of the Battle of Jutland in 1916. Jutland was in effect the one and only full scale battle between roughly equal battleship forces, there were other big-ship battles, not least Tsushima, in 1905 when the Japanese Grand Fleet annihilated the Russian Baltic Fleet but Jutland remains unique in many respects.

When war is inevitable, and even in the 21st century this still seems to be the case, then effective military forces are needed if there is to be any chance of winning. Because deterrence can fail an island like Britain needs an effective naval force (as well as an army and air-force) for self-protection. It was in defence of the realm that Britain, more specifically England, needed a sea-going force to repel a succession of invaders, Romans, Vikings, Jutes, Angles, Saxons, Dutch, French, Spanish and, in the first half of the 20th century, the Germans.

Having developed a navy for defensive purposes Britain soon learned to use its sea-going forces for more expansionist, empire-building, purposes. This was particularly true in the 17th to 19th century when the major sea powers, the Dutch and Spanish for example, were sailing the then unknown world in search of new lands to conquer and occupy. But the origins of the Royal Navy begin much earlier than 17th Century.

A surprisingly helpful source of information about Britain's seafaring history is not the historian but the numismatologist. The study of coins allows us to go back beyond written records. Using Spink's Catalogue, "Coins of England", as an example it is apparent that the ship was not a sufficiently important image for the pre-Roman Celts of England to use a boat as an icon on their coinage.

However, the Romans were obliged to sail as well as march from country to country if they were to expand their Empire and they used the Galley to do so.

One such galley is depicted on a bronze "Quinarius" issued by, Ellectus (or Allectus). As a usurper he ruled in the Colchester region of Eastern England. Spinks advises that 'this was an experimental coin associated with the fleet upon which the survival of the rebel regime in Britain was totally dependent'. Carausaius (as 'Admiral' of Portsmouth) was also a rebel leader and he too issued a coin, probably a silver dinarius, depicting a galley with a ram and eagle featured on its poop deck.

England and surrounding countries, many hostile to England at some point.

Apropos coins, the Roman name for Britain, Britannia, is still used and Britannia coins, valued at £2:00 are still struck by the Royal Mint. And talking of naming places, their name for Portsmouth was Magnus Portus; it was referred to in King John's reign, (1224) as 'Portsmue'; and the Danish Vikings called it Portesmutha.

Without coins and other artefacts to prove otherwise, the Ancient Britons were presumed not to be a seafaring nation but recent archaeological excavations in North Ferriby has uncovered coastal sites showing that at least four thousand years ago the local folk of Yorkshire were building substantial boats. These vessels were made of planks of wood sewn together and would have been a vast improvement on dug-out canoes and rafts.

Whilst a 'sewn' wooden boat may sound unseaworthy, the wooden planks would swell whilst the cord would shrink to give an excellent watertight hull that was certainly a stable and very sea-worthy craft. In this particular model there is even evidence of a mast-step, this hints at even greater enterprise, and suggests early Britons were making good use of wind and tide and were regularly cruising the coastal waters of the North Sea and English Channel.

Roman Quinarius coin

However, a few examples of sewn boats do not provide enough evidence to suggest an embryonic navy but it does demonstrate that the English were experienced sailors and coastal travellers and not just primitive farmers living off the land.

As well as using such boats for fishing or to move between coastal settlements — and embarking on a few skirmishes with local tribes no doubt — it is also likely that these early seamen were trading across the English Channel. Another sewn boat , dated to about 1550 BC, was found near Dover and was judged to be more than 30 feet in length and capable of carrying three tons of cargo. In this location, on the South East coast of England, it is possible these were seafaring men trading with their counterparts across the English Channel, whom they presumably saw as European trading partners — making the European Trading Union at least three thousand years old.

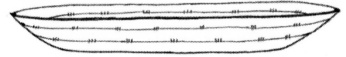

Bronze-age sewn boat circa 2,000 BC

This point is confirmed by Raymond Brown in his curious little book 'Phantoms and Legends of the Sea' in which he cites Caius Julius Caesar's own records *'De Bello Gallico'*. In this work Caesar records the help Britannia's merchant ships gave the Gauls when he, Caesar, attacked the Veneti of Gaul. The English and French were clearly at this point trading partners and allies against the encroaching Roman Empire. It remains the case that the Merchant Navy has a mutually dependent relationship with the Royal Navy.

Armed merchant ships were self-evidently the forerunner of the Navy proper. Despite this sea going adventure across the English Channel, Britannia was clearly not in a position to oppose the Roman invaders at sea when they sought to expand their empire across the Channel. But it did take several attempts for the Romans to effectively colonise Southern England; Commius circa 55/54 BC, Claudius AD 43 and Caesar in AD 56 [1]. Despite evidence of two thousand years of coastal sailing the leaders of the Ancient Britons, Cogidubnus (representing the Regneses), Prasutagus (for the Iceni) and Cartimandu (for the Brigantes) seem not to have possessed an integrated naval force capable of sea-battle against Roman sailors.

It has been argued that these ancient Brits may have taken the diplomatic approach and made peace with their new 'guests' and continued trading much as before — expecting an equal partnership perhaps. So it is possible that the English were capable of defending themselves at sea but chose not to. There are plenty of examples throughout history, and even in recent times, when a leader's choice of ally can lead to unexpected or unwelcome consequences. Britain's alliance with the United States of America, and even with Europe, is called into question by many.

All this is speculation about pre-Roman sailors brings little certainty but it gives us a useful starting point because hereafter the origins the Royal Navy can be traced with increasing clarity. The Romans, as governors of Britain, obviously did possess fleets of ships capable of sailing great distances and capable of sea battles, particularly in the Mediterranean region.

The Romans had to select landing places and Portsmouth, and in particular Portchester which lies in the far reaches of Portsmouth harbour, was one such entry point. This may not have been their first point of entry but it is a strategically sound location, with its protected natural harbour and defendable hill just beyond the landing point. The first (Roman) Admiral to use this harbour is reported to be Caius Carausis in about 284 AD. His name for Portsmouth was 'Portus Magnus' (Great Port) and Portchester 'Caer Peris' [2].

The remains of Portchester Castle are one of the earliest of an unending series of forts, castles and other defences built to protect this special place and most are still standing and well worth visiting.

So how did the Romans get to be such good sailors? The Romans learned their boatbuilding and seafaring from the Egyptians so that by 260 BC the Romans had the skills to prepare a formidable fleet of 145 oared galleys to face a Carthaginian fleet of 130. The reader will be interested to know that in this particular sea battle the Romans won – using a new secret weapon with devastating effect. It was in fact a plank of wood! This was a curious boarding plank fitted with a large metal spike to drop onto the enemy's boat. This anchored the plank in place and facilitated rapid boarding. This innovative boarding gadget was called a 'corvus', or raven, and proved decisive.

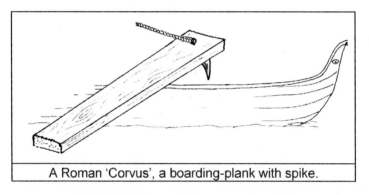

A Roman 'Corvus', a boarding-plank with spike.

It reminds us that it would be several hundred years before sea battles were fought at any great distance with heavy ship-killing guns. For now ship to ship fighting was at close quarters, basically, soldiers at sea [3].

Despite their undoubted seafaring skills, history does not judge the Romans as founders of the British navy. They left Britain a lot; a great many very straight roads such as Watling Street and Ermine Way. Apparently some 10,000 miles of roads were laid by the Romans and some are still in use. Hadrian and Antoninus left Britannia substantial walls to the North of England (but they were never very effective in keeping the Scots out of England). They left behind lots of their floor tiles and coins — mainly to puzzle archaeologists centuries later — but not a navy. So we need to go forward in time to find the foundations of the Royal Navy.

The Dark Ages defines the less well documented period following Roman exodus in about 400 AD. It would seem that after the departure of the Romans the Britons did not pursue their legacy of town planning and sanitation, road construction and fine domestic dwellings and military fortifications. All these skills were seemingly lost until the 19th and 20th Centuries. However, so far as the navy is concerned it may be assumed that the Romans would have left many of their galleys around the coast of England, boats that were either no longer required by the Roman army or no longer serviceable for sea voyages back to the Mediterranean.

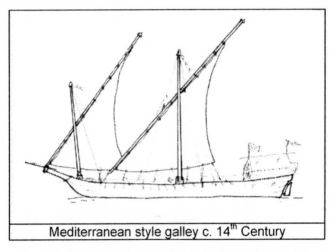

Mediterranean style galley c. 14th Century

It would be surprising if the Britons did not make use of these boats and improve their boat building skills. The simple sewn boat of two thousand years earlier was probably by now replaced by the Mediterranean style galley, a boat of similar proportions to a sewn boat and but we might guess that the galley-style boat was better suited to carrying cargo and men and better for rowing and manoeuvring over greater distances.

In 790 AD, some three hundred yeas after the Romans left, the violent pillaging by the Vikings was well underway. Incidentally, the term '*i viking*', referred to somebody who went 'plundering' – which describes this new assortment of visitors very aptly [4]. With these new invaders came the embryonic naval forces of Anglo-Saxon Kings of England. England at this time was still not a single integrated nation but great leaders were needed to deter the Vikings at sea as well as on land [5]. Athelstan of Kent and the better known King Alfred, "Alfred the Great", are credited with such leadership and there is evidence that they had some early successes against the Vikings. In 851 for example King Athelstan defeated a Danish force at sea, off the coast Sandwich in Kent, whilst Alfred is given credit for a similar victory in 882 when he also repelled four Danish ships at sea. Athelstan's victory is regard as England's first real sea battle [6].

King Alfred is also credited with building a fleet of longships — to his own design, with a higher free-board — with which he had further successes against the Danish in 882 and again in around 895/7 in sea battles in the Thames Estuary. King Alfred the Great, 871 to 899, is therefore amongst the first of many Monarchs to make a significant contribution to Britain's naval defences, ship building designs and sea battles. He came to an early conclusion that an enemy like the Danes had to be fought and defeated at sea [7]. As for the type of ship in use for these early sea skirmishes, the 'galley' was a ubiquitous style in the Mediterranean and the 'longship' in Nordic countries of Northern Europe.

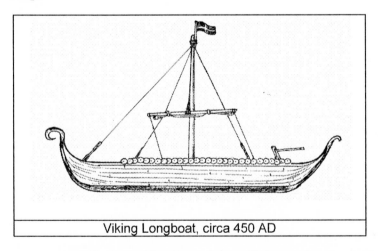

Viking Longboat, circa 450 AD

King Alfred is said to have designed his own boats – boat using technology to suite the nature of the coastal waters around England which varies considerably from sandy beeches to rocky inlets.

It is of course Nature - the coastline, the winds, tides and sea conditions - that dictate boat design. Portsmouth had many advantages so far as Nature was concerned. It was, and still is, a huge natural harbour with a narrow entrance channel leading into the Solent; it is also afforded some protection from the elements, and the enemy, by Portsdown Hill to the North side (which provides its own natural defences and upon which many forts are built — Palmerston's Follies). The Isle of Wight provides a natural barrier and funnels ships into the Solent towards Portsmouth — it also gives Portsmouth its peculiar double tides.

Here in the entrance channel Palmerston built more fortresses like Spit Bank and No Man's Land which jut out of the sea ready to repel enemy from the seaward side.

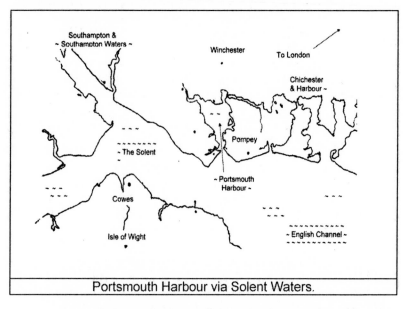

Portsmouth Harbour via Solent Waters.

It is mere speculation, but perhaps the Romans did after all leave us a naval legacy given that the Ancient Britons, after at least two thousand years of coastal navigation, were unable or unwilling to repel the Romans but some three hundred years later they had learned the fighting skills, and by then the boat-building skills, and were ready to take up arms against Viking seamen. Britain was beginning to realise the importance of sea defence and was beginning to do something about it — but with no great successes at this stage.

The Viking onslaught was unstoppable. They overran the Britons and settled here with their leaders, King Canute (1016 to 1035) for example. With them came their shipbuilding and nautical skills - as well as their money; their laws, the 'Danelaw'; and their customs. Before the arrival of the Vikings the seas around Britain played no great part in the defence of the nation but this clearly changed and the defence of the coastal waters around Britain became as important as land-based defence. The North Sea, The English Channel and the Irish Sea, had to be controlled, defended and increasingly the waters became the 'battlefield'. These sea routes were of course increasingly used for trade and transport and other peaceful purposes but even peaceful trading missions needed protection and so these coastal waters were disputed as much as the as the land itself.

By the time King Edward (1042 to 1066), "Edward the Confessor", came to the throne the need for a fleet of ships was sufficiently well established for him to organise the Cinque Ports. The Cinque Ports were sea ports on the South East coast of Britain.

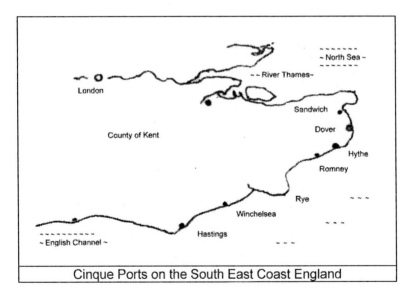

Cinque Ports on the South East Coast England

The responsibility of the Cinque Port towns was to provide ships, at short notice, to the King. This was in effect a reserve fleet. It relieved these coastal towns of other obligations such as raising taxes or providing merchant ships ad hoc. Several sources suggest the obligation was to provide a total of 57 ships - to be available for the King's use for at least 15 days per year [8]. However, if this were true the timescales were quite unrealistic because preparations for war and the conflict itself could take many months rather than a few days, during which time the owners of the ships were losing money by not trading.

For these ship owners and their towns, Dover, Hastings, Romney, Hythe and Sandwich, the status of Cinque Port was a formalised arrangement that applied more informally to most ports that had merchant fleets, ports such as Bristol, Plymouth and Great Yarmouth. At times of war all such coastal towns were under a feudal obligation to provide taxes, ships, men, food and supplies for the King's navy. The Cinque Ports merely put in place a more predictable arrangement for bringing together a fleet of suitable sea-going ships at times of war and in return these towns were given fishing rights and relieved of certain taxes.

King Edward's Cinque Port arrangement can therefore count as a precursor to a "standing navy" - rather than an ad hoc and temporary fleet of ships brought together at times of conflict or other necessity.

Next in line to make a serious contribution to an organised navy royal was King Edward III (1327 to 1377). Edward defeated Philippe VI of France at the Battle of Sluys in 1340.

Sluys but was then a fortified fortress town guarding the estuary of Zwijn and Scheldt on the seaboard frontier of Belgium and Holland. For this encounter the English mustered some 200 ships in the Mouth of the River Orwell, near Harwich on the East coast of England [9,10]. In summary, the English caught the French ships still at anchor on June 4th 1340 and despatched most of them.

Coin collectors will know that King Edward issued a gold coin, the Noble, depicting himself standing on a ship carrying a shield with fleurs-de-lys from the French coat of arms so there would be no doubt who was the victor at Sluys [11,12]. Edward's success gave him com-

Coin, the Noble, depicting Edward of ship Michael, after the battle of

mand of the (English) Channel and so began England's Hundred Years war against the French.

The Battle of Sluys is reported by some authors, Warren Tute for example, to be the first battle fought between ships – though this does not take account of the many earlier battles in the Mediterranean nor even the Battle of Dover in 1217 [13].

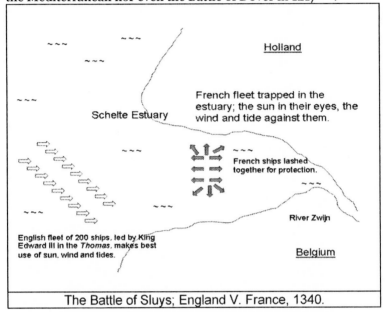

Holland

French fleet trapped in the estuary; the sun in their eyes, the wind and tide against them.

Schelte Estuary

French ships lashed together for protection.

River Zwijn

English fleet of 200 ships, led by King Edward III in the *Thomas*, makes best use of sun, wind and tides.

Belgium

The Battle of Sluys; England V. France, 1340.

The battle of Salamis in the Mediterranean was particularly noteworthy; it took place around the Island of Salamis and saved the Athenians from an intended Persian conquest of Greece.

This spectacular sea battle took place on 23rd September 480 BC with a Greek force of some 200 triremes, facing 750 Persian ships [14]. A trireme is a galley with three banks of oars, whilst sounding unwieldy it must have been a formidable sight. From this engagement there were many lessons for any commander to learn.

The commander of a fleet of warships must know how to maintain his ships in proper formation; he needs good intelligence of the local sea and wind conditions, he must avoid being trapped in narrow straits; and he must have ships strong enough to withstand a battering from the enemy as well from the weather.

This early sea-battle also demonstrated how difficult it is for an invading force to attack an enemy fleet within sight of its own bases.

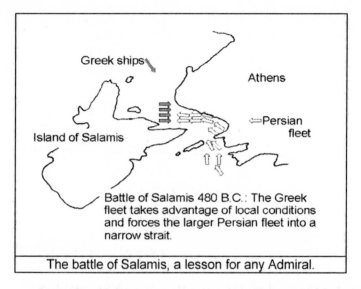

Greek ships

Athens

Island of Salamis

Persian fleet

Battle of Salamis 480 B.C.: The Greek fleet takes advantage of local conditions and forces the larger Persian fleet into a narrow strait.

The battle of Salamis, a lesson for any Admiral.

The battle of Sluys was also in sight of the French fleet's own coast and so the French fleet should have had the advantage but they were trapped, still at anchor, in a cul-de-sac. The Spanish Armada attacking the English fleet in the Channel is another example of the difficulties faced by an invading force. This makes Nelson's victories at the Nile, Copenhagen and Trafalgar all the more remarkable given that he was attacking ships who should have had the advantage. Of course not all Nelson's battle went his way; at Turk Island in the Caribbean Sea Nelson suffered one of several defeats.

We shall learn a little more about Nelson's battles in a later chapter but to return momentarily to Sluys, it may not have been the first great sea battle but it does suggest that it is one of the earliest sea battles for England and of course for King Edward III himself who was there to witness the victory. This battle also sets the pattern for naming sea-battles, which are usually named after the nearest piece of land – most famously "Jutland" not fought on the Jutland peninsular but some miles out to sea.

The Battle of Sluys also set the pattern for the method of fighting these early sea battles – they were in essence fought on land-based principles in so far as soldiers were carried on board. It was the sailor's role to bring the ships close to the enemy, touching if possible. The soldiers could then fight with bow and arrow and even swords at very close range; hand-to-hand fighting once the ships were locked together and boarded.

For several hundred years sailors and their ships were merely transporters of soldiers. In this sense ships merely replaced horses

13th Century English warship with archers mounted in the fore and after castles.

as the means of bringing opposing forces within reach of each other - until the advent of guns powerful enough to hit the enemy from a distance. In European waters the first use of guns at sea is thought to be in 1336 by Louis de Mâle in an attack on Antwerp [15]. Despite this early example it was to be about three hundred years before long distant gun battles replaced hand-to-hand skirmishing. Even by 1805 Nelson was killed by short-range rifle shot and not long-distance cannon — but as we all know England still won at Trafalgar.

King Edward III built a substantial fleet and was able to take advantage of sea conditions, the general location, the wind and tide so he was effectively prepared for battle— and perhaps he had read his history book and learned a few lessons from Salamis [16,17,18]. Edward III can therefore be credited with an early and very successful fleet action.

Control of the sea was something learned at an early stage. Adam de Moleyns, the Bishop of Chichester, as early as 1436 promulgated the importance of sea power and maintaining control of the high seas in his work 'De Politia Conservita Maris'.

From these early beginnings the concept that Britain, Britannia 'ruled the waves' and was 'sovereign of the seas' developed and it followed that the navy should later be regarded as the senior service, providing as it did for hundreds of years the 'wooden walls of England — in essence its first line of defence. King Alfred had learned from practical experience that it was better to attack the enemy's ships in their own coastal waters rather than wait and have to repel them from your own shores. In other words, take control of the seas and this will be a point expounded repeatedly in this book. In order to advance this idea of sea power the Earl of Rutland was appointed the Lord High Admiral 1391, although at this stage the title 'Admiral' defines the job, organising His Majesty's ships, rather than a rank [19].

King Henry V (1413 to 1422) was an empire-building ruler. He was a very assertive Sovereign and described by some as a "chivalric King" [20]. Keen to regain the French territories previously won by Edward II, Henry's archers won the day at Agincourt on 25th October 1415. In order to further his ambitions he re-instated a powerful naval force of warships in the form of 'Carracks'. These were huge ships for their day, sailing ships rather than galleys.

Henry paid for his Carracks from his own funds and not surprisingly invested in their upkeep. In Southampton and the nearby River Hamble, Henry built docks, store-houses, mast-houses and developed here an early naval base.

To maintain and repair these ships docks, basins and covered slipways are needed and the nearby Portsmouth harbour is credited with the country if not the world's first dry dock. A dry-dock being an opening in the shoreline into which a ship can be floated, the water displaced and the ship propped up whilst it is repaired. King Richard is reputed to have ordered a dock be built in 1194. Alternative versions claim the first dry dock was built in Portsmouth at the beginning of the 13th century; King John (of Magna Carta fame) was said to have ordered the enclosure and covering of slipways in Portsmouth (near what was HMS Vernon) these slipways were called 'exclusa'. They had apparently been dismantled by 1253. Henry VII is also credited with the world's 'first' dry dock built in Portsmouth in 1496, but this is probably another myth about the Royal Navy and its association with Portsmouth. These earlier Docks were probably a form of 'mud-dock' or 'wet-docks', no more than a ditch dug into a beach, then stopped up with an earth mound, to be dug out once work on the ship was completed – a lengthy process taking about two weeks and hardly worthy of the name dry-dock but nevertheless effective. It is more likely Deptford, in about 1578, can take the credit for the first dry dock with gates that could be opened and closed quickly and efficiently for repeated use so as to provide a watertight compound. The construction of these all-important gates follows shortly after the enclosure of a pound (a stretch of water) in the Exeter Canal which was built around this time [21].

Wretched for England, but a time of celebration for France, Henry VI lost the French territories won by his father Henry V. His reign is described as an 'ignoble reign' and his regnal dates give a clue; reigned 1422 to 1461, deposed and later reinstated 1470 to 1471; 1471 murdered in the Tower of London (a castle that is meant to protect the Sovereign seems to have a bloody history of King killing). Sadly for his family Henry's son also died, in battle, just ten days earlier. His successor was Edward IV, regarded as an able King who reigned over a period of peace — so no great developments in the military though plenty of progress in other areas of life in Britain, such as the law; in printing, (William Caxton set up his printing press in 1476) and in international trade — especially with the Hanseatic League of Northern Germany. By the time the Tudor dynasty was underway, (from Henry VII to James I, 1485 to 1603) great voyages across the vast uncharted seas were being made to discover 'New Worlds'.

For these explorations, and the associated trading that was expected to follow, ocean-going ships, rather than coastal boats, were needed.

Along with these supposedly peaceable ambitions of discovery naval forces were also making their own discoveries, not least improved fire-power. The increasing use of gunpowder and ever bigger cannon required bigger and heavier ships to carry these improved armaments and to provide protection from the enemy's cannon fire. Galleys were no longer suitable for this and the fatter, rounder merchant ships, designed to carry cargo in bulk they were the obvious solution. Having replaced the rowed Galley with the 'round' sailing ship there was now a need for a clearer distinction between merchant ship and warship. Merchant ships were used to carry heavy loads of merchandise over vast distances at a slow and steady pace, following 'trade' winds and with no prerequisite to follow a particular course whereas warships, also required to cover vast oceans, now had to carry heavy guns and large numbers of fighting men, but they needed to go where the enemy was not where the wind might blow them.

Both types of ship would have much in common so trading vessels could still be readily enough converted to a warship as the need arose. But there were disadvantages with the 'round' ship. The ships were now without oars, they were too big and heavy to be rowed. They were also much less manoeuvrable against the wind and so they could become becalmed in light winds, the 'doldrums'. Smaller and lighter though Galleys were they did have the advantage that they could be rowed against the wind or they could still make progress even when there was no wind at all; they could operate in much shallower waters and with a single lateen sail it could sail closer towards the direction of the wind (unlike a square rigged ships which has to have the wind more or less coming from astern – so galleys still had their uses but were never suitable for anything other than coastal actions.

Increasing specialisation led Henry VIII to build a number of heavyweight warships in preference to Galleys or merchant ship conversions. One such ship was the "Mary Rose" - named after his sister, Mary. She, that is the ship not the lady, was launched in about 1510 and four years later the "Henry Grâce à Dieu" was launched in Erith, South London, in 1514. The "Henry Grâce à Dieu" was more familiarly known as the 'Great Harry', it was amongst the biggest ship in the world at that time. This shipbuilding programme was of course not done in isolation, it was driven by the need to compete with other nations not least Holland, France and Spain who were building warships of similar dimensions and fire power – an unceasing "arms race" that continues to the present day. Like the arms races of the 20th century 'cold war', Henry's show of military might was intended to be a deterrent as well as an offensive force. In the years that followed Britain became so ambitious in expanding, and protecting, her Empire that a substantial Naval force was required. For the navy to be effective for both offensive and defensive purposes it had to be equal to the naval forces of any other two nations, the "2 for 1" principal, which applied right up to World War 1. This was intended maintain Britain's as "Sovereign of the Seas". The two power standard was formally introduced much later by parliament, in the Naval Defence Act 1889, when the next two largest naval forces were those of France and Russia [22].

To return to King Henry, it is of special note that Henry VIII's ships improved upon his father's ship design, which had deck-mounted guns of small calibre – people-killing rather than ship-sinking weapons, mainly of a type called "Serpentines" [23]. Henry VIII refined the use of larger guns, the development of which is discussed in another chapter but it is worth noting at this point that one of the earliest records of a ship sunk by gun-fire was in 1513 [24]. Before this critical advancement in fire-power ships were overrun by boarding parties and the ships taken as "prize".

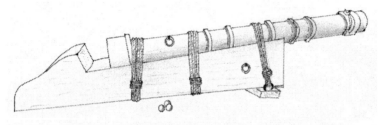

An early ship's gun, circa 16th Century.

With the advent of heavy guns a defeated Captain had the unpleasant choice of being taken as a prize or going down with his ship, not a happy choice. It remained the case however that wooden hulled ships were frequently captured rather than sunk by opposing forces. In this way a ship may well have served several (opposing) navies in its existence. In modern times such exchanges are usually through agreed sales rather than prize-taking, a second-hand Royal Navy ship is still a sought after commodity with a high resale value.

Henry's three ships - the 'Regent', with lighter guns, the 'Mary Rose' and the 'Great Harry', with heavy guns - were excellent, if ill-fêted, examples of ship development in the 16th Century.

Henry VIII came to power at a time when France and the "Holy Roman Empire" were the two super-powers. Henry hoped to regain control of France as part of his Empire and to do so he allied himself with the Holy Roman Empire – such were the Empire building aspirations of Pope Julius II that the title "Holy" seems misdirected. Be that as it may, Henry and the Pope struck an 'unholy' alliance against France. This required King Henry to strengthen his naval forces as we have seen but as Professor Rodger argues King Henry VIII had no great appreciation of the importance of sea power – he was merely building a fighting force to meet his immediate needs [25]. His big ship strategy was put to a severe test in 1545 when his fleet put to sea, or at least tried to. The now famous ship *Mary Rose* was leading the Port Division under Admiral Sir George Carew whilst the Starboard Division was led by the equally large vessel 'Great Harry' under Viscount Lisle.

The King himself came to watch his magnificent flotilla sail from Portsmouth into the Solent (the waters immediately outside Portsmouth Harbour) to meet the French. This encounter must rank as one of the Navy's bigger

...perhaps we should have closed those gun-ports a little quicker, Jack...

mishaps - described by Geoffrey Regan in his entertaining exposition of nautical nonsense 'Naval Blunders' [26]. The *Mary Rose* looked good, it was a mighty ship, with high castles fore and aft and carrying enormous supplies of men and guns. It was state-of-the-art, an awesome floating fortress. It is well known that it was over-laden with guns and soldiers wearing heavy armour. The *Mary Rose* was thus made top heavy and unbalanced. It is now evident that somebody failed to close the lower gun-ports — which are sited very near the waterline. There position would not have been a problem if they had been closed and sealed until needed for an engagement but they were left open. As the ship began to manoeuvre, the wind caught the *Mary Rose* as it was going about and a gentle list developed into a dangerous inclination. The gun ports allowed water to flood in and over it went — to the chagrin of Henry and no doubt the amusement of the French. This fine ship's place in history was assured for all the wrong reasons. It sank there and then and, as is often the case with a sudden capsize, all but 25 of the 500 men aboard were drowned; a timely reminder of the appalling impact on human life when a ship goes down so quickly.

Mary Rose is now being preserved in Portsmouth Naval Museum. So this ship, as rebuilt by Henry, did not travel very far in its long and colourful history, perhaps a total of five nautical miles!

Nevertheless, these mighty vessels were at the forefront of ship development and perhaps inevitably suffered the lessons of innovation, in this case the heavy guns and a poor understanding of displacement and inclination, see for example the naval architects Brown and Moore on ship design, centre of gravity and inclination [27]. *Mary Rose*, whilst afloat, was a formidable threat to the French but like any ship then or now it was just as much a threat to the sailors onboard.

So Henry VIII can be credited as a strong contributor to naval development, especially the use of 'ship-killing' heavy guns, but not as the 'father' of the Royal Navy, the navy was not at this time a permanent force; neither the men nor the ships were organised into a professional sea-going military entity. But before we move on the other contributors we should note that Henry VIII also made a significant contribution to some of the ancillary elements of Britain's naval forces – victualling (supplies) and navigational aids for example. And he is reputed to have established the first naval dockyards, in Portsmouth [28], Plymouth and Deptford. Trinity House was inaugurated in 1517 by Henry VIII to supervise navigational aids such as lighthouses, light-ships, beacon-buoys and (ship's) pilots. Incidentally the name of this organisation, 'Trinity' derives from the fact that the original overseers of these vital navigational aids were Christians, 'Brethren' associated with the parish Church of Deptford. Trinity House was run by the Elder and Younger Brethren and by the masters and wardens – rather more picturesque titles than the modern 'managers' [29].

This is a timely moment to consider how money was raised to pay for the King's Navy and all its accruements. A ship was, and still is, one of the biggest, most complex and most expensive piece of hardware any Sovereign, or Government, had to build and maintain. Once built, the maintenance of a warship was even more of a financial drain that the one-off expenditure of its initial construction.

We have seen that the Cinque Ports of South East England were intended to provide ships, men and equipment in exchange for privileges and exemptions from other obligations and taxes. These "obligations" derive from feudal style contributions, or tithes, in which each level of society owned dues to the higher echelons. At the pinnacle of this social hierarchy was the King who granted Knights and Barons their titles with land and estates in exchange for their loyalty and support, or more practically their men, money and equipment. At the bottom of this social hierarchy came the peasants, serfs, vassals and villains who were obligated to pay part of their "income" as tithes to their local Lords and Bishops. Such payments were usually in the form of labour or a percentage of animal and food stocks but these payments were gradually supplanted by cash in lieu of other forms of payment, these payments were later transformed into the all too familiar taxes we all have to pay.

For the poor folk at the bottom of the social order such payments rendered them close to slavery. However the distinction of servant and slave is important as we shall see in a later chapter. The slave was owned like an object, a chattel and he had no rights whilst even the humblest folk in the lower social orders of Britain had very specific rights, for example the right to till the land and graze cattle on common land, patches of which remain extant [30]. The distinction between slave and peasant will be very important when we come to slave trading.

Returning to the Cinque Ports, as we know, this was a commitment by nominated towns to supply ships and men and meant the State did not need to spend vast sums of (tax-payers') money on its own dedicated "Standing Navy". In much the same way that the current Volunteer and Reserve Naval Units allow the State to reduce full-time naval complements. However Cinque Ports system was never an entirely successful method for sustaining a navy. Neither king nor parliament can afford to wait for war to begin before deciding whether to commandeer existing merchant ships or build ships in advance of an identified need — knowing that once they have been built they are deteriorating from the moment they leave the slipway. Having identified that merchant ships were hired or commandeered for use as warships it is equally true that the navy loaned its ships to merchants on the clear understanding that they would return to the King's use as the need arose; King John for example as long ago as 1232 loaned a merchant, John Blancboilly, his ship the *Queen*. The agony of decision-making has not gone away, the Ministry of Defence still has to look into the future to estimate its requirements both in terms of technology and numbers/types of ships required for next 10 to 20 years.

By the end of the 17th century a more reliable arrangement was needed to ensure Britain could sustain a suitably efficient fleet of ships, to protect its trading interests if for no other reason. Not least amongst those others reasons was a need to reduce the sudden introduction of wartime taxes, a burden which itself could prove a destabilising force in society. The 'national debt', introduced in 1692, was the solution to fund-raising and allowed Britain to maintain a shipbuilding programme where other nations, France for example, struggled to do so [31].

Although a hundred years before the concept of the National Debt, the successful exclusion of the Spanish Armada in 1588 was due in no small way to Britain having reserve forces that could be brought into action at very short notice – in contrast to the Spanish who took many month, extending into years, bringing together a sizable fleet, about 130 men-o'-war for their intended invasion of England. Admiral Howe and the better known Drake had fleet of 102 warships. Despite this imbalance of warships Britain had the advantage of home waters whilst Spanish were obliged sail around the Iberian coast and the English Channel for months before moving against England [32].

To return again briefly to the 20th Century, a similar organisational problem arose in 1982 in respect of the disputed sovereignty of the Falkland Islands in the South Atlantic. The British Prime Minster, having previously ordained the reduction of capital ships, had to very hastily assemble the "Falkland Task-force". To do so the Ministry of Defence had to hire merchant ships, including the Luxury passenger liner Uganda, in order to bring together a large and complex fleet of warships and ancillary craft. The problems of procurement and manning haven't gone away [33].

However in both instances, Queen Elizabeth I's conflict with the Spanish and Queen Elizabeth II's altercation with the Argentines, a Merchant fleet was mustered in support of the Royal Navy's purpose-built warships. The lesson then and now is that adequate military forces must be maintained without excessive reliance upon merchant fleets and ad hoc loan arrangements.

Before the introduction of the national debt there was an extraordinary array of taxes and feudal obligations imposed on all ranks of society, from Baron to Peasant. Ship Money was self evidently the most direct system of raising funds for the navy and initially it applied only to coastal towns and ports and like many similar taxes was in lieu of goods or labour. Professor Keynon, as consultant editor of the 'Dictionary of British History', suggests that Ship Money was first imposed by Charles I in 1634" in accordance with ancient rights, Charles levied ship money from maritime towns and shires to meet naval expenses. By 1635 King Charles had extended the tax to inland counties and continued do so annually until 1640 when it was made illegal by his "Long Parliament" in 1641. It is said that his imposition of this shipping tax, without the consent of his Parliament, was one of the aggravating factors leading to his demise [34].

However, long before Charles reigned, and later lost his head, other Monarchs were raising funds in a similar fashion. Professor Rodger in his very detailed history "Safeguard of the Sea" suggests that it was common practice for the Sovereigns to raise specific taxes in this manner. Rodger records Queen Elizabeth I's budgets in some detail and explains that she had levied shipping, that is ship money, in lieu of the ships themselves, from coastal towns, and did so 'especially in 1588'. By 1603 this toll had extended to a voluntary levy on all counties in England. The incentive to pay was that these funds were to be used specifically to raise a secondary naval force for the protection of merchant ships — as opposed to the warships of the 'navy royal', the Queen's own Navy [35].

Other enterprising income-generating schemes were imposed most were so unacceptable they were abandoned or at least revamped, the Poll Tax for example. In the 20th Century a conservative Government tried to re-impose a Poll Tax; they should have remembered that a Poll Tax was first introduced in 1222 and was then so unpopular it lead to the "Peasants' Revolt", a near revolution in Britain in 1381. *"Plus ça change, plus c'est la même chose"*, nothing changes [36]. Other taxes to fall by the wayside include the well known window tax, less well known were mural tax, pavement tax and hearth tax. Some such taxes, like Stamp duty, remain in place.

During the reign of William & Mary (1689 to 1702) Lord Halifax introduced the National debt and two years later established the Bank of England, in 1694. These two initiatives allowed for a more controlled and systematic means of raising funds, levying taxes and smoothing out the fluctuations of the nations fortunes and providing much need capital for once again we were at war with the French.

To return to the navy rather than find raising; we have been searching for the 'father' of the Royal Navy and as we move swiftly down the centuries we arrive at King Edward VI, 1547, he gave us the Common Book of Prayer but not the Royal Navy. Mary I followed in1533, she earned the sobriquet Bloody Mary, with a penchant for burning Protestants, but she had no enthusiasm for ship-building — no father-figure here but at this point we shall encounter a potential 'mother' in the form of Queen Elizabeth I.

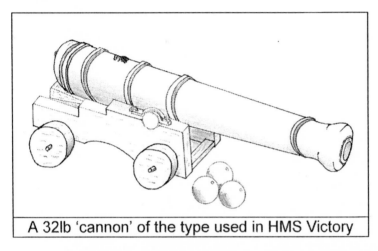

A 32lb 'cannon' of the type used in HMS Victory

The Tudor period, the 16th Century, was an exciting period. King Henry VIII's contribution to the Royal Navy was the heavy gun, the cannon . His ship the *Regent* launched 1488 was said to have carried more guns than any other ship, but this should come as no surprise, Henry was after all big man, full of superlatives, more wives, more palaces, more food more hunting... His ship, *Regent*, carried no less than 225 guns but they were not all of the largest calibre. By 1512 he, or at least his shipwrights, had resolved the problem of carrying heavy guns on a ship without making it unstable. His eponymous ship, the *Great Harry,* carried a much wider range of armaments, bronze cannon of just 2.5 inches to an 8 inch gun capable of throwing shot some 1,600 yards.

The cannon, demi-cannon, culverins, demi-culverins and the like were heavy guns and needed to be placed lower down in the ship, placed in the castles they would have rendered the ship even more top heavy and unstable.

The 'invention' making this possible was the gun port. In practice a simple matter of cutting a hole in the side of the ship, then fit a flap so that it could be shut in heavy seas. This may seem like an elementary solution but until someone had the bright idea of fitting these holes (and more importantly the flaps) guns stayed on the upper, open decks. Curiously the honour for this development is disputed. First contender is a Breton named

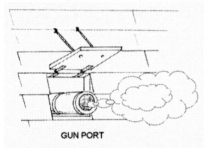

GUN PORT

Descharges in 1501. Rodger thinks this 'a plausible date but a suspiciously apt name'. The second, an English shipwright by the name of Baker, James Baker, developed their use, probably by refining loading ports already in use in the side of ships to allow the loading of provisions whilst in harbour. James Baker introduced gun ports in King Henry's ships including the *Great Harry*, launched in 1514. The fate of the *Mary Rose* has already highlighted the importance of the flaps. Both the *Great Harry*, of comparable dimensions, and the *Mary Rose* were in the Solent but the *Mary Rose* left her gun ports open – the rest is history [37, 38, 39, 40].

King Henry VIII brought his own brand of excitement – not least of which was the division between church and state and his multiple marriages. His daughter, Queen Elizabeth I (1558 – 1603) also brought her own forms of adventure, this time on a global scale. This is the age of Christopher Columbus, Walter Raleigh, Francis Drake, John and Richard Hawkins, Thomas Howard, Richard Grenville, Ferdinand Magellan. Their names have come down in history as fighters, explorers and discoverers of new worlds, there names will be found on any map of the world and of course Gerardus Mercator is remembered for the maps themselves.

So the first Elizabethan age was a time of long-haul, ocean travel. The Navy had to keep pace. As new lands, whole continents were discovered, re-discovered and fought over and as trade and plundering expanded so did the need for a navy capable of leading the way in exploration and settlement – many explorers such as Drake and Raleigh were Admirals in the Queen's pay and sailed the oceans in her name. Alternatively the Navy was there to protect merchant shipping, to defend territories and instil discipline in recalcitrant local leaders.

Like all Sovereigns, she needed money to support her empire building exploits and in doing she seems to have been happy to anticipate Nelson and 'turn a blind eye' to the sources and methods for the fortunes heaped upon her. The reader might wonder where these fortunes come from. The 16th Century was the age of Piracy and "Privateering", although the Danes, Vikings, Barbary Coast, Spanish, Portuguese, the Dutch and many other nationals were well practiced at piracy long before the English.

Piracy flourished at least in part because of the very rational sense people have for retribution and reprisal – nations throughout the world were frequently at war with each other and not surprisingly one nation would consider they were owed a debt by another – sometimes one nation did indeed owe a genuine debt to the victorious nation and its people. To recover these debts, in times of peace after the conflict, "Letters of Reprisal" were issued by the Monarchy to legitimise the recovery of debt. Equally tantalising to a Captain in search of Prize money were "Letters of Marque", this was a licence issued by Admiralty Courts at times of war permitting private merchant ships of one nation to attack ships of the opposing nation [41].

This was "Privateering" and was but a short step, an exhilarating and potentially lucrative step, from Piracy. The money, ships and properties gleaned from these enterprises were 'prizes' and like salvage, flotsam and jetsam, had to be divided by strict laws of the sea. Captain William Kidd, hanged for his piracy, claimed in defence that he was a privateer and some two hundred years after his death the. He claimed to have Letters of Marque and a French Pass proving he had legitimately taken prize from the ship *Maiden* which carrying French cargo and therefore a legitimate target for him. It was unfortunate for Kidd that these documents could not, or would not, be produced at his trial in 1701.

Like Treasure Trove "found" on land, Prizes in the form of ships or goods, acquired beyond the shoreline or at sea, belong to the Crown and its distribution is overseen by Courts of Admiralty, Prize Courts. The (European) Hague Convention of 1907 updated the principles of Prize and Salvage but the origins of distributing this merchandise, obtained by very dubious means, goes back to ancient sea laws, typically Mediterranean law, such as The Rhodian Law and The Laws of Oléron. Quaint as these codes were the Naval Discipline Acts of the Royal Navy derive from these legal precedents.

Below is an extract from these medieval statutes. They were often sensible and sometimes quite humane codes of conduct but the trials and consequential punishments under their laws were usually peremptory, brutal and harsh in the extreme.

An earlier version of chapter 24 of the original Laws of Oléron allowed the crew to immediately execute any ship's pilot who allowed the ship to founder; thus '...*if he brings a ship into a haven and it is caste ashore for lack of skill the crew shall lead him to a hatchway and strike off his head...*'! They clearly took health and safety matters very seriously even in those ancient times. The laws introduced by Richard I were based upon these pre-existing Rhodian Laws used by seafarers in the Mediterranean for centuries [42]. In contrast to the earlier version, Richard's version seems positively humane.

Modern sailors will be relieved to know that those life-threatening punishments are not to be found in the 'Pilot's Guide on Regulations for the Prevention of Collisions at Sea' and, fortunately for any modern pilot, the penalties for misdemeanours of this kind are reduced to fines or imprisonment [44].

The navy's role in Tudor period was multifarious, the navy as stated led many expeditions, it undertook survey duties, it supported and protected merchant ships and it offered protection to Britain's dependent territories.

These were obviously officially sanctioned duties but the navy itself also supplied many a pirate. It is perhaps not surprising that sailors would get disillusioned with life in the navy; its poor pay, poor food, poor accommodation, poor comrades, poor leadership and poor weather were all too often the lot of many sailors. However, if compared with conditions at home, conditions in the Navy wouldn't seem too bad.

Indeed easily tolerable and comparatively good for some if they were ex-convicts, or homeless vagabonds.

But for some sailors the freedom and excitement of piracy was just too tempting, even if hanging by the neck from the nearest yardarm was the risk and the penalty for desertion and mutiny.

> This is a copy of the Charter of Oléron of the Judgement of the Sea...
>
> A ship is in a haven and his companions say 'you have the weather' others say 'you have not the weather', the Master is bound to agree with the greater part of his companions...
>
> If a ship is lost, the mariners are bound to save the most they can...the Master is then bound to pledge some of the goods...
>
> The Master and the merchant are in great dispute, and the merchants claim from the Master their goods they shall have them...
>
> The ship arrives at another port; the mariners are not go ashore without leave of the Master...
>
> If the Master sends a mariner on any service of the ship and the mariner is hurt he is to be healed at the cost of the ship...

Richard I, 1189-1199, his Laws of Oleron

We leave the pirates for the moment because these will be discussed in more detail in a later chapter. Here we follow the developments of the Tudor Navy, new worlds, bigger ships, heavier guns and ocean going adventures. It is now time for the Stuarts (from James I to Queen Anne, 1603 to 1714). Queen Elizabeth departed this world in 1603 and she left us the rudiments of national navy.

The fundamentals of a national naval force are by now in place, large ocean going ships, ship builders, dockyards, suppliers, sources of income, but the organisation of these elements is woefully lacking; Charles I, was probably at fault here but retribution will follow, he will lose head sooner or later so he can take the blame for the poor administration of the nation's sea-going forces in the early part of the 17th Century.

The 17th Century opened with the imprisonment of Sir Walter Raleigh, of America, tobacco and potato fame, he was (sometimes) a favourite of Queen Elizabeth, although she did imprison him for having an affair with Bessie Throgmorton. He was also accused of plotting against King James I of England and again spent time, a considerable time — 13 years — in the Tower of London. Eventually, as is the way with the very contrary Kings and Queens of old England, he is pardoned, and in 1616, sent off to search for gold in Guiana. However there was a caveat, he was instructed to do so without upsetting the Spanish. Raleigh failed, he upset the Spanish somewhat, by interfering with their own looting and plundering in South America. This time Raleigh's luck finally ran out and he was executed in 1618 [45]. King James' willingness to dispatch Raleigh and allow the nation's fighting ships to dwindle to just twenty-seven ships in 1618 reflected his indifference to the navy and the poor leadership of the Lord High Admiral George Villiers, Duke of Buckingham.

Despite this neglected state of affairs the merchant navy continued to expand as exploration led to new trading opportunities. Such trading expansion would inevitably bring Britain into conflict with other like-minded nations. The usual adversaries were the Dutch, the French and the Spanish in particular. The new trade routes, and the merchant fleets that sailed them, as well as the emerging colonies acquired by Britain, needed the protection of an effective and assertive naval force [46]. But James I had problems enough on land to justify his lack of interests in the navy — he was after all the target of the 1605 "Gunpowder Plot". Guido 'Guy' Fawkes, as we all know, was the more famous frontman, for the conspirators. They were led by Sir Robert Catesby's in his attempt to remove King James, known unkindly as "the wisest fool in Christendom". So we move swiftly on leaving Guy Fawkes as the famous effigy for 5th November fireworks displays [47].

The Charles dynasty began with Charles I, 1625 to 1649. Charles married the French King daughter Henrietta Maria when she was 16 years old. Typical of this period, indeed the raisón detre for such regal marriages, this union brought political stability between the two nations. Sadly agreement between France and England was short-lived. By the end of the 17th century the English and Dutch were united under the auspices of the 1688 League of Augsburg, the 'Grand (European) Alliance' against France's expansionist policies [48].

Like his predecessors, Charles was in conflict with his Parliament and by 1649 Parliament won, and Charles lost - his head. But before his decapitation Charles introduced 'Ship Money' as a way to by-pass Parliament and to raise money directly to build ships. These ships were required at this time to protect Britain against the mighty forces of the Dutch navy. Money was also needed to provide naval forces to protect English merchant ships from marauding pirates and ships of other rival European nations — who were themselves anxious to protect their own interests from belligerent British sailors, privateers and pirates.

When Charles came to the throne he had only twenty-seven ships but by now, in the middle of the 17th Century, it was reconsidered that Britain's navy was "the largest and costliest and technically the most advanced organisation" in the land. This required leadership and control not to be found in either James I or Charles I, the Navy was not well organised. Corruption and fraud was rife. The Lord High Admiral at this time was Lord Howard of Effingham. Lord Howard had commanded the fleets successfully against the Spanish Armada so the "intolerable abuses deceits, frauds, corruptions, negligences, misdemeanours and offences", which took place under his command, were ignored — he was after all the nation's hero, he had saved the nation and petty pilfering wasn't going to tarnish his image. To give an example of the extent of this abuse, it was not unusual for an entire ship, its stores and provisions, paid for by the King, to be used as the private vessel of an unscrupulous captain who would then sell the stores and make a handsome profit - at the King's expense [49,50].

Amongst the King's own extravagancies were a number of large ships. Charles I commissioned a leading shipbuilding family, the Petts, to build him a modern warship. Phineas Pett and his son Peter were shipwrights in Deptford. They were commissioned to build such mighty ships as the *"Sovereign of the Seas"*. This particular ship was the biggest and finest ship of its day. Launched in 1637, and coincidently of 1637 tons. Not only was this a powerful fighting ship it also had ornamentation that was quite extraordinary, covered as it was with mouldings, carvings, gold leaf and sumptuous decoration. It was intended to be a statement of the King's wealth and majesty and a deterrent to the King's enemies, the Dutch in particular. The Dutch were themselves fine ship-builders and their designs were probably used for the *Sovereign*, it was said the *Sovereign* was based on the Danish flagship '*Tre Kroner*'. This Dutch ship was itself designed by the Scottish shipwright David Balfour; so no shortage of international collaboration here [51].

The Dutch might have been impressed by Charles's ship *Sovereign of the Sea*' but his own countrymen were not impressed by the ships nor the man himself. His naval career, indeed his life, ended in Whitehall on 30th January 1649 when he stepped through a window and out of the Palace of Westminster onto his place of execution.

Charles' death marks an obvious turning point in English naval history. Discovery and colonisation have encouraged the development of ocean-going merchant ships, which needed policing and protection. To provide this Britain needed a large navy, but such ships (and their shipyards) that were available were poorly managed. Nevertheless Charles' ships like the *Sovereign of the Seas* hint at Britain's intention to have command and control the high seas — so it's time to get things organised.

Chapter 2: 1650 – 1805,
Commonwealth and Kings

~~~~~~~~~~

It's 1649 and Charles is dead. Cromwell is in charge.

Thus England's Civil War was decided, we now have Oliver Cromwell as Chairman of a Council of State, later he is given the title 'Lord Protector of the Commonwealth', in essence a republican state. This commonwealth lasted just 11 years, from 1649 to 1600 when Charles II was enthroned and monarchy re-established.

The records suggest that Cromwell was at least initially a thoughtful and religious man but once in charge, power went to his head and he ran a near Dictatorship. He dismissed the "Rump Parliament" in favour of a Council of 15 members more willing to do his bidding and in doing so moved dangerously close to a Dictatorship. This was far from the egalitarian ambitions of the anti-royalists whom he led [1]. Whatever his political ambitions his organisation of the armed forces is noteworthy and commendable.

Cromwell is known for his 'Model Army' but perhaps less well known for his development of a 'New Model Navy'. It has been argued, for example by Lewis, that Cromwell, in the typical manner of a dictator, needed to control his divided nation by distraction, by generating hostility to a common enemy. Britain certainly had plenty to choose from, the French, Dutch, Spanish and Portuguese to name a few. To achieve this he imposed an aggressive foreign policy, which in turn required potent military forces. He picked on the Dutch as his antagonist. A cynical observer might note at this point some similarities with the Conservative Government of 1982. Whatever their motives, recovering the Falkland Islands from the Argentineans (the second Falkland War, 1982) was certainly a massive distraction for the nation, and unexpectedly rejuvenated the Conservative party's standing that year. American's assertive international policies are seen by some as equally chauvinistic [2].

Cromwell is credited with establishing a "permanent national, maritime, fighting force" – The Navy. The New Model Navy was permanent, that is, a 'standing fleet' like the new standing army. It was not just a temporary fleet brought together at times of war or in defence of enemy action. It remained the case however that the men themselves, the sailors including the officers, were still very temporary. Sailors were either volunteers or 'impressed' (by press-gangs). They were discharged from the navy when no longer needed. But the Navy, the fleet of ships, was now a national force and not one brought into being at the whim monarchs or by the dire necessity of merchant seamen. It was a fighting force; ships were now being designed specifically for fighting and not merely conversions of merchant ships, that is, cargo-carrying ships with guns and castles added.

This new model navy was paid for by a national tax, again not local ship-taxes charged according to an immediate need. Estimates vary as to the number of ships in the fleet in Cromwell's time. Some commentators, Warren Tute for example suggest that by 1660 there were 109 ships in the commonwealth fleet; another historian, Michael Lewis, calculates no less than 207 new ships were added to the fleet [3]. Whether it was one hundred or two hundred, it was a good deal more than the twenty-seven ships afloat in 1618, under James I.

To assert his self-proclaimed authority and his control of the high seas Cromwell appointed himself as General-at-Sea, a precursor to the title 'Admiral', and reflecting the nature of war at sea. Battles at sea were still based to a large extent on land-based fighting techniques - even though heavier guns were in use the technique was still to use short-range gunnery and hand-to-hand fighting. Ship-killing, rather than people-killing, guns were still not yet widely available and the art of long-distance gunnery was still to be learned.

Critical to Cromwell's ambition was the need to control trade and exert his authority over other sea-faring nations. To this end a Navigation Act was introduced in 1651. This was intended to secure a trade monopoly for English ships. The 1651 Act required that goods intended to be imported into England must be carried by ships owned by Englishmen, or foreigners domiciled in England (this anticipates the use of 'flags of convenience' currently used by merchant ship owners, to avoid the onerous taxes and conditions imposed by Britain). The Navigation Act was specifically intended to deter Dutch trade [4]. This was not the first 'Navigation Act' for similar enactments had been passed by a quite number of monarchs including Edward III, Richard II, Henry VII and VIII. But their parochial intentions were much the same, to cite just one example, the Navigation Act introduced by King Charles I required English subjects to use English ships when travelling abroad [5].

Whilst appearing draconian these laws had little impact in reality — the Dutch in particular had no intention of deferring to Cromwell's nationalistic flag-waving. The Dutch Admiral, Marten Van Tromp frequently sailed through the narrow seas of the English Channel in defiance of an English requirement that all foreign vessels "dip" their flag, that is, salute when passing an English ship or Dover Castle.   Instead Tromp sailed by with a broom tied to his masthead — an insolent proclamation that he had swept the North Sea clear of the English navy. Holland at that time had a naval force twice that of England so they did indeed dominate the sea for many years — until Admiral Blake carried a whip at his masthead — an equally defiant symbol that the English had 'whipped' the Dutch. But it was only after three exhausting Anglo-Dutch wars when temporary peace treaties were signed on April 15th 1654 and again April 7th 1672.

Amusing as it might be, the story of Tromp's broom carried at the mast-head of his ship does have an alternate explanation and is perhaps another of the Navy's myths – it is probably a misunderstanding of a (Dutch) tradition that any ship for sale signalled its availability for auction by tying a broom to the mast – in much the same manner that a bale of straw is still sometimes

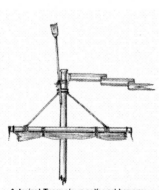

slung below a bridge in Britain to indicate the bridge is under repair. It would be surprising if Blake had confused a for-sale sign with a gesture of defiance. One assumes this to be a witty exchange between two admirals who acknowledged each other's skills, if a little begrudgingly [6].

Leaving aside the brooms and whips, if England was going to sustain fifty years of war with the Dutch she needed to organise her naval forces, Holland was after all a well matched if not a

Admiral Tromp's masthead broom;
A defiant gesture or a 'for sale' sign?

superior naval adversary. Cromwell ordained that England should protect its own trading interests – if need be by force of arms –

but the navy was in some disarray. Indeed corruption was every bit as disastrous as the plague and the fire of London which both reeked havoc in England in the middle of the century. Pepys helpfully records the extent of the naval corruption as well as the changing face of Britain as it swings between Monarchy and Commonwealth, between Protestantism and Catholicism and he also recorded in detail the two 'natural' disasters, the Plague 1665 and Fire of London 1666, in his famous diary.

That Pepys managed to survive all these phenomena is a testament to his steadfastness. Mr Pepys was born 1633 and died 1703. His tenacity appears to have been driven by three essentials; sex, money and the navy [7]. The first two preoccupations need not detain us but his life-long interest in the improvement of the administration of the navy was crucial to its development — and to his own wealth and standing in society.

The essence of Pepys' contribution to the navy was an understanding of the need to bring a professional approach to the numerous elements, branches, of what was the biggest organisation in England — employing more men, sailors, tradesmen and administrators and owning more property, ships, equipment and buildings than any other organisation in Britain.

Not all the improvements can be credited to Pepys but his involvement in matters of the navy was ubiquitous — beginning with the building of ships. Shipyards such the Deptford Yard in London were inefficiently run. Contracts relied upon the exchange of 'bribes', then a common and accepted business practice. Materials were of poor quality and much of it bought ostensibly for ship building but sold again at a profit by these entrepreneurs and without the goods going anywhere near the designated ship. Much material was wasted through poor oversight of the ship building process. Pepys introduced systems, Boards or Committees, for awarding contracts to people capable of producing what was needed whether it was a whole ship, or food supplies or other important elements, wood and rope. Thus the "Victualling Board" and a "Sick & Hurt Board" were conceived to deal with the provisioning of ships and offering some support for sailors sick or hurt while serving in the Navy [8].

One by-product of these improvements was the construction of the largest and finest buildings in England at that time, particularly in bases such as Chatham, Greenwich, Portsmouth and Plymouth. The Rope House in Portsmouth, built in 1663 was

1,000 yards long and was one of the bigger buildings, certainly the longest [9]. One of the finest and most elegant buildings of this time was the Greenwich Hospital for Sailors; this magnificent building survives but only as a naval museums and University in Greenwich (to the East of London).

Another innovation, also addressing the health of sailors, was the appointment of the first "Physician of the Fleet" in about 1654. This was of course a very sensible move given that far more men were lost through disease than were ever lost in battle. Anson, for example, in 1743 lost only 4 men in battle and 1,300 to scurvy and other diseases. However, their Lordship's first choice for the post Physician was Paul de Laune, described as "... a hapless old man of 70, who had never been to sea before and had little practical experience of treating men in battle, he died in Jamaica without anyone ever having consulted him...". Nevertheless the principle was sound and most major warships carried a physician/surgeon [10].

Changes also came within the ranks of the navy itself. Examination for officer-entry replaced the existing informal 'systems' of nepotism and patronage [11]. In 1661 a Naval Discipline Act was passed to introduce clear lines of accountability and authority; this Act was said to be tempered with 'clarity and mercy' – the humble sailor knew what was expected of him and officers had unambiguous responsibilities towards their men. The navy still had a ferocious regime of discipline but it was within a legal framework [12].

Scales of pay were introduced in 1667 when Charles II was re-instated as monarch. Other organisational developments were founded under his auspices, such as the Navy List. This was a record of all naval officers and their hierarchical position in the navy – which dictated, very rigidly, the timing of their promotion to the next rank. A system of half-pay was awarded to officers in temporary retirement so that they remained available to be re-engaged as the need arose. Half-pay was still in use until 1938 as an effective means of retaining professional naval officers, it ensured the navy could call upon officers with experience and training and it provided a career structure for the senior ranks. Half-pay also saved the nation money [13].

The numerous seaborne fights and skirmishes with the Dutch Navy in the 17th Century brought significant improvements in battle planning. Fighting Instructions, a codified system of battle orders, were introduced for the first time in 1653 along with "Articles of War" in 1661 [14]. These dealt with the formation of fleets of warships and how they were to engage the enemy. The main element of which was the line-ahead formation of warships, hence "ships of the line". Such a formation enabled warships to increase the rate of fire against the enemy. Ships now had heavy guns sticking out of gun-ports on each side of the ship and not just the fore and aft "chasers".

Now they could fire their entire gun battery as "broadsides", meaning, of course, that all guns on one side of the ship could fire at an enemy vessel — so long as that ship is sailing on a parallel course in line-ahead formation. The effect of such barrages was devastating — when such formalised engagement worked.

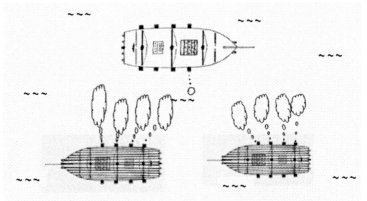

Firing a broadside from an old man-o'-war.

Bear in mind however that the warships of this period, square-rigged sailing vessels, relied upon the direction of wind to fill their sails and to set them on a suitable course — no wind, or wind blowing in the wrong direction, and the fighting had to wait. It could take several days for a fleet to get into the correct position to take advantage of the wind. This is referred to as 'having the weather gauge'. Time spent getting the weather gauge was time well spent because having this advantage meant deciding when and how to advance upon the enemy. Meanwhile, if the enemy did not have the weather gauge their fleet could do little more than sail before the wind — in a direction the advancing fleet could easily predict giving them still more advantage. Sailing with the wind is sailing 'large' and sailing more towards the wind is sailing 'by' from which comes the term 'by and large' referring to how something will generally operate under different conditions.

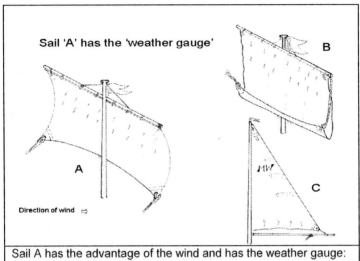

Sail 'A' has the 'weather gauge'

B

A

C

Direction of wind

Sail A has the advantage of the wind and has the weather gauge: Sail B is unable to sail against the wind. Sail C sailing into wind.

When a sail loses the wind it is 'taken aback'; to be 'taken aback' is to have the 'wind taken out of your sails' or to be unexpectedly stopped. If a sail loses its effectiveness and has lost the wind because one of its four sheets, or ropes, is broken the sail is said to be 'three sheets to the wind', that is, flapping uselessly; this phrase now refers to a drunkard not making very good progress homeward-bound.

Strict adherence to the line of battle did however severely restrict an individual Captain's freedom to respond to the events as they unfolded before him. Few Captains were brave enough to take the initiative and risk Court Martial — Nelson's fame derives from his willingness to take such risks when it meant the destruction of the enemy. Such daring, defying orders, or at least interpreting the rules flexibly to win the day, is known as the "Nelson touch". But the risks are high — if you win, you win much approbation but if you fail you lose a lot — you may even lose your head just as the unfortunate Admiral Byng did. In fact John Byng was shot. His 'offence' was rather complex and his execution was at least in part political, as is often the case. His dilemma was all too clear — in attempting to save Minorca he had to decide whether he should continue to attempt to bring his ships into the sacrosanct line-ahead (they were by now in some disarray because of poor signalling) or should he signal a general mêlée with some hope of defeating his enemy.

The fate of Admiral Matthews was on his Byng's mind as he weighed up his options. Byng was recalling that he had sat on the Court Martial of Mathews when Matthews was cashiered for failing to follow the Articles of War, accused of failing to bring his ships into line-ahead formation before closing in for the attack. Byng now found himself with the same dilemma and like Mathews made the wrong choice – at least in the eyes of his accusers.

Byng was about to be hung by his own petard - 'Article 12' of the Fighting Instructions, for which the death penalty was the only available penalty. He couldn't win – he didn't win. Byng retreated to Gibraltar, Minorca fell into enemy hands, and he was later shot for failing to do his utmost to defeat the enemy [15].

By the 1650s England had an effective naval force and was beginning to assert itself on the world stage. Spain as well as Holland had already established numerous oversees colonies and England had ambitions too. In 1655 an English naval force, led by Admiral William Penn (father to the Quaker, William Penn of Pennsylvania fame) and General Venables, confronted Spanish held territories off the coast of South America. They won for England a foothold in the West Indies with the capture of its first overseas base, Jamaica. They took control of Port Royal Jamaica, which was then a virtually uninhabited island. But this was not enough for Cromwell - so Penn and Venables were obliged to take temporary but enforced lodgings in the Tower of London [16].

As well as having ambitions in the South Atlantic Cromwell also looked to the Mediterranean. Blake was Cromwell's henchman in these enterprises. Blake established his own, and Britain's credentials, with the major forces in this area. The key players were the French, Spanish and Italians as well as the states bordering the North African coast, not least the Turks - and not overlooking the interference of the Barbary Pirates. The latter were to prove a thorn in the side of most Northern European nations for hundreds of years. They were taking slaves from all over Europe; it was apparently their most lucrative 'commodity' and it was many years ahead of the European slave trade. They were not finally eradicated until the French took control of Algiers in 1830 [17/18].

Blake's actions, in addition to his triumphs in the Mediterranean, include several actions against the Spanish seizing their ill-gotten treasures off Santa Cruz in 1657. The Spanish were at this time plundering, decimating the Incas of Peru, seizing their gold and eliminating a entire nation of people, see for example 'The Incas', by Carmen Bernard. Blake also had some success suppressing the Barbary corsairs at the Battle of Porto Farina (1654) [19].

The 1600s were a very busy time for the Navy and a very expensive time for Cromwell. His intention to create a "New Model Navy" clearly came to fruition. When his son Richard Cromwell was deposed and the monarchy reinstated in 1660 England had sufficient ships, fleets of ships, ready to take on the Dutch Navy and by now England had a much better organised navy. However Cromwell failed to pay his debts and left Charles II with a £1,000,000 debt of unpaid bills and fees. The solution was brought from Holland by William and Mary (1689-1702). They introduced the concept of the "National Debt". As explained in chapter one, the National Debt was introduced in 1693 and provided, still provides, a means for governments to raise funds at short notice in times of adversity and war. The debt/loan can then be repaid at times of prosperity. In the case of the Navy the much despised Ship Tax was no longer required.

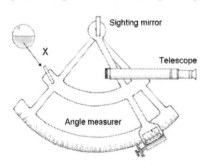

Sextant, showing the critical half-mirrored lens X.

Critical as this new fiscal arrangement was there were many other equally significant developments being refined by and for the navy of the 17th and 18th century. Navigational instruments were being improved to help the sailor cross the oceans and, equally important, to record with some precision his journey for others to follow. Several scientific instruments helped him. The Cross-staff, Back-Staff, Quadrant and finally the Sextant helped identify latitude, though not longitude. Calculation of Longitude had to wait until the Board of Longitude, set up in 1714, finally accepted Harrison's creation of the ship's chronometer in 1765.

Once again it was the Dutch who led the way with another important navigational aid, the sea chart, maps of the coast with depths of coastal waters. It seems rather extraordinary that the British seaman had relied upon their enemy the to provide them with the most accurate charts of their own coastline! For Britain to break its reliance on Dutch cartography Pepys, under the orders of Charles II, issued an Admiralty Order in 1681 assigning Captain Greenville Collins to the task of surveying the British coastline. He published his first edition "Great Britain's Coasting Pilot" in 1693. This heralded the introduction of the Branch of Hydrography and the Admiralty Charts of coastal waters, buoys and sea depths. The first Admiralty Charts were published in 1801, and a leading light in this work was Alexander Dalrymple the first British Hydrographer. Known for his meticulous work these and subsequent Admiralty Charts remain esteemed throughout the world [20].

Another vital navigational aid is of course the compass, two types were in use, the magnetic and the gyro (until the age of satellites). The first points to magnetic North the other to true North. The invention of the first is lost in history but the second type was invented and perfected in the early 1900s. During the 17th and 18th century mariners were learning to understand and make predictable allowances for the difference, or 'variation' between magnetic and true North. The Azimuth compass assisted in this. As anyone who uses a map will tell you this variation is now published on all decent maps and includes an indication of the predicted variation over the coming years.

Other less fundamental inventions demonstrate the slow but steady progress of the navy from man-o-war to the modern battleship navy. These include a primitive man-powered submarine invented by the Dutch engineer Cornelius van Drebbel in 1621. A workable diving suite was invented by an Englishman, Andrew Becker 1715 and the Diving Bell by Edmund Halley 1716 and we shouldn't move on without mention of flag signalling.

Flags have been used for signalling between ships for hundreds of years, if only for the basic necessity of distinguishing friend from foe. Britain's numerous battles with the Dutch stimulated a need for improved flag signalling.

By the time of the Third Dutch War in 1672 battles at sea were becoming long distant; guns could fire over greater distances so each fleet needed a system of communication, to make the commander's orders known to all his ships as the battle was unfolding. It was no longer possible for him to anticipate every possible outcome and issue orders in advance. Until 17th century command was by word of mouth – the Admiral called together his Captains and gave his orders according to the sequence of events he was expecting. Signalling thereafter was a very primitive — fire a gun and raise a flag into an agreed position on one of the three or four masts, this advised the Captains to follow the agreed sequence of manoeuvres. If the battle didn't go according to plan then all was lost. Improved signalling might have saved Admiral Byng.

Code flags 5 and 3; 'Prepare for Battle'.

So important was signalling that Professor Rodger suggests, in his latest book 'Command of the Ocean', that Britain ultimately lost the American War of Independence because of poor signalling by Admiral Graves in the crucial Battle of Chesapeake Bay (1781).

Admiral Blake issued the first volume of Sailing & Fighting Instructions in 1653 and thereafter flag signalling became ever more complex. Coded books were issued, often changing with every change of Admiral until Admiral Lord Howe revised the system by introducing a numerical system, flags numbered one to ten could be hoisted to provide hundreds of combinations listed in numerical codebooks. Thus the two flags 5 above 3, read as code 53 — "Prepare for Battle". Rather more popular than Code 53 was the invitation to come aboard for drinks — the blue and yellow striped 'Gin Flag'.

Captain Home Popham improved the numeric codification by assigning individual letters as well as code words to each numbered flag. This would allow any Captain to create a new message not already listed in the numeric codebook. It was this form of code that Lord Nelson used in his famous signal to the fleet – "England expects every man to do his duty" [21].

Mention has been made of improvements to guns, and this was just as well given Warren Tute's long list of sea battles in the 17th and 18th centuries; the British navy was involved in no less than thirty-three sea battles between 1627 and 1710. So these improved guns were put to the test very frequently. Henry VIII's had refined the casting system barrel making but improvements were needed to make guns stronger and cheaper. Improvements came in the metals used; to the precision of the bore, the length of the gun, its calibre (that is, how large the bore was) and how long the gun barrel was as a ratio of the bore.

The two ship killing guns favoured by the British were the Demi-Cannon and the Culverin. The former would have a calibre (length) of 8 whilst the Culverin around 32 times the size of bore. The Demi-cannon was the heavier weapon firing a metal ball of 32 pounds whilst the Culverin fired an 18 pound projectile but it had a longer barrel and was more accurate than the cannon [22].

As we have seen, the overall organisation of the navy was brought into some order in Pepys time. It is said he created the 'Admiralty' and re-created the 'Navy Board'. In the broader picture control of the Navy was gradually moving from the King himself as Lord High Admiral to Parliamentary control with the monarch's role increasingly titular. It remains the case that Queen Elizabeth II holds the highest rank in the Navy, Lord High Admiral, but she is no longer expected to go to sea to lead her ships into battle — which is just as well because she no longer has use of the Royal Yacht Britannia.

Peter Kemp summarises this historic role of the Lords Commissioner very concisely - although the full title of the administrators is less than concise — 'Lords Commissioners for the Executing the Office of Lord High Admiral'. Very helpfully the title carries its own job description. Whilst the King held the highest office, with decreasing influence, the Admiralty comprised Lords, Politicians and Judges, who sat on a variety of Boards and Courts to administer the Navy and Naval justice.

It remains the case that the higher ranks of Admiralty, First Sea Lord, is as much a political position as a military one, in so far as the most senior ranks in all armed forces, the Chiefs of Defence Staff are answerable to the 'Defence and Overseas Committee' which is chaired by the Prime Minister.

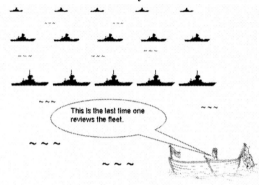

A rowing boat;
No substitute for the loss of HM Yacht Britannia.

Commissioners were first appointed in 1628 by Letters Patent. The duties of the Lord High Admiral's office were twofold, Naval Courts (of Justice) and administration over the Navy. The administration of the Navy was delegated to the Navy Board, which comprised subsidiary Boards of Victualling, and the 'Sick & Hurt Board'. This structure remained extant for some two hundred years, until 1872 when the whole service was brought under the control of a single Board of Admiralty. To complete the story of the Navy's administration, the Lords Commissioners and the Admiralty ceased to exist in 1964 when the Admiralty was integrated into a single military organisation the 'Ministry of Defence', responsible for all three services, Army, Navy and Air Force [23].

If Pepys was a leading light in the advancement of the navy in the 17th century then Anson is worthy of mention for his contribution in the 18th. George Anson was a very successful Admiral as well as a skilful administrator. The highlight of his success was the capture of the French fleet at Cape Finisterre off the North-West coast of Spain in the Bay of Biscay on 3rd May 1747.

Once ashore, he married Lady Elizabeth York, was raised to the peerage in 1748 and was appointed First Sea Lord. Under his direction the Fighting Instructions/Articles of War were redrafted; standardised uniforms issued to Officers; like Pepys he set about tackling the inefficiency and corruption in the Royal Dockyards; he also introduced a new Corps of Marines. Anson brought some sense and order to the 'rating' for ships-of-the-line according to the guns (cannon) they carried, thus a First Rate ship carried 100 or more guns, a Second rate 84 to 100 and so down to a Sixth rate carrying less than 32 guns. Only the first three were expected to form the line of battle, hence the term battleship or ship of the line, the remainder had scouting, signalling and communication roles [24].

The Navy eventually became the 'Royal Navy' by Royal Proclamation of Charles II. Curiously, and typically English the Royal title came at a time when the navy was no longer royal it was virtually a civil organisation, though the monarch remained and still remains its titular head [25].

Whatever the case, hereafter the navy royal shall be referred to as the 'Royal Navy'. But what exactly had the Royal Navy been doing to earn its title. As mentioned earlier in this chapter, Warren Tute lists no less than thirty-three naval actions between 1627 and 1710, the most significant being the three Dutch wars, 1652, 1664 and 1672. Having eventually established something of a supremacy over the Dutch the Royal Navy then joined our former Dutch adversary in actions against the French - such is the nature of European politics [26].

The Royal Navy was even busier in the 18th century, Britain was dealing with America's fight for independence and France's ambitions to control much of Europe, Britain also had its own Empire to build, control and protect.

Britain lost America but learned some valuable lessons. The names of the sailors learning those lessons are now familiar to any naval historian, Hood, Rodney, Nelson, Cornwallis, Collingwood — some were later to become part Nelson's elite 'band of brothers'. The principal lesson to be learnt was promulgated by General George Washington who stated that "in any operation a decisive naval superiority is the basis upon which every hope of success must ultimately depend...". Britain was nowhere near that position of superiority; she stood alone against America. When France, Spain and Holland joined the war, against Britain, there was little hope of reversing America's push towards autonomy. For Britain the distances were too great. It has been estimated that a naval force loses 10% fighting efficiency for every 1,000 nautical miles travelled. Whilst this might not be an accurate recollection it does reflect the considerable logistical problems of waging war over such vast distances. The destruction of the Russian Fleet by the Japanese, at Tsushima (1905), was a salutary reminder of this lesson. Even Britain's (2nd) Falkland

War in 1982 was matter of considerable logistical organisation with little hope of back up once underway.

However, back in the 18th century the Royal Navy did have some successes across the Atlantic. In the Seven Years War against the French 1759 was the Royal Navy's year. Taking their forces up the St Lawrence River to Quebec was an excellent example of combined-service operations by the two leaders, Major-General James Wolfe and Vice-Admiral Charles Saunders. Every advantage lay with the French, not least because they were defending their bases and the British forces were a long way from home. The French troops easily outnumbered the British Army/Navy forces but their moral was poor. The French Governor finally capitulated on 18th September 1759 and Quebec fell into British hands, and was not long before the whole of Canada was back under British influence. Brigadier-General George Townsend commended the Royal Navy thus, "...*it is my duty to acknowledge how great a share the Navy has had in this successful campaign...*", (Quebec, Seven Years War) [27].

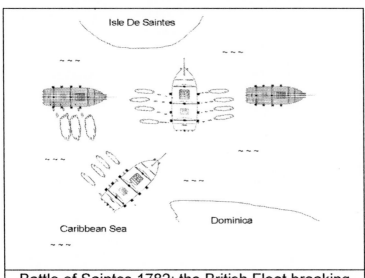

Battle of Saintes 1782; the British Fleet breaking through the American line, firing broadsides Port and Starboard as they go.

The Battle of the Saints 12th April 1782 was another success, in this case much farther South, in the Caribbean Seas. Admiral Sir George Rodney commanded the British fleet with thirty-six ships of the line at his disposal against Vice-Admiral Comte de Grasse's thirty-two ships.

One significant feature of this engagement was the change in Fighting Instructions allowing Rodney to break away from the line-ahead formation. No longer was he constrained by the need to maintain a single line of battle parallel with the enemy. Instead, he sailed through the middle of the enemy's line, allowing his ships to fire broadsides.

This breaking of the line was of course used to masterful effect by Nelson. Rodney won the day – such sea battles usually lasted only a day or so - but he was later criticised for not following up his victory by chasing the remnants of the French fleet and destroying the lot. Much the same criticism was to vex Jellicoe a hundred and thirty years later after Jutland [28].

As the 18th century draws to a close in this chapter the Royal Navy's contribution to the Empire is not forgotten and will be described in another chapter and so will the Royal Navy's exertions against Napoleon. This will be discussed in the chapter on Nelson since he claims several famous victories in that theatre of war.

At this point we pause to reflect again on the birth of the Royal Navy. One is bound to conclude, somewhat whimsically, that Queen Elizabeth I was its mother; Samuel Pepys its godfather, its moral guardian. Charles II named it and might claim rights. Perhaps the Royal Navy has a Royal father in Charles II; or was it the commoner, Oliver Cromwell, who created the New Model Navy, which Charles merely renamed ... we shall never know for certain because we now move on to the 19th century.

Chapter 3: Royal Navy & Empire

~~~~~~~~~~~

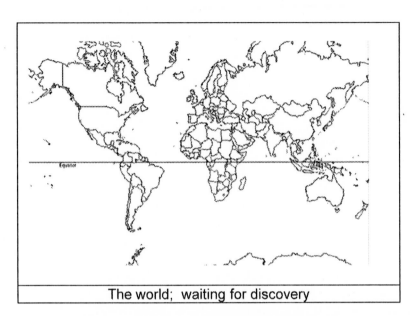

The world; waiting for discovery

The first two chapters established that Britain had a decent navy and in this chapter we explore that many uses to which it was put. In the name of trade the navy was inextricably linked to the expansion of Britain's empire. Britain was rather slower than other European powers in exploring new continents and trading routes. The Dutch and Spanish were well established in some regions such as South America, the Spanish Main as it was referred to. This was long before Britain was in a position to take part in this predatory expansion.

The Royal Navy's role in the rise of the British Empire was vital for the exploration, navigation and discovery of new worlds and opportunities and it was something of a race between outward looking nations searching for opportunities beyond their own borders. Inevitably, these newly discovered lands required charting and mapping; for several centuries the (British) Admiralty's charts were used throughout the world, the first being issued in 1795 and by 1833 some two thousand charts had been drawn up [1].

As land was discovered and charted the Royal Navy had several duties; setting up defensible positions, escorting and protecting traders and repelling usurpers. Indeed usurpation has kept the Royal Navy busy right into the 21st century. The unlawful encroachment by the Argentineans on to the Falklands Islands being a more recent example directly affecting Britain. Whether Britain should ever have owned the Falklands Islands in the first place is a matter of conjecture and outside the remit of this short treatise. Suffice to say that until the 20th Century it was the norm to use force of arms to take and occupy territory. Now even the mightiest of Nations have their actions moderated by the intervention of the United Nations.

Whatever the arguments now, the taking of lands in this manner was merely an extension of principles applied at home throughout the ages. As an example of this state of mind, Captain Cook (of Pacific Ocean fame) found justification for his actions in Judge Blackstone's interpretation of the law as it then stated [2]:-

"Anyone who owned land but did not exploit it forfeited his claim to it"

Cook thus described Australia as 'Terra nullis', land of no-one!

The Royal Navy was used in this aggressive and outmoded approach to oust other empire builders and establish its own dominion. In this way lands, whole countries, could change control many times, large tracts of America, Africa and India had a kaleidoscope of flags as land was won and lost by competing Empires.

During the occupation of these various lands the Royal Navy's role was sometimes diplomatic. The Falkland Island once again serves as a useful example of just this point. Britain had always maintained a ship, HMS *Endurance* an Ice patrol and survey vessel, and a small contingent of Royal Marines. This served as a peaceful but clear presence to remind others of Great Britain's intention to maintain ownership and control. Whether intentionally or not those signals became blurred with talk of removing this naval presence and Argentina sailed in to take possession. Keith Speed, former navy Minister explains the details in his book 'Sea Change' but his point is made by quoting (Solzhenitsyn) [3];

"...The threat lies not in the capabilities of its enemies but in the indifference of the West....".

Since the Government of the day had demonstrated considerable indifference to the Navy's diplomatic, restraining and deterrent roles it was then faced with using the Royal Navy in another of its roles – attack.

However, before attack there is sometimes an opportunity for an intermediate role, that of gun-boat diplomacy. In the control of its Empire it was sometimes necessary, as judged by Britain, to assert its intentions authoritatively and so the concept of gunboat diplomacy emerges. This could mean, literally, a shot across the bows of an aggressor's ship or merely a show of force, more assertive than a mere presence but short of direct conflict. It was important such shots missed otherwise an act of war was perpetrated compelling a reaction; so long as the shots missed the 'enemy' could choose to interpret this as a warning. The Royal Navy's White Ensign was itself a potent symbol tending to pacify without the need to demonstrate firepower. But it was only a potent symbol if it could be backed up by considerable military strength and for many years this was the case [4].

These roles are all related to control by force but the Royal Navy posses other skills, its ships and personnel can equally useful in much more peaceful actions. A naval presence shows Britain's continued interest in the well being of its overseas territories and with a flexible amphibious force, it frequently could offers aid and relief in times of disaster [5].

But, as we saw with the Falklands Islands, a battle is sometimes the only course of action short of capitulation. In this battle role the Royal Navy has rather a lot of experience, it is after all what the ships and guns are for.

This chapter is about the role of the Navy in the expansion and maintenance of the British Empire. As we have seen in other chapters Britain's earliest experience of empire was as part of another nations', the Roman, Dutch and French. It may be argued that because Britain was subject to so many invasions that it developed, through necessity, into one of the more belligerent nations of the world. Had we been left to go about our peaceful occupation tilling the fields and tending our flocks perhaps England would never have become *Great* Britain, less still an Empire; but it's too late to test that theory.

If Britain was slow to learn how to defend itself it certainly learned the rules for defence and conquest with astounding thoroughness. The traditional view of the Romans is that they invaded Britain but modern research may suggest that their presence was welcomed by some leaders in Southern Britain and Roman's presence may have peaceful colonisation rather than subjugation but this view needs to be confirmed by future research and analysis of the evidence. Meanwhile Rome, always regarded as the first known conquerors of Britain, began taking a serious interest in Britain in about 55 BC. This was based upon Julius Caesar's intention to restrict any interest Britain might have in Gaul. 'Gaul' described a large part of Europe including France, Germany and the Netherlands. Rome intended colonising this region and wanted no interference from Britain.

Archaeologists tell us that the ancient Britons, pre-Roman folk, were building sea-worthy boats in Dover capable of carrying heavy loads. This suggests Britain already had substantial trading interests across the narrow English Channel, probably increasing its own trading interests to the annoyance of the Roman Empire. It is reputed that a full invasion force of 50,000 men, led Aulus Plautius, invaded Southern England, in 43 AD. This was the start of the Roman conquest of Britain, which lasted about 400 years. For those 400 years Britain was part of an empire rather than the head of one. The Romans finally retreated back towards Italy circa 446 AD [6].

With the vacuum left by the Romans the Germanic hoards took their chances and in 5th Century Britain became a target for the Angles and Saxons, giving us the Anglo-Saxon races of Southern England, driving the Celts to the far corners of Britain. Britain was still then divided into numerous separate and divided kingdoms and again it's possible that the Angles and Saxons arrived from Northern Europe with the agreement of certain leaders and arrived as traders and settlers rather than invaders. This revised view of Britain's history is explored by Francis Pryor in his book 'Britain AD'.

If the Angle and Saxons were in Britain by invitation, the Vikings waited for no such bidding, they were out and out villains the very name Viking means 'to plunder' and the 8th Century the Vikings were sailing in their familiar longships from across the North Sea to begin their raids all around the coast of England, Wales, Scotland and Ireland.

Until this point Britain appears to have demonstrated little resistance to these aggressive incursions, which may lend weight to Francis Pryor's view that weren't invasions in the first place.

Whatever the case, over the next two centuries Britain began to show its mettle and was learning some necessary skills, especially sea-faring skills, to repel the Viking's constant pillaging.

Alfred the Great, 871 to 899, is said, amongst other claimants, to be the first King of all England. Alfred is reputed to have built a fleet of ships capable of engaging Viking forces off the coast of Kent as we saw in chapter one. But this embryonic navy was not sufficient to deter the Danish Vikings for very long. In 1016 King Canute ruled all England and once again Britain found itself part of another nation's Empire, this time the Danes [7].

A succession of Kings ruled Britain but the Normans were on the horizon; 1066 and the Battle of Hastings is looming. The Normans crossed the Channel to shoot an arrow into Harold's eye, allegedly but doubtfully - probably yet another myth. Like modern newspapers, the Bayeux Tapestry's depiction of the Battle of Hastings is to be regarded with some suspicion. But whatever it might suggest about King Harold's eye it is true that the Normans had subdued the Anglo-Saxons and commenced another, Norman, Empire under William Duke of Normandy (William the Conqueror). There are many interesting byways one could follow in tracing Britain's pre-Empire education. One interesting lesson not taken up by the British in subsequent law was principle of 'murdrum'. Essentially this was a tax, or fine payable by the local community, known as the 'Hundred'. The principle was this; if a Norman was slain and the slayer not produced for trial the hundred in which the killing occurred was required (by the Norman rulers) to pay a substantial fine. The fine could be avoided if it could be proved the dead person was not in fact a Norman. This sounds like a useful weapon to have in one's armoury but the more typical form of reckoning was reprisal in kind – lots more killing in revenge; with this mind murdrum seems the more humanitarian option [8].

Norman Kings and later the Plantagenet Kings, 1154 to 1399, including Henry II; Richard I; King John, and many other illustrious English Kings ruled Britain, and with their French connections, their Empire stretched from Scotland in the North to the Pyrenees in the South. But this was an Empire based upon royal connections and by 1204, during the rule of King John, Britain lost most of its possessions in France.

France soon became a frequent adversary of England. Not least in this perpetual discord was the "100 years war" from 1337 to 1453. This did bring a moment of glory, albeit a very brief moment, for England — when Henry V won the Battle of Agincourt, in 1415, and with this victory came a renewed English claim to the French throne.

From Agincourt; the V sign

This lengthy war did make one small contribution to modern life; the two fingered salute. It is now a well known reference to the English archers' skilled use of two fingers when drawing a bow (and arrow) on the battle fields of Agincourt. This salute was made famous by Winston Churchill WWII as a defiant V for Victory gesture but it has since reverted to its original use as an obscene gesture, used frequently by football supporters as their fortunes ebb and flow.

We have reached the 15th Century and still not much sign of a British empire, except for a brief entitlement to the French throne. Access to the French throne does remind us that an empire could be built upon Royal marriages and political alliances as well as through invasion and conquest.

The first elements of the British Empire began with the union of those lands immediately adjacent to England (Wales and Scotland), this was of course after England had itself become a unified nation. England's own unification under Alfred the Great, circa 886, was extended to Wales in 1536 and to Scotland in 1603. Union with Ireland came in 1800, by which time Britain had won and lost its American colony.

Before Britain could build its own empire it still had to release itself from yet another yoke, this time the Dutch royal house, in the form of William of Orange. It is true some English Noblemen invited him to take the throne. But this was a political move, a voluntary alliance, to avoid a catholic monarch following James II's conversion to Catholicism.

After a period of Dutch rule the next royal house was that of the Hanoverians, 1714 to 1910, beginning with King George 1 in 1714. To complete this rapid synopsis of royal dynasties, the Hanoverian dynasty was followed by the House of Windsor - who remain the current monarchs. Each contributed something to the expansion, or retraction, of the Empire but this is to skip the early development of the Empire's rise and fall.

As we have seen before going on to conquer various parts of the wider world Britain could claim to have at least nominal control of several European states. In the 12th century the Plantagenets, Henry II and Richard I, ruled a large Angevin, French Empire and again in the 15th century the King of England, Henry V was again briefly King of France, from 1422 to about 1453. From 1714 to 1837 the Kings, but not the Queens of England were also Electors and later Kings of Hanover (Germany). Britain's claim to France and the French Crown was through one of a number of offensive conquests, as at Agincourt on 25th October 1415, but she lost the last of her French possessions, Calais, in 1558.

However it was in this manner that Britain was beginning to signal an intention to extend its boundaries, to take control of foreign territories, if not by marriage or negotiation then by force. For this Britain would need a substantial Army and a Navy.

But before we leave this early history of Britain there are two naval engagements worth discussing in a little more detail as they presage things to come and good news is always welcome.

King Athelsat of Kent is credited with defeating a Danish force off the coast of Kent in 851 AD and some record this as the first naval battle in English history. 500 years later, 1340, and Edward III was tiring of the damage done by French raids into coastal towns like Portsmouth and Southampton. Warned of a possible invasion Edward took a naval force across the English Channel - this was in the days when Kings led their armed forces into battle. Edward had the wind and sun behind his ships and he took full advantage of conditions. The records tell us that the King

'in his ship Thomas gave the signal to commence battle, at midday on 24th June 1340. With trumpets blaring they bore down on the French fleet which had failed to leave the estuary in which they had anchored overnight. Only the few ships able to cut their moorings and slip into the open sea avoided the bloody battle that was the first true

> *sea engagement for the English navy, even though*
> *it was in sight of land and fought mainly by arch-*
> *ers and hand to hand sword-fighting. The French*
> *"Grand Army of the Sea" was soundly beaten and*
> *England was again in control of the English*
> *Channel'.*

This was the Battle of Sluys (1340) [9].

Trade, the commodities bought, sold or stolen and the wealth this generated, was the driving force behind empires. Britain was evidently trading around Europe before the Roman visited but international trading across oceans did not begin until seaworthy ships and competent sailors with navigational skills were available. This brings us to the age of exploration and discovery. For England this was the age of the Tudors, from 1485 Henry VII to 1603 Elizabeth I. Incidentally, the title 'Tudor' comes from the Welsh name Tudur and in particular Henry VII's grandfather, Owain Tudur a Welsh squire who claimed to be a descendant of a Welsh Prince.

Many of the territorial discoveries of this time will be disputed. The British Empire was always in something of a fluid state. Lands, territories and colonies, came and went and those nations that formed elements of the Empire had various statuses within the Empire, Colonies, Dominions, and Dependant Territories. Those few Dependent Territories are now more politely referred to as 'British Overseas Territories' and there are now only thirteen remaining as the residue of the British Empire [10].

As this book is about the origins of the Royal Navy it is of little consequence who *first* discovered the various lands later occupied by Britain, whether North America, South America and Australia and so on. They were found, come upon, by various Europeans and may well have been found or occupied by others before but the British came and conquered. It is acknowledged that many lands said to have been *discovered* were in fact occupied by indigenous peoples but they were dismissed by early European explorers as primitive and lesser mortals not capable of harvesting their own lands, nor capable of working with modern tools and technology – rather overlooking the obvious fact these indigenous people were surviving quite well until Western civilisation brought, disease, conflict and massive shifts to the existing social order.

To begin the expansion Christopher Columbus discovered South America in 1492 whilst in 1497 John and Sebastian Cabot made their way to North America. Sir Frances Drake, in 1557, sailed around the world and Sir Walter Raleigh made his first expedition to South America in 1559. Two hundred years later and Captain James Cook is also sailing around the world "discovering" Australia but not *Terra Australis Incognita* the supposed continent in the Antarctic region which is what he was actually looking for. However Cook was not the first European to do so. William Dampier probably got to Australia before Cook, indeed Cook may have used Dampier's notes to re-trace his steps. Dampier's contribution to empire is discussed in the chapter on piracy because young William was something of buccaneer as well as an accomplished navigator but even he may not have been the first European to discover Australasia.

In many cases the British were following in the footsteps of Dutchmen such as Abel Tasman who, in 1642, gave his name to the Tasman Sea, between Australia and *New* Zealand. The Maoris and Aborigines were of course already sailing around the Pacific Ocean long before these the adventurers found themselves there. The Spanish explored and plundered South America, especially Peru. As we now know they wiped out the entire indigenous population of Incas, which until Spanish arrived, had been a highly developed and sophisticated society but they unable to resist the blandishments and aggressive plundering of the Spanish. The gold stolen by the Spanish was of course a great attraction to other marauding nations not least the British who took every opportunity to relieve the Spanish of the plunder by intercepting their homeward bound treasure ships. These fabulously ladened ships fuelled the privateers, buccaneers and pirates who merely sought to relieve these ships of their cargoes – an easy profit if they succeeded.

Many of the voyages of discovery were under the auspices of the Admiralty at the behest of the Monarchy. Queen Elizabeth I and George II were keen supporters of exploration and the expansion of empire. These explorations were often led by naval officers, Captain Cornwallis and Captain Cook being excellent voyagers on behalf of the Admiralty. William Bligh's fame, or infamy, is mixed. He sailed on a voyage of discovery around the Polynesian Islands in the Pacific Ocean in a converted merchant ship renamed Bounty. By his petty tyranny he drove his crew to mutiny -

despite the risk of being hung as mutineers, as several eventually were. Bligh is equally famous for his recovery. After being cast adrift from the Bounty on 28th April 1789 he sailed to safety some 4,000 miles in a small launch – his navigation skills were beyond reproach but his leadership seems to have been appalling. A hundred years before William Bligh, William Dampier seems to have been of similar character; also masterful navigator but a hopeless leader of men. No doubt many sailors will still recognise this challenging combination in their officers [11].

As Britain's overseas interests grew to embrace all parts of the globe the Royal Navy had two rather contradictory roles so far as slavery was concerned; it supported and protected the Merchant Navy and its trading routes on the one hand but challenged slave trading on the other — even though slavery derived from the imperative of trading, without slaves many enterprises would fail. The Navy might therefore find itself in conflict with merchant ships carrying slaves — yet also find itself defending ships carrying the products of slavery, silk, cotton, sugar, tea, coffee and so forth and indeed it may well have been the Navy that originally open these opportunities for trading in the first place.

But the navy's role in such matters should be neutral, the Royal Navy operates as an instrument of parliament — so it is to be presumed that it can't be said to take a moral position on trading, slavery or any other 'political' matter. It is the Royal Navy's purpose to do its duty – as defined by parliament and Admiralty, or the Ministry of Defence as it now more prosaically called.

Meanwhile, exploration continued unabated and undaunted by the hardships; to the North (the Arctic Regions) Britain was searching for a North-West passage, between Canada and Greenland, a route across the top of the world. Roald Amundsen, sailing in the ship *Gjöa*, finally fought his way through on August 27th 1905. It had taken 400 years of searching to find a way through the icepacks. The Arctic Ocean is littered with dozens of islands and waterways and these mark the names of explorers and the course of their progress; Frobisher (Bay), Hudson (Bay), McClintock (Channel), Beaufort (Sea), Amundsen (Gulf) and so forth. In many cases these points also mark the demise of those brave and hardy seamen.

Sir John Franklin was one such brave, or perhaps foolhardy Captain. He gave his name to Franklin Strait off Prince of Wales Island and he is immortalised in song and story for his courageous attempts to find a way through the Arctic Ocean, into the Bering Strait (between Siberia and Alaska) and on into the North Pacific Ocean. His wife Lady Jane Franklin and the Admiralty, who had commissioned the exploration, offered a huge reward in an effort to discover his fate. The many, unsuccessful, searches added to his fame and the mystery of his disappearance [12].

Had the journey been any easier than it proved, it would have opened a new route into the Pacific and the trading opportunities on the West coast of America – without the need to go South into the Antarctic region and the almost as equally hazardous Cape Horn with its violent and stormy winds. The Panama Cannel, via the Caribbean Sea, is now the preferred route from the Atlantic into the Pacific Ocean.

Long before the North-West passage was identified, Britain already had territorial interests requiring the protection of the Royal Navy. John Cabot, a Venetian working for the English, had sailed across the Atlantic, in the ship *Mathew*, and discovered North America, Newfoundland in particular, in 1497. He thought he was on the other side of the world in Japan, but this error of navigation didn't prevent him claiming the land for England, although out of loyalty to his own country, he actually planted a Venetian flag when he went ashore. He retraced his steps back to England and reported a plentiful supply of fish, Halibut, Sole and Cod.

The English set about exploiting these fishing grounds, as did the French and Portuguese and not for the last time, English fishermen needed Royal Navy Protection - as they did 500 years later in the 1976 "Cod-war" between Iceland and Britain. Cabot had also reported signs of human habitation but as was usual in the days of empire-building such information was of little relevance – except in judging just how much resistance could be expected.

Thus America was being opened to European expansion and formed an early element of the British Empire. Expansion into America was primarily a matter of entrepreneurs looking for new trading and money-making opportunities or settlers running from famine (Ireland for example) or religious oppression (England for this example). Sir Walter Raleigh took advantage of these American opportunities; Raleigh was a successful entrepreneur but not a successful coloniser. He failed to colonise Virginia but did bring back to Britain, to Queen Elizabeth I, Potato, Tobacco plants and exotic hard-woods. The Pilgrim Fathers, escaping religious intolerance, endured the hardships of the Atlantic voyage and mastered the adverse conditions of this inhospitable land. They established settlements in Plymouth, in 1620, but it is not to be overlooked that this was on lands already occupied by the Massachusetts Indians.

George III, or rather his incompetent Prime Minister Lord North, forced the imposition of too many taxes upon these pioneers. On 16th December 1773 the American colonists had had enough and disgorged a cargo of tea into the Boston harbour. The Boston "tea-party" heralded the end this bit of the Empire.

But before America gained full independence there were some interesting and instructive naval encounters between this fledgling nation and Britain. In Chapter two we noted the St Lawrence River engagement here we look at the Battle of Chesapeake Bay. The French, who rarely needed much prompting to take up arms against the English, were helping the Americans in their struggle for separation from the motherland. A French fleet, commanded by De Grasse, was anchored in Chesapeake Bay, at 10 am September 5th, 1781, when the British men-o'-war hove into view. The British were led by Admiral Graves who managed to miss an excellent chance to trounce the French. Being an Englishman he politely waited while the French weighed anchor and made for Cape Henry and the open sea.

De Grasse obliged by bringing his fleet into an orderly line-ahead formation. It was not until 4 pm, when the two fleets were sufficiently well-ordered and formed into two parallel lines, that battle commenced. Once again those restrictive Fighting Instructions stifled any initiative Graves might have shown. This apparent lack of initiative on the part of the British fleet was of course due to Graves' technically correct insistence on sticking to the line-ahead rules of engagement. Some blame must also lie with his poor quality signalling between ships. First blood went to the British but despite the presence of battle-hardened Captains like Drake and Hood the French were soon causing grievous damage to the British vessels, although the French suffered more casualties. This was a clear victory for the French/American naval forces and it allowed reinforcements to reach Chesapeake. Achieving command of the sea at this time was seen as a turning point in favour of America's War of Independence [13].

To quote David Thomas (Battles & Honours); 'Graves was indecisive and lacking in resolution, he seemed reluctant to engage too closely and this brought about a spasmodic battle lasting several days. Graves held a council-of-war and, deciding that his ships were in a poor state of repair and lacking bread and water, he retired to New York to refit. This left de Grasse in command of Chesapeake Bay, The way was clear for Cornwallis's defeat and surrender a month later and with that the loss of the American colonies' [14].

The settlement of North America was largely a matter for merchant seamen, settlers and for trading companies willing to invest in the most doubtful of enterprises. There was no significant role for the Royal Navy.

South America was quite a different matter. In the southern part of the Atlantic Britain was challenging Spain's hold on the "Spanish Main" in the Caribbean. If British expatriates were seeking to settle and trade with the locals in North America the Spanish appeared to take quite a different approach in the South.

In 1511 The Spaniard Vasco Núñez de Balboa was sailing the Pacific Ocean and reporting his finds and by 1532 Fransisco Pizzaro determined to trace the gold, sliver treasurers rumoured to be so plentiful in the mountainous lands of Peru. Here the Incas came into fatal contact with the Spanish. By 1572 disease, slaughter and the disruption of a delicately balanced social order and a long established agricultural life pattern was wiped out by the Spaniards - the Incas civilisation ceased to exist.

The contrast between the Inca civilisation and the European's behaviour cannot be more striking and should be a salutary lesson to expansionist nations even in the 21st century. The following commentaries are a reminder to all that Empires were built at the cost of many human lives and destroyed many perfectly well ordered societies.

In Cuzco the capital of Inca Dynasty, on Sept. 18, 1589, the last survivor of the original conquerors of Peru, Don Mancio Serra de Leguisamo, wrote in the preamble to his Will the following:-

"We found these kingdoms in such good order, and the said Incas governed them in such wise that throughout them there was not a thief, nor a vicious man, nor an adulteress, nor was a bad woman admitted among them, nor were there

*immoral people. The men had honest and useful
occupations. The lands, forests, mines, pastures,
houses and all kinds of products were regulated
and distributed in such sort that each one knew his
property without any other person seizing it or oc-
cupying it, nor were there law suits respecting
it..."*

To take just a single example of the Spanish approach to
this well ordered society, the following quote describes Pizzaro's
execution of one of the last surviving Inca leader, thus:-

*"Pizarro invited Atahuallpa to a peace parlay,
then seized and imprisoned him. He demanded the
fabulous ransom of a room filled with gold and
silver. This, incredibly, the Incas delivered. Still
Atahuallpa was not released. Instead, he was
brought to trial on charges of murder, sedition,
and idolatry, and condemned to death by fire, [de-
spite] the protest of Pizarro's (own) most influen-
tial advisors."*

Of this event William H. Prescott, an American historian, wrote

*"....The persecution of Atahuallpa is regarded with
justice as having left a stain, never to be effaced,
on the Spanish arms in the New World......"* [15].

Such barbarity provides a timely reminder that the dominion of one nation over another can never be fully justified. However, the British Empire was enlarged without quite the same persistent and gratuitous violence. It is assumed that the British Empire was intended to increase trade and to provide military bases
for the British. Ultimately this depended upon a degree of coop-
eration from the indigenous populations, whether American, African, Indian or Oriental.

Having noted the appalling conduct of the Spanish towards
the Incas it is interesting to note the English Parliament's (stated)
sense of fair play and equal rights for the Indians in North America. The reader can draw his own conclusions as to the veracity of

Lawrence James' research (The Rise & Fall of the British Empire) and whether Parliamentary intent ever translated into Colonial deeds across the Atlantic. Parliament's stated position in respect of the indigenous American/Indians is reported as this:-

> "...in the eyes of the British Government such creatures were subjects of George III and as long as they kept his laws they had the right to expect protection. From1763 onwards the King's ministers and their officials in North America endeavoured to fulfil this obligation, particular protecting the Indians from the legal chicanery practised by speculators. By contrast the colonial merchants sought to hinder the Government's efforts. A means to cut through the tangle of conflicting rights and claims was finally devised in the summer of 1774 – the Quebec Act, but it only led to rebellion..." [16].

To return to the Spanish and their ill-gotten treasure, the British were very keen to relieve them of this gold; but not with any honourable intention of returning it to its rightful owner. No, this was the age of Pirates.

Piracy grew alongside empire building — when traders and settlers were discovering new lands but before naval forces were in place to protect them. It took the determined efforts of both the British and American Naves to control piracy, though it still remains a dangerous scourge especially in the Southern Oceans. But with sufficient numbers of pirates arrested and dispatched pirates were under some sort of control and allowed the expansion of empires to continue unabated.

America had been won and lost (possibly following Graves defeat at Chesapeake Bay), and this is acknowledged in the Treaty of Versailles, 1783. But by this time Canada had been ceded to Britain, under the Treaty of Paris, 1763 and Britain continued to increase her 'interests' in the South, particularly the Caribbean islands.

On the other side of the South Atlantic European empires, including Dutch, French, German as well as Britain, were variously and voraciously carving up Africa. Many of these possessions changing hands several times before establishing firm links and 'ownership' by any particular empire. Often land was gained through warfare – either defeat of the indigenous people or their current overlords. In some cases parts of a nation were swapped in deals between oppressing nations. One such rather obscure deal was struck between Britain and Germany in 1890 when Britain ceded Heligoland (a small island belonging first to Holland then Germany) to German in exchange for Zanzibar (Africa). Britain again took control of Heligoland for 7 years immediately after WWII.

Parts of China were similarly divided between those nations that had participated in the defeat of China during the Opium Wars in the latter part of the 19th Century. It was as recent as 1997, 1st July 1997 to be more precise, that Britain's control of Hong Kong returned to China after a 99 year lease-agreement lapsed, brining to an end Britain's spoils from the Opium Wars.

Different territories had different values within the British Empire. Some were primarily staging posts, bases or harbours, whilst some territories had a mutual dependency with Britain; Malta and Gibraltar in the Mediterranean and the St Helena islands in the South Atlantic for example. Others, such as the Caribbean islands provided a rich source of income and profit for the early settlers, mainly through sugar plantations, they gradually became less significant for their wealth generation and more useful as British bases, but the benefits to the Caribs is surely doubtful, the benefits were almost entirely in Britain's favour. South Africa was both an important trading nation and also provided important naval bases (Simonstown amongst others) when the Royal Navy operated in the Southern Oceans.

India was however quite another matter. It was said to have been the jewel in the crown of the British Empire. Its history as a British colony is long and complex and will not be reiterated here. Suffice to say the East India Company [BEIC] and Robert Clive, later Baron Clive of Plassey, dominated the development of India as part of the Empire. Early trading was through the BEIC and they had their own armed forces sanctioned by Britain. But control gradually moved from the BEIC, and Local Princes, to direct rule from Britain during Queen Victoria's reign, hence her title Empress of India. Whilst Britain's interests in India were primarily trading this trade was again more beneficial to Britain than to the Indian sub-continent – trading tariffs ensured this.

Control and protection of trade and trading routes was through the BEIC who, with the support of the British Government, created its own armed forces. In 1612 the BEIC organised a naval force, which pre-dated the Indian Navy. Its title changed over the years, the Surat Marine, the Bombay Marine, the Bengal Marine and latterly the Indian Navy. It was in essence a branch of the Royal Navy, in particular the East Indies Squadron, a position confirmed in 1891 when the Indian Marine was permitted to use the title Royal Indian Navy.

One of the earliest actions of this naval force was in January 1615 at Surat, in the Gulf of Khambhat to the North of Bombay. Briefly put, this was action against an old adversary of Britain, the Portuguese, and the Indian Navy performed well; the Portuguese were defeated with a loss of 350 lives. The Indian Navy continued to be well occupied defending trade and coastal bases from French, Portuguese, Dutch and even Russian interference in Britain's interests. And, as everywhere else in the Southern Oceans, piracy was also a constant blight.

In 1759 the Bombay Marine Service was in action against the French headquarters in Pondicherry, on the Southern tip of India. The frigate BMS *Protector* after two years of creditable action was finally lost in a gale during the siege of Pondicherry.

The Indian Navy's actions were not always defensive nor where they confined to the Indian sub-continent. In 1810 five ships of the Bombay Marine took part in the capture of Mauritius and they assisted in the conquest of Java (Indonesia). Later still the BMS played a prominent part in the First Burmese War 1824-26 with some fierce naval engagements on the Irrawaddy (Erawadi) off the Southern coast of Burma (Myanmar).

The many conflicts between Britain and the indigenous population were usually fought out in land-based confrontations. The Calcutta incident, more familiarly known as the 'Black Hole of Calcutta', in 1756 – this is the incident in which 75 British soldiers perished overnight. Or the Indian Mutiny, in 1857, which was the Indian Army's response to Britain's (allegedly but unlikely) imposition of cartridge shells 'contaminated' with pig-fat. These were matters for Army engagements rather than the Navy. Even so the Navy did provide additional Naval Brigades as man-power and sailors served often ashore with distinction. In First World War the Royal Indian Marine, as it was by then known, did invaluable work in the Persian Gulf and during the British advance up the Euphrates and Tigris Rivers and in defence of Egypt [17].

The Royal Indian Marine can also boast a first for the Royal Navy. That is, the first deployment of a steam ship, the *Diana*. She was owned by the East India Company and used by them in the First Burma War 1824. However, as is often the way, there are other contenders for this 'first'. In this case another steam ship '*Comet*', was ordered by the Admiralty in 1821, but this was a tug rather than a warship. The *Diana* however was a small, armed troop carrier and it was operated, in the Rangoon Region of Burma in the 1820s, under the command of Captain Frederick Marryatt (later to become the author of sea novels such as "Mr Midshipman Easy" [18]. The first use of a steam ship in combat goes to the British built ship *Karteria* in 1826 it was owned by the Greek and used in the Greek War of Independence [19].

And so the Empire expanded Eastward. In the Far East Britain was developing trading links with China and Japan and finding uses for its new territories in this area including the vast lands of Australia and the many small islands dotting the Pacific.

Australia was claimed for Britain by Captain Cook, although as noted earlier he referred to this land rather disparagingly as 'Terra nullis' during his voyage of the Pacific Ocean in 1768 and he was not the first Englishman to set foot here, William Dampier certainly preceded him. Britain gave Australia the curious function of prison overflow, a penal colony. New South Wales was described, more portentously by the Governor, Lachlan Macquarie, as a "Penitentiary Asylum on a grand scale". It exemplifies the various methods by which new lands were settled. As we know Britain transported many convicts to Australia as punishment, a form of banishment and hard labour but it was also seen a means of improving the mind and spirit of convicts, to deter them from crime and put them to good use opening new opportunities for Britain. Many of those sentenced to serve their time in Botany Bay started their journey from Portsmouth so the town acquired recognition as the 'Mother of Australia'.

These new lands and the banishment were intended to be a punishment, but for some it was an opportunity for entrepreneurial enterprise. A lot of those banished were no more than petty crooks, not hardened criminals and murderers as many may suppose, so once they were released from their enforced duties they put their new found health and skills to good purpose. In other parts of the developing colonies, America for example, craftsmen went to find their fortune, or death, as skilled labourers, whilst some were itinerant, jobless and cashless folk looking for mere survival. Many were slaves and not a few were servants, whose duties rendered them near slaves. Technically a servant was contracted and given a (very) small wage and they had a set time limit to their servitude, after which such servants would be free to make their own way in the new colonies. By contrast a slave was regarded as a possession, like a piece of furniture or mechanical equipment.

Australia's (own) naval defence dates from about 1866 when Queen Victoria's Government ordered coastal defence craft to be built. By 1892 South Australia had what was called a "cruiser". It was only a 920 ton cruiser - at a time when cruisers were typically 3 to 5 thousand tons. So this ship would more be accurately described as a "sloop". Nevertheless this mini-cruiser served in the RN during the Chinese Boxer rebellions at the end of the 19th Century [20].

It is with the Boxer uprising we shall finish this brief survey of the Royal Navy's role in empire building.

Battle honours were won by 11 ships of the RN during the (re-)capture of Peking 14th August 1900. The "Boxers" were a secret society, the 'Society of Righteous and Harmonious Fists' or 'I-ho chuän'. Under the guise of physical fitness training they plotted against the British and other nationals. This was part of the infamous opium wars. The Boxers laid siege to various legations in Peking and were relieved by forces supported by Naval Brigades [21].

Despite this action Britain had no intention of annexing much of China, just a small coastal region known as Hong Kong Island and the Kowloon peninsula. Hong Kong was one of the great sea ports of the world with two immense natural harbours, Deep Water Bay and Tytam Bay, it remained a British naval base for 99 years. The Dockyard closed in 1959 and Hong Kong was returned to China under the terms of the original lease on 1st July 1997. China, being a Communist, country has agreed a fifty-year extension to Hong Kong's capitalist system [22].

Other than this important far-east base, Britain's clear intention was *not* to bring China into its already expansive empire. Instead Britain's aim was to open trade routes. But once again Britain *was* willing to use force to ensure these new oriental trading 'partners' kept its markets open to Europeans and of course to Britain in particular.

Britain had two products to sell in China, Opium and Cotton in exchange for tea. The East India Company enjoyed a monopoly in the production of Opium, which apparently the Chinese people clamoured for — to the chagrin of their rulers. Not only did the Chinese Emperors, the Manchu Dynasty for example, not want their people imbibing this drug, they were equally scornful of trading with foreigners whom they saw as barbarians, whatever they might want to buy or sell. The First Opium War in 1839-42 and the Second Opium War in 1856-58 were (successful) exercises in intimidation of a nation (China) still functioning without the tools and weaponry available to Europeans. China capitulated to the terms of several treaties, the Treaty of Nanking in 1842 and the Treaty of Tientism in 1858 for example. These ensured Britain got her way, trading rights and Hong Kong as a British Base - until that is the popular uprising by the 'Boxer' rebels.

In 1856 Japan followed China into the world of international trade, but did so under threat of British intimidation.

One exciting diversion for the Navy was the capture of pirates, they were still operating with impunity in the Far East in the mid19th Century, but now there was a pirate's bounty on their head - £20 alive, £5 dead. The clear intention was to sweep the coastal waters, rivers and estuaries of these unauthorised 'traders' The Royal Navy found this (financially) rewarding work and excellent practice in small ship manoeuvres.

Before we leave this part of the world we need to remind ourselves of the Yangtze River episodes. In the middle of the 19th Century Britain could very readily demonstrate her Navy's mighty naval fire-power and quickly subdue any resistance to its Imperial might; but things were very different by 1949.

When the Second World War ended the British, along with the Americans, tried to reassert their control and influence in China, but after this war the world had changed irrevocably. Within a few years the Chinese Communists had driven out the Nationalists and with them all foreigners and so it returned to its former isolation. For the Royal Navy there was one last dramatic episode; the second Yangtze incident. The British Frigate HMS Amethyst, pennant number F116, was trapped up the Yangtze, or Ch'ang Chiang, River between Nanking and Shanghai.

HMS *Amethyst* had to try and make a dramatic withdrawal. To do so it had to run the gauntlet of Chinese gunfire. HMS *London* a 10,000 ton cruiser, accompanied by HM Ships

Consort and *Black Swan*, went to her aid but the *London's* size in the confines of the river was to her disadvantage and she was beaten back by shore batteries. Eventually the *Amethyst* made her own way through the barrages and but then ran aground off Rose Island where her remaining crew swam to the shore and made their way overland to Shanghai. Her Captain, Lieutenant Commander Bernard Skinner was killed and for his sacrifice was "mentioned in dispatches". In all twenty-three of her crew were killed and are buried in a Shanghai cemetery.

To demonstrate a peculiarity of war the records tell us that whilst Lt Cmr Skinner got a 'mention', Simon the ship's cat, a black and white tabby, received more than just a mention; this cat won the Dickin Medal for his contribution to the Yangtze action. Like his human counterparts, he stayed at his post to do his duty and continued to keep the rats at bay despite being wounded in the course of this untimely withdrawal. A lesser cat might have realised the game was up and moved onto a new owner. He was the first cat to be awarded this (animal) honour [23].

The *Amethyst* was the last foreign warship to be in Chinese inland waters without the permission of the Chinese government. This brought to a gallant close the history of foreign intervention in China.

Chapter 4: Pirates and Press Gangs

~~~~~~~~~~~~

Some authorities suggest the Golden Age of Pirates — swashbuck-ling, sword wielding brigands and buccaneers of the high-seas — was just 30 years at the beginning of the 18th Century. Other writ-ers, Peter Earle for example, trace piracy over two and half centu-ries [1]. In fact piracy remains a problem to the present time and still costs lives but not to the same extent. Piracy is now confined largely to the Southern Oceans whereas in the 18th Century no ocean-going trader was free of piracy. This chapter will look at the black side of the Royal Navy; problems of pi-racy, of press gangs and, the ultimate offence in the Royal Navy, Mutiny.

John Rackham "Calico Jack"
His pirate flag, circa 1720

Greed and an an-archic disregard for au-thority drew many sea-men, including sailors from the Royal Navy, into piracy. It is equally true that poverty and harsh living conditions at sea would have per-suaded many to take to this risky business. A pirate's life may have been carefree and bounteous but it was usu-ally a very short life; John Rackham for example spent just four short years plundering before being caught and hanged in 1720. A pirate had many enemies including his fellow outlaws; his "cap-tain"; other pirate ships plus the rest of the law-abiding sea-faring world and of course the navies of Britain and America.

Piracy flourished for a number of reasons not least because sea-faring nations were usually at war with each other and cared little about enterprising sailors who unofficially furthered their own objectives – especially if it was against ships from an enemy state. Indeed piracy was not always unofficial and illegal. There were ways in which enterprising Captains could fill their own cof-fers — so long as their sovereign also saw some profit.

Letters of Marque and Letters of Reprisal gave some legitimacy to "privateers". The first, Letters of Marque, were issued to private persons, rather than to armed forces, at times of war. It gave authority to the holder to seize the property of a belligerent state with whom the authorising nation was at war. In this case the privateer was acting on behalf of the sovereign in order to undermine the enemy and this was seen as an extension of the armed forces, but they acted quite independently of the Navy proper. In Britain's case the usual adversaries were either France or Spain.

Letters of Reprisal followed after a period of war. In this case the issuing nation was giving authority for a victim of war to seize property to the value of goods and materials lost to the enemy at times of war. These Letters of Reprisal were very valuable assets and could be handed down, father to son, over several generations [2,3].

If there was little difference between a privateer and pirate there even less difference between a pirate and buccaneer. The very marginal difference perhaps was that pirates had no 'rules of engagement' and would happily take on ships of all nations where buccaneers tended to avoid attacking ships from their own nation and were that much closer to the concept of 'privateer' with Letters of Marque. But this was a slim, and in most cases, invisible difference. With these rather flexible arrangements in place it is not surprising that the distinction between a privateer and pirate became blurred – to the advantage of the pirate.

The 'Jolly Roger' flag was used by pirates to declare their presence and their bloodthirsty intentions. The name derives from "Joli Rouge" (pretty red), in the typical English manner of misreading and poor translation of French terms. In this case a description of a red flag sometimes flown by pirates and originally made reference to a red flag flown by most navies about to go into battle, a declaration of engagement. In much the same way that a White Ensign declared the presence of the Royal Navy a Jolly Roger sent a chill into the hearts of the bravest sailor, but there were no rules of engagement here; you could be murdered on a whim.

This emblem became sufficiently notorious for many crews of merchant ships to submit to boarding and looting in the hopes that the pirates would spare their lives. There is no doubt that pirates were very savage and thought little of killing and maiming their hapless victims. This reputation meant that in many cases the mere appearance of a Jolly Roger flag was sufficient to deter opposition.

There was however one form of violence that is more myth than reality that is, to 'walk the plank'. As depicted in many pirate films, a wooden plank was secured over the side of the ship, the gunnels, the victim was blindfolded and induced to walk towards the end of the plank whereupon the plank was lowered and the man inevitably fell into the water − at which point the pirates would begin shooting at the hapless soul. There are one or two examples of its use, in 1769 one George Wood confessed that as a pirate he had forced men to 'walk the plank'. In 1822 a Cuban pirate forced a merchant seaman, by the name of Captain Smith, to take the same deadly stroll but this form of torture, murder, was apparently rarely used [4,5].

Like many villains, pirates had their own sense of justice − but it was rather arbitrary and probably depended more upon their humour and state of drunkenness than any sense of fair play. To cite an example, Edward England was the scourge of the Caribbean and African coast in 1718, but his sense of fairness was his undoing. He was put ashore by his own crew in favour of a more ruthless leader the likes of John Rackham. Rackham, known as "Calico Jack" for his colourful coats, he plundered the West Indies about the same time as England. Rackham is remembered for his love a lady pirate, Anne Bonny. According to Daniel Defoe he was totally pre-occupied by this lady, and his love for her was probably *his* undoing for he was captured in 1720. Survival as a pirate seemed to require a total disregard for humanity [6].

Given the rarity of female pirates it is worth noting the Anne Bonny was an Irish woman who ended up in the Bahamas and left her husband in favour of the pirate Jack Rackham. Bonny's attentions again wondered in the direction of another young 'man' who was in fact a female sailor. He, more correctly she, was a battle-hardened English soldier, she left the army and went to sea dressed as a cabin-boy. Her name was Mary Read. The pair were soon companions and were described as "lionesses in battle". They were sufficiently bloodthirsty to be sentenced to be hung with Rackham and others of his crew. They both sought to escape the death penalty by pleading leniency on the grounds of pregnancy. The British Courts proved to be humane in their attitude towards the unborn children and both had their sentences commuted to imprisonment. So much for equal opportunities, perhaps a misplaced chivalry was at work here. Peter Earle is of the opinion that these two women were amongst a small number of female pirates (as opposed to concubines of pirates) in the Caribbean [7].

Meanwhile the merchandise stolen by these pirates, male or female, were usually divided in agreed proportions according to their status. This went some way to ensuring pirates didn't kill each for their portion. Seeing the distribution of gold and silver and jewels shared in this manner was a great temptation for law abiding but impoverished sailors to swell the ranks of the marauding crew and abandon their honest ship-mates to their doom.

The business of piracy flourished until legitimate traders and travellers tired of their interference. The Royal Navy set about their downfall but it was not an easy task. Conditions for sailors in the Navy were dreadful, with poor pay, poor food and harsh discipline. The potential for mutiny amongst the law enforcers themselves was ever-present and it was not uncommon for sailors to transfer their loyalties from one service to the other. Occasionally the reverse would happen and pirates, in exchange for a pardon, would become the hunters.

One character who demonstrated the fluidity of roles was William Dampier (1652 to 1715). Dampier started his naval career enlisting as a seaman and then worked a while on the Caribbean islands. From the outset he was looking for adventure and having tried of logging and with the weather conditions against him he was forced to join company with a group of buccaneers. He claimed in retrospect to be 'with them' rather than 'of them'. Whatever the case he seems made his money and moved on. He is credited with circumnavigating the world no less than three times. But his adventures and his breadth of experience seems not to have taught him how to get the best out his crew. As Captain of the *Roebuck* in 1699 (and some 70 years before Captain James Cook 1754 to 1817) William Dampier set forth on an expedition into the Pacific Ocean to explore and chart such lands as he might discover. Dampier was an accomplished navigator and journalist and his findings are recorded in the frequently republished work 'A Voyage to New Holland' (Australia) 1703. But he was a poor manager of men and trouble dogged him from the outset. He was ultimately judged by Court Martial to be '*not a fit person to be employed as Commander of any of Her Majesty's Ships'.* He was evidently a more successful pirate than Commander but his legacy as navigator, observer/naturalist and diarist has been somewhat over-shadowed by other adventurers like Captain Cook and Captain Bligh [8].

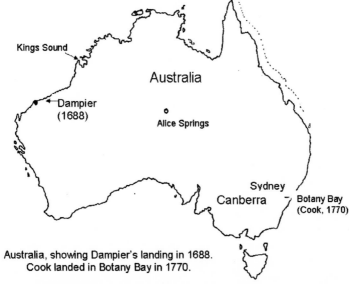

Australia, showing Dampier's landing in 1688.
Cook landed in Botany Bay in 1770.

Enterprising and adventurous as pirates and buccaneers were they had to be stopped — but pirates were difficult to intercept, the oceans are vast and pirates could steal any ship best suited to their purpose, fast sloops and frigates. These could often outrun the Navy. However, if pirate ships could outrun the Navy the Navy could easily out-gun the pirates, so the pirates needed the advantage of speed. Pirates also had the whole of the Southern Oceans with its infinite numbers of small islands to hide amongst. It was a "Cat & Mouse" game in which the Navy cruised the islands off the Caribbean Seas hoping to catch their prey in their lair. Douglas Botting describes very graphically the manner in which the Royal Navy (and the American, U.S. Navy) hunted down these marauders – but at times the chase was farcical, a complete shambles, not least because the Pirates were often caught unawares, caught literally napping or very drunk and were then easily led into traps. Captain Ogle, H.M.S. *Swallow* lured one of the ships of the bloodthirsty Bartholomew Roberts', *Great Ranger*, into one such trap.

Douglas Botting paints the picture [9].

> *"... by 11 am the Great Ranger was within musket shot of the Swallow. Incredible as it may seem, it was not until this point that the captain, James Skyrme, to his horror realised that both he and Roberts had made a terrible mistake. Suddenly with speed and precision the Navy ship turned to starboard, ran out her lower guns and let fly a devastating broadside. This turn of events seems to have befuddled the pirates. For a moment they dithered. They hauled their pirate flag down. Then they hauled it back up again. Rather than flee they decided to fight. They fired a return broadside at the Swallow. They stood on the poop deck wildly swinging their cutlasses in an optimistic gesture of aggression. Skyrme urged his men to board the Swallow but they could not bring themselves to take this drastic and dangerous step and by 3 pm it was too late... ten pirates lay dead, twenty wounded, the Great Ranger dismasted and beyond fighting or fleeing, Skyrme struck his flag and asked for quarter."*

Skyrme, Roberts and dozens of pirates were brought to trial – a surprisingly fair Vice-Court Martial in the British-held Cape Coast Castle, in Ghana on the West coast of Africa. Those able to prove they had been forced into piracy – as many were – were set free the others hung. In all 74 men were acquitted; 54 sentenced to death; 17 committed to the Marshalsea Prison in London and 20 sentenced to seven years hard labour (none of these survived this ordeal).

The Royal Navy was kept very busy chasing pirates and even when they did manage to bring pirates to justice that justice was sometimes rather perverse, as in the case of HMS *Ruby* and the Pirate 'Captain' Bannister. Captured by the *Ruby*, Bannister was acquitted at his first trial and managed to escape from confinement while awaiting re-trial. He didn't take the hint that this might be a good time to change his ways and went sailing off to more piracy — however his luck ran out six months later when

HMS *Drake* finally caught up with Bannister. This time he was brought to trial, convicted and hung [10]. A great many Royal Navy warships were sent out to hunt pirates ships but they frequently failed to intercept them, what successes they had usually involved capture of the crew on land. HMS *Greyhound* was an exception, like the pirate's own sloops it was light and fast, in fact it was light enough to be rowed in shallow, coastal waters or in windless condition; this came as something of an unpleasant surprise to some pirates.

As Peter Earle describes, the hero of the hour was the Captain of the *Greyhound*, Peter Solgard and the action takes place, in June 1723 not in the more usual hunting ground of the Caribbean but off Long Island, New York. Captain Solgard located the pirate leaders, Charles Harris and Edward Lowe. The usual exchange of signals preceded the clash, the pirates raised their black 'pirate' flag assuming the *Greyhound* would give way; when it didn't the pirates then raised a red flag – a universal signal for battle and their intention to give no quarter. In the exchange of gun fire the pirate were getting the worst of it so they took to their oars. In the past this had allowed them to outmanoeuvre the warship and to retreat to shallow waters but on this occasion the *Greyhound* also took to her oars and kept up the chase, coming between the two pirate ships and raking both ships with broadsides. Harris and twenty-five of his crew were caught – and later hung. Lowe however took advantage of nightfall and escaped as darkness fell.

This marked a turning point and in Peter Earle's commentary it looked as if the war against piracy was won [11]. But, despite the Royal Navy's successes, piracy remained a serious problem into the early years of 19th Century. By this time America decided it must deal with piracy once-and-for-all. In 1823 (a full one hundred years after HMS *Greyhound*'s successes) the United States commissioned the West India Squadron, an anti-pirate fleet, which over the next two years routed the pirates. Interestingly two tactics used by the U.S. Navy were small flat-bottom boats used to get close into shore and decoy merchant ships secretly armed with heavy cannon. These were precursors to the Landing Craft and Decoy ships, important weapons used by the Royal Navy in both World Wars. The decoy boats were referred to as "Q-ships", this time aimed at defeating German submarines.

The U.S. Navy did not however deal with piracy once-and-for-all; in 2003 the International Maritime Bureau's reported that that was a 'black year for piracy'. There were no less than 445 pirate attacks recorded, in which 100 passengers and crew paid with their lives.

As ever, it is the presence of naval forces that have ensured such attacks are reduced if not curtailed but as this chapter has indicated the distinction between ships operating within international maritime laws, privateering, outright piracy and even mutiny were somewhat blurred in Tudor and Stuart times. It is perhaps not surprising that Royal Navy sailors occasionally deserted their ship to offer their services to a pirate ship, despite the inevitable and deadly consequences. For some it was the safer option given the bloodthirsty nature of pirates, it may well be sensible to throw your lot in with the outlaws and live to see at least a few more days and possibly spend them carefree, drunk and relatively rich if you earned a share of their bounty.

For some sailors, to be a pirate was merely reverting to old habits given that many sailors in the Royal Navy were already convicted criminals needed to make up the numbers to man His Majesty's Ships. It should be emphasised this refers to sailors in the 18th/19th Century and not the 21st; sailors of this age are very professional and law-abiding – most of the time.

Recruitment was always a serious problem, a sailing ship required several hundred men to work the sails and man the guns and a fleet at war may well have fifty to hundred or more ships-of-the-line. So, many thousands of men were needed. A variety of solutions were available to ships Captains. Officers were enlisted by way of recommendation, patronage and personal influence — until qualifying examinations and a more structured intake system was introduced — typically the sons of gentlemen entered the service as Captain's Servants but this was gradually supplanted by the Naval Academy (Royal Naval College) so that officer-recruits had basic training before putting to sea. Pepys initiated the principle of a professional examination for all officer entrants but nomination by officers was only abolished, transformed from 'nomination' to mere 'recommendation', in 1913.

As for the 'other ranks', the men needed to fill the ships and undertake the labour, far from taking a qualifying examination to join the ship, there was an open invitation for anyone to volunteer their services and if men didn't volunteer in sufficient numbers then there were quite a few other methods for getting men on board His Majesty's Ships. Queen Elizabeth recognised the importance of manning her ships with experienced seamen so she devised a cunning plan — to add extra Fish Days to each week; as well as fish on Fridays, in deference to Catholic custom and practice, she also instigated extra days when no meat was to be eaten. This had the effect of increasing the sale of fish and the need for fishermen to catch the fish; this in turn increased the pool of experienced seamen capable of working a man-o-war when required to serve in her Majesty's ships.

This system didn't last for long and by the 18th Century the core crew would be volunteers, experienced sailors who will have joined the Navy as 'Boys'. These boys were usually orphans, waifs and strays or young lads in trouble with the law; they would have been 'volunteers' but it is unlikely they had much choice. Nevertheless, they would have adapted to a life at sea would become the most experienced and dedicated section of the crew. Typically at the time of Nelson's Trafalgar for example volunteers might account for about 15% of the crew and boys another 8%. That leaves a big gap to fill and at this point the Captain turned to impressment, a precursor to conscription.

Impressment was virtually legalised kidnapping. Much as people might imagine, a group of sailors, a Press Gang, marched into a pub or bar, snatching several unwilling drunkards and dragging them back to the ship.

One has to presume this was how Lieutenant Andrew Miller operated; so successful was he in acquiring ships' crews his name became synonymous with the Royal Navy itself, sailors might still refer to themselves as being in the 'Andrew'.

Whilst the experience of being pressed might feel like kidnapping in reality there were rules about which men were to be 'pressed'. Indeed the very term impressment refers to a fee paid in advance for services to be rendered and therefore implies a contract of sorts. Accepting this small fee was known as 'taking the King's shilling' and indicated your willingness to join the Andrew, or more typically the Army. The rules were that only seafaring men were to be taken and the Press Gang must include a commissioned Officer, usually a Lieutenant. It was therefore not unusual for Press Gangs to board merchant ships homeward bound and take for the Royal Navy a proportion of merchant seamen. Such men might have already spent six months at sea and must have been dismayed if they caught the eye of the Lieutenant. To the 23% volunteers and boys can now be added about 50% pressed men.

Next to join ship might be foreigners and not infrequently mercenaries from the very nations Britain was at war with. French sailors were a typical example and they fought alongside Nelson at Trafalgar. About 12% of the crew might be foreigners and some of them will have been 'pressed' into service but we still don't have a full ship's complement so things are getting desperate for the Captain and for the Admiralty.

The next group of men were in some ways the most controversial and certainly caused great resentment amongst the ship's crew. The 'Quota Men' derived from the Quota Acts of 1795. Each County in England had to supply a proportion of men for sea duty according to the size and population of the County and a reward or bounty was to be paid to these 'quota men'. Not surprisingly if other men had volunteered or been pressed by Andrew Millar for just a shilling and to add to the injustices they usually had to wait many months for their wages. Such men were inevitably unhappy to see quota men bribed, with quite large sums of money in some cases, into joining the ship.

Along with the unwelcome quota men, who were largely landsmen with little idea of life at sea, also came even more undesirables. Debtors, 'rogues and vagabonds' and convicted criminals, who were directed to serve on His Majesty's Ships; they had a choice — prison or ship. Given the choice, some actually preferred prison.

Finally the quaintest group of nascent sailor was 'My Lord Mayor's Men'; typically this might be a gentleman from a 'good' family who found himself in trouble and wishing to avoid embarrassment to his family would 'go to sea' to keep out of harms way until the coast was clear [12].

All these unhelpful solutions were only in place at time of war and were replaced by Conscription, or National Service, for Hostilities Only service (HO). Conscription applied to all eligible young men and in that respect was fair and equitable and all would have received basic training before going into their designated service, Army, Navy and latterly the Air Force.

With such a diverse group of inexperienced men to work the ship a rigid discipline was necessary if the ship was to function as an effective fighting machine and Royal Navy ships were by reputation potent and awesome fighting machines. With such a disagreeable and reluctant band of men working the ships many must have been very resentful; conditions on board could dreadful and discipline was at time harsh. Even so it was comparable with life ashore and in many respects may have improved the lot of many — with regular food, (irregular) pay, free health care (albeit in a rather primitive form) and the opportunity to travel and see the world if they were lucky. Nevertheless life on board ship was not easy.

Desertion and mutiny was always a potential threat to good order and discipline but the Articles of War (see appendices) would tend to suppress any thought of indiscipline. The Articles of War on board a Royal Navy ship assumed the proportions and gravity of holy writ. It served as the law and *axis mundi* of life in His Majesty's Ships. It was read at least once a month, usually when church was rigged on Sunday, and when punishment was inflicted. The Articles were originally established in the 1650s, amended in 1749 by Act of Parliament and again in 1757. It is a daunting document to ponder, especially the number and type of offences that were punishable by death [13]. To cite just one Article No.19:-

'If any person in or belonging to the fleet shall make or endeavour to make any mutinous assembly upon any pretence whatsoever, every person offending herein, and being convicted thereof by the sentence of the court martial, shall suffer death: and if any person in or belonging to the fleet shall utter any words of sedition or mutiny, he shall suffer death....according to the nature of his offence by the judgement of a court martial.'

This was a substantive deterrent but a good Captain, one that engendered loyalty, could keep a ship happy despite the common hardships. Captain James Cook, of the Pacific discoveries, was one such Captain; Nelson was of course another. Conversely others, like William Dampier of the *Roebuck* and William Bligh of the *Bounty*, were the worst possible men to lead a crew of such mixed backgrounds. Bligh, and far too many like him, bred discontent in the most loyal of men and it might be said between the Admiralty's poor overall management of their sailors' welfare and the incompetence of individual Captains it is surprising there were not more men ready to jump ship, desert or worse still incite mutiny.

There have been many mutinies in navies throughout the world and quite few in Her Majesty's Royal Austalian, Indian and Canadian Navies. There are however surpsrisngly few mutinies recorded in the Royal navy — perhaps a cover-up but it is more likley most Captains got the balance between authority and humanity about right.

Those few mutines involving British warships include the following as mentioned in various books listed in the bibliography and on various World Wide Web sites. They are described in some detail here as it demonstrates the enthusiasm with which the Admiralty pursued offenders – although it is to be noted with some chagrin this energy was lacking when it came to sailors' well being and even their basic pay [14].

Mutinies in the Royal Navy:-

1   HMS *Bounty* 1789; On the morning of April 28th, 1789, led by Master's Mate Fletcher Christian, twelve crew members staged the now famous mutiny, capturing the ship, and setting the Captain, Lieutenant William Bligh and his loyal supporters adrift in the ship's launch. This was the first of three mutinies during Bligh's career. The second was at the Nore in 1797 and the third was the New South Wales mutiny whilst he was their newly appointed Governor. On this third occasion he was himself arrested and returned to England.

2   HMS *Blanche* 1797; An incident aboard the frigate *Blanche* saw Nelson, the diplomat, intervening to settle a dispute between the newly appointed Captain Henry Hotham and his crew. Hotham had a reputation as a tough disciplinarian and the crew refused to accept him. An American sailor, Jacob Nagle, recorded the event:

"Hotham came on board on 7th. January 1797, had the officers armed on the quarterdeck and all hands turned aft to hear his commission read at

*the capstan head. They all cried out, 'No, no, no.'
He asked what they had to say against. One of the
Petty Officers replied that his ship's company
informed us that he was a damned tartar and we
would not have him and [we] went forward and
turned the two forecastle guns aft with cannister
shot.*

"*...He then went in his boat on board Commodore
Nelson's ship and returned with the Commodore's
first lieutenant. When on board he ordered all
hands aft. He called all the petty officers out and
paraded them in a line on the quarterdeck. 'Now,
my lads, if you resist taking Captain Hotham as
your captain, every third man shall be hung.' The
crew flew in a body forward to the guns with
match in hand, likewise crowbars, handspikes,
and all kinds of weapons they could get hold of
and left him, Captain Hotham and the officers
standing looking at us. They consulted for a
moment and returned on board Commodore
Nelson's ship.*
"*In the space of half an hour the Commodore
himself came on board, called all hands aft, and
enquired the reason of this disturbance. He was
informed of Captain Hotham's character, which
was the reason that we had refused him.
" 'Lads', said he, 'You have the greatest character
on board the Blanche of any frigate's crew in the
navy. You have taken two frigates superior to the
frigate you are in, and now to rebel?' 'If Captain
Hotham ill treats you, give me a letter and I will
support you.' Immediately, there was three cheers
given and Captain Hotham shed tears, and Nelson
went on board his ship....*"

3   HMS *Hermione*, 1797 was the worst
year for the navy because a mutinous trend
seemed to spread through the service and it
resulted in serious outbreaks at Spithead (near
Portsmouth) and The Nore (the ports in the

Thames estuary) which led to courts martial and a number of hangings. It also saw the worst case of mutiny at sea when the crew of the frigate *Hermione* rebelled against the officers, killed the Captain and eight other officers, took possession of the ship and committed the unthinkable act of surrendering it to the enemy. What drove the crew to such extreme action that mutiny became murder and could even be regarded as an act of treason?

Captain Pigot of *Hermione* was a tough disciplinarian, a "martinet" who provoked his men into taking matters into their own hands and risk hanging rather than serving under such a brutal master. Pigot had ordered sail to be shortened but didn't like the way the topmen had performed and threatened to flog the last two men who descended from the rigging. In the ensuing panic, two men fell to their deaths on the deck below and to compound the cruelty of his threat, Captain Pigot ordered the bodies to be thrown overboard. It was hardly surprising that, during the coming night, loose cannon-balls were rolled around the deck as an ominous warning that mutiny was impending.

However, the navy could not simply sit back and do nothing. A raid by the frigate HMS *Surprise* recaptured the *Hermione* from the Spanish and many of the mutineers were rounded-up, court martialled and hanged. No-one emerged from this with any credit but it served to highlight the fact that there were many aspects of the service that needed urgent attention.

4   Spithead and Nore 1797; The Spithead mutiny in April 1797 did lead to general improvements in conditions His Majesty's Ships. The Channel Fleet under Lord Bridport mutinied and refused to weigh anchor. There was no violence and no-one was hurt but sixteen battleships, the main defence of the kingdom, remained at anchor until a list of grievances were

examined by the Admiralty who, within a week, granted the first pay-rise since 1658 and agreed to better food and provisions. All the mutineers were pardoned. But, the mutiny spread to The Nore where it appeared to some to be a more sinister, politically motivated affair. Here, the mutineers demanded more shore-leave, regular payment of wages, fairer distribution of prize money, removal of unpopular officers and changes in the Articles of War but, this time, they went too far. On the face of it, such demands seemed reasonable enough but the mutineers attempted to blockade the *London* merchant trade and this provoked both the Admiralty and the government to act against them. For a while it looked as though other British warships were going to engage them and the mutineers soon realised that they were in trouble and, one by one, the ships surrendered including the flagship HMS *Sandwich* where the mutiny had started. The mutiny achieved nothing and Richard Parker, the leader, was hanged along with others who were seen as activists. Many more were flogged or imprisoned. A refusal to obey orders was one thing but attempts to disrupt the nation's trade was quite another. It should also be noted that Richard Parker joined the Navy as a debtor rather than a volunteer and provides a very good reason why Quota Men and criminals were not the best source of manpower for the Navy.

5   HMS *Marlborough* 1797; Contemorary records provide the following commentary: "...this ship being known to the commander-in-chief to have been among the most disorganised at Spithead, had been ordered to take her berth in the centre, at a small distance from the rest of the fleet. It, however, had so happened that a very violent mutiny in her had broken out at Beerhaven, and again during the passage, which had been suppressed by the officers, but chiefly by the First Lieutenant. The very object too of this mutiny was

to protect the life of a seaman who had forfeited it by a capital crime. A court-martial on the principal mutineers was immediately assembled; and one was no sooner sentenced to die than the commander-in-chief ordered him to be executed on the following morning,

"and by the crew of the 'Marlborough' alone, no part of the boats' crews from the other ships, as had been usual on similar occasions, to assist in the punishment,"

On the receipt of the necessary commands for this execution, the captain of the *"Marlborough"*, Captain Ellison, waited upon the commander-in-chief, and reminding his Lordship that a determination that their shipmates should not suffer capital punishment had been the very cause of the ship's company's mutiny, expressed his conviction that the *Marlborough's* crew would never permit the man to be hanged on board that ship."

Receiving the Captain on the *Ville de Paris'* quarter-deck, before the officers and ship's company, hearkening in breathless silence to what passed, and standing with his hat in his hand over his head, as was his Lordship's invariable custom during the whole time that any person, whatever were his rank, even a common seaman, addressed him on service, Lord St. Vincent listened very attentively till the captain ceased to speak; and then, after a pause, replied, -

"What do you mean to tell me, Captain Ellison, that you cannot command his Majesty's ship the 'Marlborough'? for if that is the case, sir, I will immediately send on board an officer who can."

The captain then requested that, at all events; the boats' crews from the rest of the fleet might, as always had been customary in the service, on executions, attend at this also, to haul the man up; for he really did not expect the "Marlborough's" would do it.

Lord St. Vincent sternly answered: *"Captain Ellison, you are an old officer, sir, have served long, suffered severely in the service, and have lost an arm in action, and I should be very sorry that any advantage should be now taken of your advanced years. That man shall be hanged, at eight o'clock to-*

morrow morning, and by his own ship's company: for not a hand from any other ship in the fleet shall touch the rope. You will now return on board, sir; and, lest you should not prove able to command your ship, an officer will be at hand to you who can."

Accordingly, at seven the next morning, all the launches, ready and armed, proceeded from the "*Prince*" to the "*Blenheim*," and thence, Captain Campbell having assumed the command, to the "*Marlborough*." Having lain on his oars a short time alongside, the captain then formed his force in a line athwart her bows, at rather less than pistol-shot distance off, and then he ordered the tompions to be taken out of the carronades, and to load.

At half-past seven, the hands throughout the fleet having been turned up to witness punishment, the eyes of all bent upon a powerfully armed boat as it quitted the flag-ship; every one knowing that there went the provost-marshal conducting his prisoner to the "*Marlborough*" for execution. The crisis was come; now was to be seen whether the "*Marlboroughs*" crew would hang one of their own men.

The ship being in the centre between the two lines of the fleet, the boat was soon alongside, and the man was speedily placed on the cathead and haltered. A few awful minutes of universal silence followed, which was at last broken by the watch-bells of the fleet striking eight o'clock. Instantly the flag-ship's gun fired, and at the sound the man was lifted well off; but then, and visibly to all, he dropped back again; and the sensation throughout the fleet was intense. For, at this dreadful moment, when the eyes of every man in every ship were straining upon this execution, as the decisive struggle between authority and mutiny, as if it were destined that the whole fleet should see the hesitating unwillingness of the "*Marlborough's*" crew to hang their rebel, and the efficacy of the means taken to enforce obedience, by an accident on board the ship the men at the yard-rope unintentionally let it slip, and the turn of the balance seemed calamitously lost; but then they hauled him up to the yard-arm with a run, - the law was satisfied, and, said Lord St. Vincent at the moment, perhaps one of the greatest of his life, "Discipline is preserved, sir!". This dreadful sentence was again and again inflicted, and in all cases of insubordination the crews were invariably the executioners of their own rebels; but never again was the power of the (naval) law doubted by any one.

6   HMS *Danae* 1800; On 6th March 1800 it sailed from Plymouth on a cruise to the westward and at about half past nine on the 14 March when most of the officers were in bed, the marine officer came to the captain's cabin to inform him that there was a mutiny on the deck. He attempted to get up the after-hatchway but found that it was blocked by twenty men, and when he was stunned by a cut to the head, they were able to secure the remaining hatches. The Captain distributed a few muskets and cutlasses to about forty loyal men who were still in their hammocks in hopes that the mutineers would be forced by the weather to stand out to sea. Unfortunately the wind changed and the following morning the ship was able to reach Conquet in Finisterre where a large number of French troops came on board and took possession. Capt. Proby, his officers and the loyal members of the crew were honourably acquitted of blame at a court martial on board the *Gladiator* on 17 June. On 12 June the *Indefatigable* captured the French privateer *Vengeur* which had sailed from Bordeaux two days previously for Brazil. The 200 men on board were taken to the Mill prison in Plymouth and on 24 August, while they were about to be marched to Stapleton prison, Lieut. Neville Lake, who had been first of *Danae*, spotted one John Barnett who had been a principal ringleader of the mutiny. In other circumstances he would probably have escaped detection since he was from Jersey and spoke perfect French. Barnet was tried by court martial on 2 September and sentenced to death. At half past ten o'clock on 9 September the prisoner was taken to a platform on the forecastle of the *Pique*, and after he had prayed for some time he was run up to the fore-yard arm. The body remained hanging for an hour and was then taken to the Royal Naval Hospital.

7   Invergordon 1931. Incident in the British Atlantic Fleet, Cromarty Firth, Scotland, on 15 September 1931. Ratings refused to prepare the ships for sea following the government's cuts in their pay; the cuts were consequently modified.

8   HMS *Apollo* 1958. The most recent alleged mutiny is rather

obscure, the only reference found for this incident is a note that "Captain Michael Lumby was sent out to investigate the mutiny". The incident is recorded as taking place in 1958; the ship then named Apollo was a small minelayer – its unlikely that such a small ship with an equally small crew would find itself so ill-disposed as to mutiny without support from other big-ship crews. Until further information comes to light this will be discounted as another naval myth.

This chapter has looked at the less glamorous and sometimes ignoble side of the Royal Navy, in the next chapter we review the progress made in the ship construction.

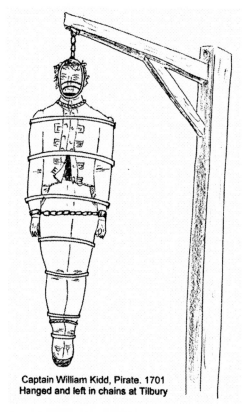

Captain William Kidd, Pirate. 1701
Hanged and left in chains at Tilbury

The end of Captain Kidd and the end of this chapter.

Chapter 5: 1805 - 1900,
Steam and Steel

~~~~~~~~~~

The Royal Navy is now a well-established fighting force, cruising the world oceans and patrolling the Empire. Year by year its ships have improved, from square-rigged, sailing men-o-war to metal-plated vessels, with ever bigger guns. This chapter looks at that transition; from sail to steam, from wood to steel. Most of these developments took place in Queen Victoria's reign, 1837 to 1901.

The first ironclad warships were built in 1850s and the last all-wood sailing ship built 1858. This heralded the beginning of steel ships. The transitional period included 'combination-ships', iron plates on wooden hulls and steam plus sails, and these curious combinations continued for some time. But wooden hulls and sails had had their day and with them went the "wooden walls of England", Nelson's legacy of 100 years of peace in Britain because she had a strong naval force policing the world's oceans.

The last battle between sailing ships was at Navarino Bay. British, French & Russian forces allied against Greek & Turkish forces. For the record, the allies won the day.

If Navarino was the last battle between sailing ships then the North American encounter between the 'Merrimack' (rebuilt by the Confederates as the 'Virginia') and the 'Monitor' (for the Unionists) was the first battle of ironclads. This was a sea-going adventure during the American Civil War and took place in 1862. The Royal Navy did not take part in this first all-metal affair.

As for the result this, then novel, encounter; the Unionists withdrew after several hours exchange of heavy gunfire. A draw some say. The outcome may be in doubt as it often is in battle. Whatever impact on the opposing forces this exchange of fire marked the end of centuries of wooden sailing ships as warships [1].

This was now a time for experimenting with new ideas. The Russians amused us with their completely round ships. They were revolutionary ships, pun intended, and a novel interpretation of the earlier meaning of 'round' i.e. a Cog-type ship rather than Longship. The 'Novgorod' and the 'Admiral Popov' were sent out on their first trials in 1874 and steamed up the River Dnieper but were quickly overtaken by the tidal flow and swept out to sea –

literally in a whirl. The crew were quite unable to steer these circular monsters in a straight course. They were in fact better suited as fortresses and so they were anchored as ostensibly as floating forts but they were also a huge success as a tourist attraction. The French version of a circular ship, in 1798, was even more peculiar; it was intended to be powered by several windmills but their first Iron-clad the *Gloire* preceded Britain's efforts and goaded them into building bigger and better protected ships, starting with *Warrior*.

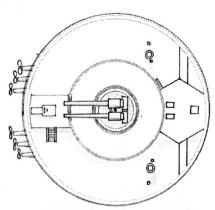

The Russian ship, *Poppoffka Novgorod*, 1873.
A single gun turret with an uninterrupted sweep but incapable of being steered in a straight line.

Britain's early trials were less amusing than the Russian's round ship. H.M.S. *Warrior*, built in 1860, might be considered the first true modern warship although other ships content for the title first all iron hull, the Warrior was the first iron-hulled warship. Canal boats, including the *Vulcan* for example, were the first passenger carrying boats to be made of iron, and the first ocean going ship was the *Aaron Manby*. Another contender for first warship is the East India Company's *Nemesis* built 1839.

Initially ironclad ships were not a success, at least not for the Royal Navy. The metal in use then was too brittle and quite unsuited to conditions expected of a Navy warship, far too brittle in cold weather and apt to shatter when pounded by gun fire. Experience had taught the Admiralty that a wooden warship could absorb an enormous battering and still remain afloat.

To return to the *Warrior*, her claim to fame is the use of armour plating, in that sense it becomes the first 'battleship' of modern times. But as it had only one gun deck it was more accurately described as a 'frigate', although at the time it would have made short work of any First Rate, three-decked, wooden-hulled battleship that preceded her.

Propulsion was the next consideration for the Navy. James Watts is given the credit for inventing the first practical steam engine and these were adapted to work side-mounted (and sometimes stern-mounted) paddle wheels. The age of paddle wheels as a main means of propulsion lasted just thirty years, 1815 to 1865. However, they remained in use for the Navy well into the middle of the 20th Century, certainly in Portsmouth Dockyard where tugs with paddle wheels were seen daily moving warship around the harbour. They were powerful and highly manoeuvrable vessels.

Several ships were built in combination, it could be said this was the age of combination ships, steam and sail, wood and iron, large and small calibre guns and so forth. HMS *Warrior* is the prime example of combination building – steam and sail. It produced some curious arrangements trying to allocate positions for the guns so they that wouldn't hamper the rigging and vice versa.

The next quandary for the navy was whether to stay with paddles, now a tried and tested system of propulsion, or go with the new and innovative screw propeller. Amongst its earliest proponents in 1836, and the man with the better design for this device, was the Englishman Francis Petit Smith but the Swede John Ericsson also worked on a similar if less successful screw in 1837. The practical demonstration between the *Ratler* and the *Alecto* is well known, in truth the Navy had already decided to go with the screw but the demonstration was a worthwhile publicity stunt. No doubt there were many die-hards within the Royal Navy that would need convincing and the *Ratler's* success was very convincing. For those unaware of this little piece of sea-borne history on 30th March 1845, the *Ratler* was roped to the *Alecto*, end to end; both set their engines full steam ahead to produce a most entertainer tug-of-war.

The screw propeller won and is now fitted to all ships in preference to a side-paddle [2]. In 1825 Captain Samuel Brown invented or at least experimented with a twin bladed propeller fitted to the bows but this was something of a novelty and propellers ended up at the stern; although bow-thrusters are now frequently fitted to the forward end of larger ships to help manoeuvre them.

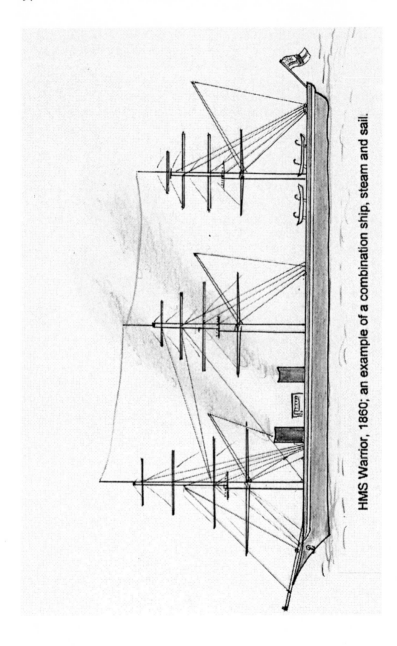

HMS Warrior, 1860; an example of a combination ship, steam and sail.

Not unusual for this organisation, the Admiralty had shown considerable tardiness in accepting the screw propeller, in preference to side-mounted paddle wheels or indeed sails [3]. Innovation often comes slowly to the Royal Navy; In 1837 Sir William Symonds, Surveyor to the Navy, was advising that a screw propeller would make her majesty's ships impossible to steer. Perhaps he had in mind the circular Russian ship *Novgorod*, which was nearly impossible of steering in a straight line despite six propellers — although it was building on the work of British ship designers developing shorter wider warships to give a more stable gun platform, the Novgorod took this idea to its extreme. The Russian Royal Family must have been pleased with the results because a third circular ship, the *Livadia*, was built as their Royal Yacht [4].

Royal Navy's ships, the '*Devastation*' and the '*Thunderer*' were the first of the Royal Navy's battleships built without rigging, in 1872. They were not a great success because the Royal Navy in its traditionally conservative manner had chosen to use mussel-loading guns rather then the modern (1860) breech-loading system. On January 2nd 1879 the *Thunderer* had a serious accident. The 12" gun blew up while being loaded, causing the death of two officers and nine ratings and injuring many more. The Admiralty finally accepted the common wisdom of breech loading guns in 1881.

Although the Royal navy was sometimes slow in its procurement process the Navy was nevertheless amongst the first with many innovations. To be fair this was a situation the Admiralty couldn't really win – they could choose to be the first to innovate and risk costly and sometimes foolish mistakes or keep with tried and tested equipment and end up facing superior forces with the latest equipment.

The fate of HMS *Captain* explains the dilemma. HMS *Captain* was designed and built to have a full set of sails with all the accompanying masts and rigging and had a lower gun deck with turret mounted guns – it solved the problem of having large guns capable of a wide sweep without fouling the rigging. Sadly what seemed like a reasonable compromise failed, because the lower deck was too low; the freeboard, the height of the ship above the water line, was so low that water washed into the ship and it soon capsized.

By 1841 the Royal Navy was using steam power, one of the earliest examples was a steam driven paddle-boat, a small sloop, sent out as part of a squadron to mount a blockade of the Chinese coast. Paddle driven ships had a definite advantage in coastal waters because they could manoeuvre in the shallow waters of estuaries and rivers. Conversely, the screw propeller and steam-engines could be fitted in much larger warships such as the HMS *Agamemnon* in 1850. But at first these engines were not popular with naval officers — because the coal dust and soot fouled the spotless decks!

For the Royal Navy a number of other fundamental issues were tackled in this 'combination ' era, such as the optimum size and number of guns for a ship; how those guns should be mounted, in fixed barbette or rotating turrets; how those should be loaded, via the mussel or breech-loaded (i.e. whether to load at the front, open-end which a time wasting and slow affair, or fit breech-opening mechanism - also time consuming and without a strong, a gas-tight fit very dangerous). Armour plating was also a vital consideration. As guns and the shells they fired became increasingly powerful so the ships carrying them had to be bigger and stronger and they had to be defended against the onslaught by the enemy's equally potent armaments. In later chapters we shall see how those issues were resolved and revised with experience.

Other inventions were clearly more immediately and obviously successful from the start, including the use of steel for ships' hulls. From about 1870 steel production made its use cheap and viable for whole ships hulls and not just specialist machinery parts. The Navy has to thank Sir Henry Bessemer for inventing, in 1855, a system for turning pig-iron into steel by using a 'tilting converter' and blasting air through it. To the Navy's benefit he specialised in gun-making.

This period of innovation, 1850 to 1900, with all its triumphs and disasters is now called the pre-dreadnought era. It could be seen as preparation for the "dreadnoughts" to come at the turn of the century.

Before we leave this golden age of invention and innovation we can look at one last experiment in the 19th Century that of the ram. In common use in ancient times it was fitted to galleys as the main offensive weapon. Rather surprisingly the ram came back into favour again after the Battle of Lisa (20th July 1866). This battle is special because it is the only recorded fleet action between ironclad, steam-driven warships. This particular combination was used for just a short period of time and is therefore a rather obscure and unrepeatable record to hold. It is also remembered for the Austrian's use of the ram mounted on their ship the '*Erzherzog Ferinand Max*'.

The *Max*' rammed and sunk the Italian ship '*Re d'Italia*' and did so very quickly indeed.

Everyone seemed to ignore that fact that the Italian ship was unusually vulnerable to almost any form of attack, because it was stopped dead in the water. Nevertheless the idea of a ram as weapon regained credence as in Admiral Sir George Elliot's commentary in his "Treatise on Future Naval Battles and How to Fight Them (1885)". And so it was with considerable enthusiasm and excitement, the Admiralty embraced the prospect of a ship-killing weapon at very low cost; rams were fitted to many ships over the next 20 years. Their rise and fall was swift.

After a number of accidental rammings, of friendly ships, during ship manoeuvres they were removed and the ram returned to its place in history. This is one idea Sir George probably wishes he had not pushed — an example where Admiralty caution would have been the better option. It is to be acknowledged however that given the opportunity, any Royal Navy ship in a position to ram, and with no other effective means of attacking a ship, will still steam full ahead and ram the enemy, many enemy submarines were attacked in this manner.

It follows the aggressive tradition of the Royal Navy to slow down the enemy at all costs - even if it means the loss of your own ship (and of course the sailors on board) to do so. Several actions have been won with such single-minded aggression against the odds. The sinking of the German ships *Bismarck* and *Graf Spee* serve as excellent examples; both German ships were merely dented by much smaller Royal Navy forces but both ended up at the bottom of the sea.

Besides his ill-fated ideas about the reintroduction of the ram Sir George had a rather better idea in advocating the use of the torpedo. In fact he might have been studying the French *la jeune école* (the 'new school' of naval development), led by Admiral Théophile Aube in the 1880s. Their thinking was that the torpedo was the preferred weapon of sea warfare – rendering big ships useless. To some extent they were to be proved correct but it was not until the combination of aircraft and submarine combined forces that the big ship was finally rendered obsolete [5]. But for the time being the torpedo was definitely a better option than the ram, one might even see the torpedo as ramming at a distance; with the added bonus that your own boat is not endangered, usually. One curious historical note in respect of both torpedoes and rams was the American ship CSS *Hunley*, named after the financier HL Hunley and built at the height of their civil war.

The *Hunley* was an early submergible boat, crewed by a small group of men turning a crank-handle. This was a very simple but nonetheless workable version of a submarine and was used by the American Confederates with some success. It carried a bomb, referred to as a torpedo, fixed to the end of a spar in the form of an extended ram; the object was to ram the enemy ship, in this case the *Housatonic*, and withdraw before the torpedo detonated. In the first part of the engagement the *Hunley* was successful but failed in the second part, withdrawing safely. The sub' never made it back to base. On Wednesday 17th February 1864 it sank with all hands, including Captain George E Dixon. This ranks as the first example of a submarine sinking a warship and of course many such attacks were to follow. This was the end for rams but just the beginning for torpedoes.

The Royal navy's first attempt at submarine was the *Resurgam* which was steam powered lozenge-shaped affair. It sank while on tow in 1879.

Meanwhile weapon of choice for submarines, the torpedo, was also under development. The towed version of the torpedo was invented by Commander Fred' Harvey RN and the autonomous, self propelled version was refined by Robert Whitehead - from whom the Royal Navy bought two in 1870 . In brief, one of the key developments of the torpedo was the counter running propellers - to stop the torpedo going round in circles, and here follow two more 'firsts'.

The first Torpedo boat was HMS *Lightning* (Torpedo Boat 1, TB1).

The first use of a self-propelled torpedo in combat was by HM Frigate '*Shah*' against the Prussian ironclad *Huascar* in 1877.

Torpedoes *should* be safer than ramming, especially when the torpedo is not tethered to the vessel delivering the explosive. But that is not always the case....the crew of HMS *Trinidad* will testify that it is always possible for your own weapons to turn against you. The date and location give provide a clue as to cause of the following mishap. In March 1942 an Arctic convoy, PQ13 spotted three enemy destroyers. HMS *Trinidad* fired, or at least tried to fire, three torpedoes; so bitterly cold were conditions that two torpedoes froze in their tubes but the third went off alright, however as soon as hit the icy waters of the Artic the oil froze in its gyroscope and motor, this caused the 'fish' to change course considerably, so much so that it reversed course and struck *Trinidad* herself. *Trinidad* managed to limp on to Murmansk for repairs [6].

Although a wide variety of surface ships carry torpedo tubes the torpedo is usually associated with submarines, because the torpedo is ideally suited to this vessel. It can be fired above or below the surface making it an ideal weapon for sub's, which would otherwise need to surface to fire deck-mounted guns. Of course, in modern times torpedoes are supplemented by guided missiles, which can also be fired from surface ships or from the depths.

The development of a sub-surface boat was a long and fascinating one. The essentials for a submarine are an enclosed tube, an adequate supply of air for the men inside; a means of propulsion; a method for sinking below the surface and, more importantly, a method to bring the boat to the surface again and finally - as they are primarily used for warfare - a weapon system.

A variety of clockwork and mechanical devices were tried and tested by many brave souls, who not infrequently sacrificed their lives in the name of progress and research, before the Navy the saw an acceptable solution. This came with the Irish-American John P. Holland's version. His early trials began in 1878 and the first successful version came in about 1900. Once the Admiralty had satisfied itself that a viable, submergible vessel was available they began building their own 'Holland' class submarines.

In fact submarines were initially so despised by naval commanders that the First Hague Conference had a motion attempting to outlaw them. This failed to stop their development and use but it was not the only time efforts were made to resist their introduction. In the end the Submarine, with Whitehead's torpedoes, became an inevitable if loathed weapon in the armoury of every nation's fleet. They now form a pivotal role in any modern flotilla. Advances in sub-marine vessels continue unabated.

The journal New Scientist on 17th September 2005 reported that from the earliest forms of submarine, operating at depths of few fathoms, to the nuclear sub's, operating at depths of around 700 metres, there are now submersible vehicles capable of reaching the deepest ocean rifts at steel-crushing depths of 11,000 metres.

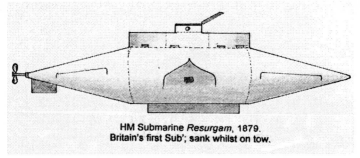

HM Submarine *Resurgam*, 1879.
Britain's first Sub'; sank whilst on tow.

Inevitably all these developments required the Navy to think about the *types* of ships in a fleet. At the beginning of the 19th century the battleship, the First Rate man-of-war was the centrepiece with a variety of lesser sailing ships in attendance. By the turn of the century a much broader range of warships could be considered.

The front-line Battleship; the middleweight Cruisers; fast but lighter Frigates and the torpedo-carrying/submarine destroying "Destroyer"; the submarine plus numerous small coastal boats such as sloops, corvettes and launches. Within a decade or two Aircraft carriers would also form a central role in the fleet. In addition, there were a variety of other specialist boats to consider such as landing craft, the river gun-boats, Monitors, and so forth. We now have all the essential components for a really good ship, made of steel, armour-plated, steam-driven and with big, breech-loading guns. In the next chapter we shall see how all this new technology was brought together to provide the Royal Navy with its latest gun platform.

Chapter 6: 1900 – 1950, Dreadnoughts

~~~~~~~~~~

The Royal Navy's primary role was and remains to protect the Crown and the people of Great Britain and to do so by force of arms if necessary. Admiral Viscount Jellicoe's in his book "The Grand Fleet" published in 1919 summarised the four purposes of the British Navy thus:-

1. To ensure for British ships unimpeded use of the sea....
2. In the event of war, to bring steady economic pressure on our adversary by denying him use of the sea...
3. In the event of war, to cover passage and assist any army sent over seas to protect its communications and supplies...
4. To prevent invasion of this country, and its Dominions, by enemy forces.

As we have seen throughout this book a battle ship was needed to achieve these aims. The Greeks used Galleys and the Vikings their Longships. Eventually most Navies shifted to the Man-o'-War sailing ship. The Royal Navy's choice was the First Rate, 100-gun vessel as their ship-of-the-line, ships such as HMS Victory.

But the old wooden man-o'-war, after several hundred years of service was to be supplanted. Merging the technology of the 19th Century gave us a "dreadnought", *the* battleship.

Tradition has it that the Royal Navy's first Battleship HMS Dreadnought heralded the age of this class of ship, the "all-big-gun" ship, although in reality there had been a number of iron ships before the dreadnought. The very name "Dreadnought" defined the class as well as the era. The dreadnought era was a surprisingly short period of time, from 1906 when Dreadnought was launched to 1956 when the last RN battleship, Vanguard was scrapped. None survive in Britain, even as museum pieces. It is sad to reflect that HMS *Victory* survives after 250 years but HMS *Vanguard* survived just 20 years. HMS *Vanguard*, like the *Hood*, was a beautiful warship if a little anachronistic by 1950. Some will regret that important ships aren't 'listed' as heritage monuments with the same enthusiasm buildings.

However this chapter is not about the demise of the Battleship instead this chapter gives an overview of this ship type; its birth and development in the first quarter of the 20th Century.

Sir John "Jackie" Fisher (later Lord Fisher) had to make a number of decisions when ordering his ships. Fisher was of one of the triumvirate of Admirals, Fisher, Jellicoe and Beatty, famous for the role they played in the Battle of Jutland 1916 but that was some years ahead.

At the turn of the century one decision Fisher considered but set aside was the French school of thought, the *la Jeune école*, which strongly supported the use of the new torpedo as a primary weapon. In fact Fisher was to revise his thinking fairly soon and realised that the torpedo, along with the submarine and later still the aeroplane, would be the more significant weapon platform in future sea battles. But for the moment, Fisher was to bring to the Royal Navy and its administration the same vigour and challenges as Pepys had in the 17th Century and Anson in the 18th.

Fisher was intent on sweeping away the old and bringing in the new. In his decision to go for the dreadnought class he was following not the French but the Italian School, Vittorio Cuniberti's ideas on 'the new type of armoured ship'. Cuniberti advocated large ships capable of high speed and carrying only larger calibre guns the 'all-big-gun' theory [1].

Fisher directed the building of his version of the large armoured ship in 1906 and as anticipated its construction rendered obsolete all earlier battleships [2].

Those commanders who saw the all-big-gun ship as the ideal battleship will no doubt have had recent events in the Pacific in mind. Russia had a most disastrous encounter with the Japanese Fleet at Tsushima (aka Tshushima or Tsou-Shima) on 27th/28th May 1905. At Tsushima the ships were engaging each other at very long range, 19,000 yards in the early stages of the battle, this rendered medium calibre guns useless (4 to 8 inch guns for example)[3]. So what Fisher wanted was big guns; after all that's what a battleship is for — to fire the most powerful guns they can devise (and afford) and render the enemy's ship unusable.

His choices in respect of guns were:- Their size, or calibre; whether they were to be muzzle-loaded or breech-loaded; how many guns and of what sizes - and how they might be distributed on his ship — that is to say the guns could be mounted on the centre-line of the ship, so as to be able to fire both sides or they could be paired-up one on each side; he could choose fixed barbettes (with guns swivelling within fixed mountings) or a turret (in which the whole gun, men and machinery moved as the turret rotated). He could also make other choices about the type of shell to be fired from the guns, including their shape and their content, high explosive, armour-piercing, star or shrapnel (incidentally, this type of shell was named after Lieutenant-General Henry Shrapnel circa 1793), its precursor was the Langrel and both were shells filled with bits of iron which would cut rigging, or people, to pieces.

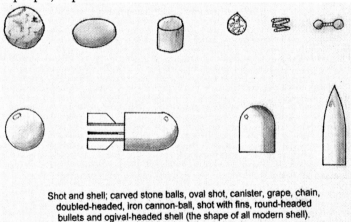

Shot and shell; carved stone balls, oval shot, canister, grape, chain, doubled-headed, iron cannon-ball, shot with fins, round-headed bullets and ogival-headed shell (the shape of all modern shell).

Some choices were inevitable, such as the matter of "rifling", curved grooves in the barrel. In the age of simple ballistics, (rather than guided weaponry), the bigger the gun the farther their range and the bigger the shell the greater the damage (to the enemy, one hoped).

From these decisions others would follow about the hull itself; its size, shape, engine power, ship's complement, accommodation, distribution of armour plating and so on [4]. One problem he would not have had to ponder was the colour – always battleship grey, unless at war when camouflage was needed.

The design team, headed Sir Philip Watts set to work to produce the first modern warship of the 20th Century. Their aim was to realise the newly appointed First Sea Lord Admiral Fisher's dream of a "high speed, all big gun ship, and a ship so well protected as to be able to "disregard the enemy's small calibre armaments" [5].

Admiral Fisher's dream-ship was to be named HMS *Dreadnought*. It was built in Portsmouth Royal Dockyard. The keel was laid on 2nd October 1905 and, in something of a race against the American's ship building programme, it was launched in just four months on 10th February 1906, astonishingly quick for a boat of its size, its complexity and innovation. Sea trials began on 3rd October 2006 [6].

Her statistics are given in a little detail and will serve as the benchmark for other big ships mentioned in this book. It was of course all-steel, no wooden parts to the hull, other than the wooden planking covering the main decks, with no rigging (for sails). This was not to be a 'combination' ship.

It was 527 feet long, 82 feet wide, giving a length to beam ratio 6.5 to 1 (compared to 7:1 for galleys/longships and 3:1 for the 'round' sailing ships). Her draught was 26.5 feet. Displacement 17,900 tons standard and 21,845 with full load.

The final decision for her armament was ten 12" guns (for "ship-killing"); plus 27 x 12-pounder guns, that is 3" guns for protection against torpedoes and torpedo boats. Armoured protection varied according to the most vulnerable parts of the ship and again compromises had to be made as to the overall weight and best speed (and always cost). Armour was thinner on the decks, thickest around the guns and at the water line. It varied from 3" up to 11" in thickness and added as much as 5,000 extra tons in all [7].

The significant decision here was the use of big guns, when 12" was the largest available, and with no secondary weapons. 6, 8 or 9 inch guns could have been fitted – the design committee, with First Sea Lord Sir John Fisher as its President, chose what they referred to as design 'H' and this gave them ten 12-inch guns. With the benefit of hindsight the size and distribution of guns would vary as battleship classes developed and improved in later years.

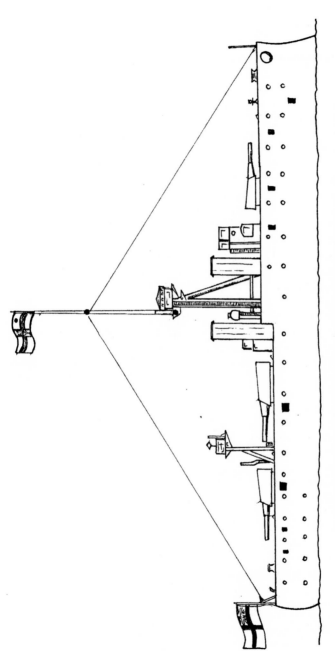

HMS Dreadnought circa 1907, 500 feet in length and carried 10 x 12 inch guns.

Some records state HMS *Dreadnought* had 5 Torpedo tubes but Admiral of the Fleet Viscount Jellicoe of Scapa GCB OM GCVO records that in 1914 it had four torpedo tubes. With a rank and title like that he should know — Jellicoe would have noticed if he had five not four tubes on his ship [8].

As for speed, this ship was given 18 Babcock & Wilcox Boilers with 4 Parsons turbine engines. The 'Turbine', a system of fan-blades to increase the efficiency of an engine, was invented by an Englishman, the Honourable Charles Algernon Parsons in 1884. He also built and trialled the first turbine-driven steamship the *Turbinia* in 1897 [9]. As for the *Dreadnought*'s turbine engines, they produced 23,000 hp. For fuel it carried 2,400 tons of coal and 1,120 tons of oil (her engines were partially oil-fired). It had four propellers and could maintain a speed of 21 knots and operate for 5,000 miles at an average speed of 18 knots. HMS *Dreadnought* had a complement of 700 to 773 men according to peace or wartime conditions.

This combination of firepower and speed made her the best ship of her time and any country aspiring to have an effective naval force would need to follow suite. It took just another fours years for them to do so. There were two major effects of the building of *Dreadnought*; the first is that it rendered all other battle ships obsolete, the second point followed from the first. It meant that if Great Britain were to remain pre-eminent it would have to maintain its advantage by building a completely new fleet of these monsters because Britain's fleet was rendered as obsolete as every other nation's. Far from having a clear lead there was now parity, it was just a matter building ships better and faster than the opposition.

Britain struggled to hold the advantage. Many countries including Germany, America, Japan and France built Battleships and to better designs than Britain's first *Dreadnought* – once again the problem of leading with innovation gave others the advantage of learning from your mistakes and building-in refinements from the outset. In 1909 Britain abandoned, at least in theory, the Two-Power standard she had set herself in the Naval Defence Act 1889, instead the Royal Navy would be compared directly with the most obvious naval threat at the time - The German High Seas Fleet. The irony was that in 1914 by adding to its own fleet numbers the number ships being built in British yards (albeit for other navies but which could be withheld and used in the Royal Navy) the two-power standard was still in place.

Willmott revaluated the issues in his book, "Battleship" [10]. He seems to conclude that Fisher in his autocratic manner threw away the lead Britain had. Whilst his drive and energy had brought the *Dreadnought* into being his abrasive and tight control of design and development stifled further innovation and meant there was no improvement to later classes. Willmott is quite scathing about Fisher's next generation of battleships, the Indefatigable "*representing no real improvement over the Invincible class*". He went on to heap yet more obloquy upon Fisher's approach...

"....*in fact, criticism of Fisher on this particular point can be made quite simply and very bluntly: the Indefatigable class represented one of the worst classes, if not the worst class, of capital ship laid down before the First World War, and represented the totally irresponsible squandering of the lead that had been won by the rushing of the Dreadnought to completion in fourteen months...*" [11].

Like many heroes their image can become somewhat tarnished once the glory of the moment passes and history observes their deeds with dispassionate vision and hindsight. But as Shakespeare put it [12] "... the evil men do lives after them; the good is oft interrèd with their bones..." so let it be with Fisher, he did after all gives us the *Dreadnought*.

HMS *Dreadnought* provided the nation with some entertaining moments. On February 10th 1910 the Foreign Office received a telegram advising the Captain that The Emperor of Abyssinia was in town and wished to inspect the pride of Channel Fleet, HMS *Dreadnought*. A group of dignitaries were suitably entertained and at the end of their tour they tried but failed to convince the officer escorting them that he should accept the Order of Abyssinia. It was only later that they learned from the press that they had been duped by a group of literati dressed in fine robes and talking gibberish through a duly sombre interpreter [13].

Despite 'squandering of the lead' the following figures give some indication of Britain's continuing intent to remain 'sovereign of the seas', but this was by now a declining ambition.

Willmott provides the following distribution of forces as at the 1st August 1914. It is to be noted that there were other fleets in being, for example the Austro-Hungarian fleet included three dreadnought class battleships and the Japanese two [14]. This simplified table does not of course give any indication of the relative qualities of each ship or class of ship.

Type	Britain	France	Russia	Germany	USA
Dreadnought	22	2	-	15	10
Pre –"-	40	20	10	22	23
Battlecruiser	9	-	-	5	-
Numbers of battleships held by five leading naval forces					

War, the Great War, came on 4th August 1914, by which time HMS *Dreadnought* was eight years old so an elderly ship by ship standards but it was still afloat and earning her keep in the main Battle Fleet, the 'Grand Fleet'. HMS *Iron Duke* was by then the flagship and HMS *Dreadnought* was Vice-Admiral Gamble's flagship for the 4th Battle Squadron [15].

The *Dreadnought* did see a little action, but very, very little action. Whilst patrolling in the North Sea it *saw* one submarine but failed to engage it, her second chance for action came at 12:30 pm on 4th February 1915 when the *Dreadnought* was alerted to the presence of a submarine. The Officer of the Watch Lt Commander Piercy sighted a periscope. Jellicoe records the events in the following manner:

> "...Captain Alderson at once altered course direct for the submarine, increased speed, followed and rammed her ... the bow of the submarine came out of the water and her number, U 29 was plainly visible. She sank immediately HMS Blanche (an escort) passed close by the ship and reported a quantity of wreckage, one article of clothing and much oil and bubbles on the surface, but no survivors..."

Jellicoe went on to say of Captain Alderson, "The *Dreadnought* was admirably handled...." [16]. All with that fire power and ramming was still the most useful weapon on that occasion. *Dreadnought* never fired its big guns in anger!

Despite the intransigence of Fisher, battleship design did progress by degrees; Admiral Sir Percy Scott was a leading light in gunnery and gunnery 'fire-control'; fire control was a shift from the local control of guns by the gun Captain to a centralised, co-ordinated direction-finding system.

The following table very briefly summarises some of the changes and developments in battleship design between *Dreadnought*, the first, and *Vanguard*, the last.

Statistics	Dread-nought	Iron-Duke	Malaya	Hood	Van-guard
Launched	1906	1910	1915	1920	1944
Ratio, length to breadth	527 x 82 = 6.5:1	620x90 = 6.8:1	640x104 = 6:1	860x105 = 8:1	814 x 107 = 7.5:1
Guns, main, calibre/inches	10 @ 12"	10 @ 13.5"	8 @ 15" 12 @ 4"	8 @ 15" 12 @ 5"	8 @ 15" 16 @ 5"
Displacement, Standard	17,900	25,000	31,100	42,100	42,500
Speed, knots	21	21	23	31	29.5
Horse-Power	23,000		75,000	144,000	130,000
Comparison of British battleships					

For comparison HMS *Victory*, at the time of Battle of Trafalgar in 1805, was 186 feet long at the gun-deck; beam 51 feet giving a ratio 3.6. It displaced about 3,500 tons. Her maximum speed in fair weather was about 8 knots and it carried 104 guns, "cannon", ranging from 12 to 68 pounders.

For those more familiar with passenger ships, the *Q.E. 2*, the Cunard cruise liner, not the warship, is 963 feet long and 105 feet in the beam giving a ratio 9:1. *Q.E. 2's* displacement is about 67,000 tons. Her engines produce 110,000 shaft horse power, s.h.p., giving her a speed of 28 knots. *Q.E. 2's* armament is probably restricted to a few small-arms for the Captain's use in case of mutiny or piracy.

For further comparison, a modern Destroyer, the Duke class Frigate (HM ships *Kent, Portland, St Albans*) have a displacement of about 3,500 tons. These ships are 436 feet long by 50 feet beam, giving a ratio 8.7:1. with a published speed of 28 knots.

Armaments are now guided missiles and torpedo systems rather than ballistic guns, although most RN ships now carry at least one 4" gun (114mm) such as the Vickers Mk8 and several rapid-fire guns such as the "Goalkeeper" or "Phalanx" for close quarter protection when all else fails.

These small but impressive rapid-firing weapons (Goalkeeper) are fully automated and can fire up to 4,000 rounds a minute – designed to bring down in-coming missiles that have evaded other counter-measures. Contrast that to the Spanish Armada in 1588, their rate of fire was sometimes as slow as one round per *day* for some cannon (mainly due to the time it took for the heat to be dissipated between rounds) [17].

Interestingly some torpedoes such as the Mk 24 Tigerfish torpedo are still wire-guided as envisaged in 1866 by two of the earlier innovators of this type of under water weapon. Captain Luppis of the Austrian Navy and Commander Fred' Harvey RN both developed torpedoes requiring a tether to control the torpedo whilst Robert Whitehead is credited with the development of the self-propelled, or "locomotive" torpedo in 1868. Credit should also be given to the American Winfield Sims USA who invented an electric torpedo in 1882 [18].

The table above shows the improvements to the battleship over its short life span. Displacement tripled, the extra weight providing thicker armoured protection and heavier guns. The ratio, length to beam, increased from 6 : 1 for the *Dreadnought*, extending to 8 : 1 for the *Hood*. With these fine lines, similar to the very elegant passenger liner *QE2*, HMS *Hood* was regarded as Britain's most powerful and fine-looking warship in the 1920s.

The speed of these ships in the hundred years between *Dreadnought* in 1906 and modern Destroyers has increased very little — according to published figures.

Speed has stood steady at 20 to 30 knots; a speed that appears not to have increased very much in the intervening years perhaps because of fluid dynamics, an extra knot in speed would require a disproportionate increase in motive power and therefore cost.

The Ministry of Defence's "Royal Navy Handbook" reports that the new Destroyers Type 45 (*Daring* D32 to *Duncan* D37) will have a "speed of 29 knots" [19].

We now move on to follow the life of one particular battle-ship, HMS Malaya — for no other reason than it was the Battle-ship in which the CPO Powell served and to whom this book is dedicated and serves as an example of the life and role of such ships.

Chapter 7: HMS Malaya's Story

~~~~~~~~~~~~

HMS *Malaya* was a gift to the British Government; a very large and most useful gift from the Federated Malayan States, and was a welcome addition to the Royal Navy's fleet of battleships when tensions between Great Britain and Germany were mounting — in the early years of the 20th Century.

The next two chapters tell the story of a battleship from slipway to breaker's yard, the boredom, the tensions, the excitement and the fear. Like the rest of this book it is not in minute detail but is intended to give an impression of the manner in which a ship plays out its role in a fleet.

HMS *Malaya* was designed by Sir Philip Watts and built by Armstrong the shipbuilders in Newcastle-upon-Tyne, UK. The initial cost of building Malaya was £2,945,709 - although modifications in the 1930s - affecting about 60% of the ship's structure, cost a good deal more, at nearly £11,000,000. The keel was laid down October 1913 and it was launched on 18th March 1915 and finally completed in February 1916. It was commissioned in time to join the 5th Battle Cruiser Fleet at Scapa Flow in the Orkneys where the British "Grand Fleet" was based [1].

By 1916, when Malaya was launched and ready to work-up or 'shake-down' (preparing the ship for sea and action), war with German had been declared, on 4th August 1914, so her first sea trials were not just theoretical and tedious practices, they were very real and in anticipation of imminent contact with the enemy's equally powerful navy.

HMS *Malaya* was one of five of the "Queen Elizabeth" class battleships. Each was a floating fortress, a huge vessel protected with heavy armoured plating, up to 14 inches thick in some places, but this was to prove not heavy enough as Admiral Beatty was later to exclaim. Intended to be a stable platform for the heaviest of guns the Malaya weighed 31,000 tons.

This modern class of ship had oil-fired boilers, at a time when many ships were still using coal. The boilers provided power to steam turbines capable of producing 75,000 horsepower and a speed of 24 knots, not as fast as cruisers or destroyers, which could reach speeds of about 30 knots, but this was part of the compromise. Her speed gave way to a lot of very big guns and heavy armoured protection, designed to stand and fight not just reconnoitre or scout ahead of a fleet. The *Malaya* was a colossus at 600 feet long and 104 feet in the beam, and with a draft of 33 feet. It was mounted with eight 15" guns, twelve 6" and eight 4" guns plus other smaller armament such as four x 3-pounder guns, and Lewis guns, that is, rapid-fire machine guns; it also Torpedo tubes below the water line. Here we can see the move away from Fisher's all-big-gun formula to mixed armaments, a more flexible and pragmatic approach catering for a variety of scenarios.

Malaya was modified in the 1920s and again in the 30s when these armaments were modernised including changes to the torpedo tubes, the 6" guns plus the fitting of an aircraft launch-catapult [2].

The larger calibre guns were of course for ship to ship fighting or shore bombardment, the smaller guns for anti-aircraft and close-quarter fighting if the need arose for example against submarines and smaller vessels encroaching too close to the *Malaya's* sea space. These refinements made *Malaya* one of the newest, fasted and heaviest armed capital ships in the Royal Navy at the high point of Britain's fondness for big-ship design. It was fitted-out as a flagship – meaning that it could accommodate the admiral in charge of a squadron or an entire fleet.

From the ship's first log, now held at the Public Records Office [PRO] in Kew, West London we know that, with the assistance of a ship's Pilot, the *Malaya* left Armstrong's shipyard Tyneside, North-East coast of England, on 4th February 1916 and moored at a deep-water birth before leaving the Tyne on Thursday 17th to make her way to North Scapa Flow in the Orkney Islands. It arrived in this desolate Scottish bay on Friday 18th February and immediately joined the fleet in daily exercises [3].

Scapa Flow is a very remote location with little to occupy an off-watch sailor but at this time the bay was full of ships. The Grand Fleet was base here as a strategic location to cover the North Sea and access to the Atlantic, here the Fleet lay in readiness to take on the German High Seas fleet, if and when it put to sea.

As if by way of an early warning, and a timely reminder of her purpose, on Monday morning the 21st February at 11:50, only two weeks after her arrival, the *Malaya* spotted a floating mine. Mines, whether floating or fixed to the sea-bed, contact or magnetic, were a serious threat to any ship — including the very ships that laid them if they didn't keep a careful record of where they were they had left them!

So this was a small but potent omen of the dangers they were to face and no doubt gave real purpose and determination to the endless exercises the fleet was always engaged in. Small arms were put to immediate use and the mine was sunk. Typically, the ship's log is succinct;

"...passed a floating mine... mine sunk...".

The ship's lookouts didn't need the Navy's notorious disciplinary code to keep them alert after this souvenir of the enemy's recent visit, it was a salutary reminder of their proximity.

Despite this minor drama the routine of the fleet and HMS *Malaya* followed a pattern. Cleaning ship and painting ship were frequent duties – a matter of safety as well as hygiene and time-filling. During this period of preparation our ship raised steam most days and put to sea, if only for a few hours, to practice gunnery; to set the compasses; practice action-stations; practice keeping station — manoeuvring the Fleet as group of ships. One of her logs shows the ship fell out of her correct position in the fleet during such an exercise but we need not dwell this minor lapse in navigation, that's what practising is for.

It's time to meet some of the sailors. The ship's complement comprised nearly 1,200 men and the first Captain of the *Malaya* was the Honorable Algernon Boyle M.V.O. The man in charge of the 5th Battle Cruiser Squadron [5th BCS], to which the *Malaya* was attached, was Admiral David Beatty. In command of the whole Grand Fleet was Admiral Viscount Jellicoe in his Flagship Iron Duke. He was responsible for managing the entire fleet and all its subsidiary squadrons and flotillas. Back in London, in the Admiralty, Earl "Jacky" Fisher was reinstated as First Sea Lord; he was responsible for translating the Government's political ambitions into a naval strategy.

We shall hear more about these three heroes, Fisher, Jellicoe and Beatty. Like them, Captain Boyle's moment of glory came when he took part in the "Battle of Jutland".

Many volumes have been written about this encounter between the two most powerful battle fleets of the time. This battle was special because of a number of factors, namely it was at a time when Radar and even aerial reconnaissance was in its infancy (manned balloons were still being floated skyward to get a better view over the horizon). So the ships needed to actually see each other before engaging in any fighting; armaments were "ballistic" so again the ships needed to be in sight of one another so that shells could be "lobbed" to and fro, there were no guided or self-propelled missiles at this time.

Aircraft cover was very limited and took no part in this action. The impact of these factors meant it was the last of the traditional naval actions. A battle of fleet against fleet; ship against ship; and therefore very much a matter of leadership – man against man – John Rushworth Jellicoe against Reinhard Scheer. This required both men to have some understanding of how the other might plan and execute engagement of his ships; it was therefore a matter of experience, confidence and courage. Such battles, and more obviously those battles between sailing ships, were dependent upon natural elements such as visibility, daylight, fog, wind and the general weather conditions [4].

Future battles could rely on electronic surveillance, guided weapons, submarines, air-cover, even satellite-cover and all the other paraphernalia of modern electronic warfare but in 1916 fog, or night-time darkness, was enough to bring the biggest of ships to a virtual standstill and to miss each other within yards.

Submarines and aircraft spelt the end of "big ships" and those battle fleet engagements which were on a spectacular scale. A Battleship was to become far too vulnerable to torpedo attacks and aerial bombing and so a modern fleet comprises at its centre not Battleships but Aircraft Carriers and Submarines. But we are still in the early part of the 20th century. Towards the end of May 1916 the German High Seas Commander Admiral Scheer took his Fleet to sea with the intention of some off-shore bombing of Sunderland but he was spotted by Admiral Beatty.

On 31st May 1916 Captain the Hon. Algernon Boyle's moment had arrived. HMS *Malaya* was part of the 5th Battle Squadron, which comprised HM Ships *Barham*, as flagship, *Malaya*, *Valiant* and *Warspite*, the ships of the 5th BS were commanded by Rear-Admiral Evan-Thomas. This battleship squadron was itself attached to the Battle-Cruiser Force [BCF] commanded by Vice Admiral David Beatty in the Cruiser Lion [5].

Beatty's Cruiser Squadron was the first to engage the German ships in the North Sea. This was part of the Jellicoe's strategy; to draw the German High Seas Fleet into something of a trap by encouraging them to think they were taking on a lesser force of Cruisers. Beatty's objective was to draw the Germans into a full-scale battle by leading them towards Jellicoe's Grand Fleet further to the North so the trap could be sprung.

It was at the commencement of this momentous battle that Admiral Beatty exclaimed those damning words ... *"there seems to be something wrong with our bloody ships today... "*. He was of course referring to the inadequacy of his ships' armoured protection. What made him exclaim in the manner was the sight of ship sinking very quickly; first he thought it was a German ship sinking then dawned the awful realisation it was one of his own ships, *Queen Mary* going down within minutes of being hit by Admiral Hipper's German Battlecruisers.

Rather proving the point that Britain was not learning the lessons as quickly as Germany, despite Beatty's outburst in 1916, HMS *Hood* was also inadequately protected from high arcing shells. HMS *Hood*, the pride of England, sank after just three shots from the *Bismarck*, on 24th May 1941 in the Atlantic — and that was another legend in the making during the next world conflict.

Back to 1916 and still in the North Sea, Jellicoe's masterplan was beginning to bear fruit. The *Malaya's* log records with the usual brevity and understatement;

Wed 31st May 1916, Position Lat. 56.43N Long. 3.21;

"Course and speed as required for engaging the enemy".

With this short entry the Battle of Jutland was about to unfold. It was the task of the Assistant Paymaster on board the *Malaya* to make a written record of the action as it unfolded. Commander B. R. Coward R. N. transcribes the events of the evening of 31st May thus [6]:-

"...4 o'clock the Barham opened fire at the enemy on our Port bow;
    4:02 Valiant Fires
    4:10 Warspite fires.
    4.25 Malaya fire A or B Turret (the largest 15" guns)
                    at a range of 20,000
yards.

4.58 Altered course 16 points and followed Battlecruisers.
4.59 (German) salvo fell about 50 yards over us..".

The writer continues to describe the German's all too accurate firing and by 5.05pm he reports that the Germans

"... have got our range exactly now.. [their] salvo 20 yards short of us...". He continues, "... [they have] straddled Valiant and ourselves. We are outlined against a bright yellow horizon but they are nearly hidden in the mist ...".

At 4.58 pm when the squadron altered course the British 5th Battle Squadron is taking the full brunt of the German battleships and both the *Barham* and *Malaya* are hit.

A writer on the *Barham* hints at the turmoil with the following commentary

"... All of us worked on incessantly like automatic machines ... scarcely conscious of what we are doing... the roar and shriek of the guns never ceased, and those who were in the proximity of the guns were so deafened by them that they were deaf for days to come... there was no doubt that our firing was very accurate and we must have caused a considerable amount of damage". Barham's writer continued *"... after some time though the Germans began to score some hits and the first shock which struck our ship was a sensation one is not likely to forget for many a day... we realised we were in an extremely tight corner ... terrific salvos were being fired at us in rapid succession ... so quick and fast were the shells coming that it seemed at one time that nothing short of a miracle could save us... the din of explosives crashing on the water all around resounded in the very bowels of the ship in the most extraordinary way..."* [7].

However by 5.30 in the evening the 5th BS had managed to extricate itself and by opening up the range led the German High Seas fleet towards the British main forces to the North - where the balance of fighting power would more equal.

The bait is taken and the Germans, with Admiral Scheer as command-in-chief, are giving chase and thus a unique Fleet action between modern battleships is just minutes away.

Admiral Sir R H Bacon records Jellicoe's decision making in these crucial minutes thus [8]:-

31st May 1916; ".... at 6.14 pm the firing was located as coming from the direction of the starboard wing division, and a signal was received from the *Lion* giving the bearing of the enemy battle fleet. Instantly Sir John (Jellicoe) walked quickly to the standard compass, at which Captain Dreyer was watching the steering, and gazed intently for twenty seconds in silence at the compass card. Nelson had six hours to dispose his fleet. Jellicoe only twenty seconds. Nelson knew that in England there was a reserve fleet equal in numbers to his own. Jellicoe knew that the whole sea strength of England was arrayed in this battle...

....in those twenty seconds the fate of the Empire most probably hung in the balance...".

Jellicoe's decision was to deploy to Port thus intercepting Scheer's fleet as they advanced towards their own home base and with no idea that they were about to be pounced upon by the Grand Fleet.

By 6:23 pm on the same day, 31st May, the two battle fleets were within firing distance and the battle began. By midnight it is finished.

The end of this particular confrontation, which lasted less than one day, was indecisive. The Germans sank more of our ships and caused more British casualties, so they claimed a Victory. Not least because the British were so slow in publicising their action that the German Press made the first pronouncements — in Germany's favour of course. Inevitably this led the British people to think their Grand Fleet had been defeated and a good deal of public acrimony followed. However, the Germans chose not put their High Sea Fleet at risk and it never went into battle again during World War 1. So the British also claim a victory.

The Battle of Jutland has now passed into distant history, it is the stuff of legends and a great many words exchanged trying to unravel the detail of each side's actions. Jellicoe and Beatty have each come in for criticism.

In the final analysis Britain continued to rule the waves, in the North Sea anyway.

The *Malaya*'s small but not insignificant part in this momentous battle was to be positioned near the rear of the main fleet and to take a wrong course (not for the first time!) at the end of the day when the Fleets had disengaged. The Germans were heading for a safe haven, towards the Horns Reef passage and on to Heligoland. It was by now dusk but the British were still looking for the German Fleet — in the hopes of coming to a more decisive conclusion. Having fallen out of station HMS *Malaya* spotted the German Fleet making its escape ...... but failed to signal this information to the flagship [9].

Without that vital piece of information Jellicoe could only guess where the Germans were heading. He didn't guess quite accurately enough to re-engage them. In fact their paths had actually crossed within a few miles of each other at about 9 pm. It remains a matter of conjecture as to whether or not the *Malaya's* omission changed the course of history.

Nonetheless Jellicoe had succeeded in confining the German High Seas Fleet to its bases and the *Malaya* spent the rest of the war patrolling the North Sea.

Between the wars 1918 to 1939 the *Malaya* followed peacetime routines, based in Portsmouth as part of the torpedo training establishment. The ship's crew, albeit a much reduced complement, were kept busy on training exercises, manoeuvres; watchkeeping, re-quipping, painting-ship, cleaning-ship; evening prayers; ... the endless routines of a ship not doing what it is designed to do — fight. It was the job of a Captain to keep his crew busy, to keep them physically and mentally alert and to minimise discontentment. This meant hard work but lots of competitive activities – sailing and rowing ("pulling" as the Navy call it), sports especially boxing and swimming — although it should be remembered that not all sailors could swim, swimming was not always a prerequisite of joining the Royal Navy. The armed services provided many competitors for World and Olympic events. One very popular past-time is the board game Ludo or "Uckers" as it called in the Navy. Uckers is not yet an Olympic game — yet, but given the farcical array of competitions now on offer the Royal Navy may one day lead a winning team in Uckers. Until it ranks among the Olympian Sports it will remain just a very popular game with the Navy.

Thus a ship passes time, until in 1925 the *Malaya* went into dock for a major refit, this continued intermittently to 1934 and cost a staggering £11,000,000 – six times the original cost of building her. Modifications included changes to the torpedo tubes; redirecting the trunking of the forward funnel into the after one; new turbines; changes to the bridge and control towers and eventually an airplane catapult system was fitted. Before the deployment of purpose built aircraft carriers large battleships and even supply vessels carried small bi-planes for reconnaissance and for siting fall of shot when the big guns were being fired. Whilst planes could be catapulted off a battleship the unlucky pilot had to land — ditch — in the sea and then be hoisted back on board his ship [10].

Thus modified the *Malaya* was ready for duty when the next major conflict arose – World War 2 of course – in 1939. But before 1939 the *Malaya* had other brief moments of adventure as we shall see in the next chapter.

Chapter 8: HMS Malaya's Log

~~~~~~~~~~~

This chapter summarises the life a battleship in the Royal Navy in the first half of the 20th Century. It has been compiled from the ship's own log now held in the Public Record Office at Kew in West London and from the various sources listed in the bibliography.

1912	Conceived by the Malayan Government
1913	Agreed with Britain
20/10/1913	Built by Armstrong
18/03/1915	Launched
February 1916	Completed, trials, shakedown and Commissioning.

Commanding officer's HMS *Malaya*:

07/11/1914   Engineer Commander
23/06/1915   Cpt – Lt Com Guy Coleridge
28/11/1915   Cpt Hon. Algernon Boyle MVO - to 1918
xx/01/1918   Cpt Louise Woollcoombe MVO
14/05/1919   Cpt. Henry Buller MVO
27/09/1919   Cpt – Vice Admiral Sir Edward Chorton KCMG
08/03/1937   Cpt JN Sparks
25/05/1937   Cpt. FA Buckley
16/12/1938   Cpt Ian B.B. Tower DSC. (died in air raid 14/10/40)

20/05/1940 Cpt AFE Palliser DSC   [Mr Powell also joins ship 21/4/40]
03/05/1941 Cpt C Coppinger DSC   [Mr Powell discharged 17/9/41]
xx/03/1942 Cpt JWA Waller ADC
xx/11/1944 Captain WH Fallowfield

Details from the Navy Lists, Public Records Office, Kew.

The name 'HMS *Malaya*' may have been allotted to two ship of the RN; the first being the Battleship and the subject of this history. As for the second, some ex-matelots recall serving on a Cruiser in the 1950s. But here some obscurity creeps in; Mike Critchley makes no reference to a Cruiser named 'HMS *Malaya*' in his catalogue, British Warships Since 1945. As a second ship with this name is not relevant to this Log the minor ambiguity can wait for another edition.

David Thomas's 'Battles and Honours' lists all battle honours for the RN. The battle honours for listed for HMS *Malaya* all relate to the Battleship and not any subsequent ships of that name [1]:-

Battle Honours: HMS Malaya
1 Jutland Battle Honour 31st May 1916 in 5th BC Squadron under Beatty.   2 Atlantic Convoy Campaign honour 1939 - 1945   3 English Channel Campaign Honour 1939 – 1945   4 Malta (Mediterranean) Convoy Campaign Honour 1939 – 1945   5 Mediterranean Campaign Honour 1939 – 1945
From D Thomas, Battles & Honours

The *Malaya* also took part in the Bombardment of Genoa but no battle/campaign honour was granted for this action. Nor, according to Thomas, was this ship awarded a Battle/Campaign Honour for Operation Neptune. Neptune was of course the Royal Navy's contribution to the Normandy landings in France (WW2); this is despite suggestions to the contrary in other commentaries; see for example Haines & Coward's Battleship, Cruiser & Destroyer [2].

As previously stated, the following information was collated from the ship's Logs and from a number of authors as listed in the bibliography. Here are summarised a few notable incidents in which HMS Malaya had a direct interest:

1916 Jan   *Malaya & Valient* join Grand Fleet at Scapa Flow [3].

1916 Feb 18th   5th Battle Squadron including *Malaya* with Grand Fleet at Scapa Flow. [4]

1916 Jun 9th   *Malaya* at the rear of Fleet at Jutland; they sight German Fleet but fail to report it to Jellicoe in Iron Duke See for example Bacon's biography of Jellicoe and Howarth's "The Dreadnought" for *Malaya's* contribution to Jutland battle [5, 6].

1934 change of guns.	Major Refit; airplane launcher added and
1936	Refit ends.
1937	Collision between *Malaya* and *SS Kertsono* [7].

On the evening of Saturday 6th February 1937, at 18:15 hours to be precise, HMS *Malaya* was involved in a collision with the Dutch merchant ship SS *Kertosono*. This peacetime incident took place fifty miles off Oporto (Porto) on the Atlantic coast of Portugal. The Merchant ship SS Kertosono was outward bound from Genoa (Genova, Italy) to London (UK) - and by ill luck *Malaya* was crossing her path. Incidentally, we know from the records that the *Kertosono* was carrying Tea, Coffee, Copper and Tin to Britain. The Captain of the Malaya at this time was Capt. F.A. Buckley RN. We also know from the records, in particular those produced for the Court of Enquiry, that conditions at sea were, to quote Admiral 'Jackie' Fisher's observations, "lumpy".

In fact "lumpy" disguises that fact that conditions were very poor indeed. Lieutenant Gerald Cobb, the Navigating Officer's record tells us that it was;

> *"...very foggy; at 18:15 hours on 6/2/37 the wind was "...SSW force 6, sea 45°F (a little above freezing point) with a swell from the Westward, visibility 2 cables, engine revolutions at 102, giving a speed of 7.1 knots and on a course set at 180°..."*.

In these cold, windy and murky conditions the two ships met - unexpectedly, with no Radar to give advance warning. To quote another author, *"a ship stranded in fog is like a blind man tapping down a strange road at midnight"* [8]. But at sea there are certain "rules of the road" to help the "blind" Captain make his way safely. This is much like the Highway Code for cars on the road; see for example the International Regulations for Preventing Collisions, and the Admiralty Manual of Seamanship.

The basics were, and remain the case, that ships are to pass each other Port side to Port side (left to left). So, in the event of poor visibility the rule is that both ships automatically slow down; stop unless it is clear how to proceed; and then they are to move slowly to Starboard — to give a greater chance of passing Port to Port.

On this occasion it seems the two ships were heading almost head-on with the *Malaya* estimating the *Kertosono*, from the sound of the fog-horn, to be "fine off the Port bow", that is a little to the Malaya's left. The *Malaya* stopped for four minutes then proceeded to move to Starboard, to the right, presuming to give the *Kertosono* a wider margin. In fact the *Kertosono* was probably going too fast for the conditions and moved (incorrectly) to her Port, to the right, bringing them onto a collision course. They inevitably collided at 18:33 hours when the *Kertosono* hit the *Malaya* on her Port side. The details of this unhappy incident are given in the Public Record Office Admiralty archives under reference ADM178/131. This is a record of the Enquiry at the Royal Courts of Justice Admiralty Division under Mr Justice Bucknil. On the 9th July 1937 he concluded that neither of the ship's captains appreciated the true position, speed and direction of the other ship; he also states that in his opinion neither captain was negligent but

> *"... under these circumstances I am unable to see clearly any reason why different degrees of blame should be established, and I find both vessels equally to blame...".*

What in fact this High Court Judge (on Appeal) had decided was that the original Court Martial had wrongly concluded that the greater blame lay with the *Kertosono*. Thus in the calm, warm glow of the Courts of Appeal, in the Strand, London, and after five month's of deliberations, the fate of both seamen is decided — men who had to make decisions in an instant in the stormy conditions off the coast of Portugal on that rough and foggy night in February. The contrast couldn't be more stark but such is justice.

The punishment for each captain and the crews is not recorded within this final judgement but at an earlier hearing the chairman of the Board had gently admonished the Captain of the Malaya and suggesting that Captain Buckley

> *"...exercise greater care in future..".*

This seems a fair if rather understated admonition.

As for the fate of the ships; the *Kertosono* was towed, listing heavily, into Lisbon and the *Malaya* was ordered to Portsmouth for repairs. The PRO records show that the *Malaya* stoodby the *Kertosono* for two days until conditions at sea were good enough for tugs to come and rescue her and take her in tow. At which point, at 0805 hours on the 8th February, the *Kertosono's* Captain made a final radio call to *Malaya* to thank Captain Buckley thus;

> *"...Today another tug is coming and I will try to go to Lisbon. Have you much damage. I thank you so much for your help and kindness and say goodbye and good voyage...".*

Happily no-one died in this collision, the ship is repaired and time moves on. It is now September 1939 and the Second World War is about to begin. Declared on 3rd September between Britain and Germany. So, for the second time in the 20th Century global war is again upon us.

1939   Dec 4th Mon.*Doric Star* sunk by Graf Spee
1939   Dec 17th Sun *Graf Spee* scuttled in River Plate, in Beunos Aries
1940   Jan 1st   *Malaya* leaves Gibaltar for Halifax, to act as escort to merchant ship convoys.
1940   Jan 14th   From Halifax put to sea at 1242hrs, 10 knots, took station in convoy.

1940   Jan 15th   Merchant vessel in the convoy the *"Imperial Transport"* develops mechanical defect.
1940   Jan 18th   *Malaya* sights ship's navigation lights and sets an evasive zig-zag course.
1940   Jan 19th   Ship's log records "snow blizzard"
1940   Jan 21st   *Malaya* sights ship *"Jess Mursk"*. Malaya's Speed is 16 knots.
1940   Jan 21st   *Malaya* back in Halifax.
1940   Halifax Escort Force; Rear Admiral Bonham-Carter in HMS *Malaya* [9]
1940   Feb 2nd   *Malaya* providing Battleship escort to UK for Canadian Convoy TC3.

1940 Feb 7th   *Malaya* sights "*SS Aquatania*" Cunard liner acting as troop carrier .

1940 Feb 2nd   Malaya anchors at Greenock (UK) Log also records that *HMS Hood* and *HMS Warspite* here in Greenock and practicing a lot of gunnery drill.

1940 Feb 15th   *Malaya's* Flag at "half-mast" for Ratings lost in *HMS Suffolk*.

The ship's log records that on the 15th of February the *Malaya's* flag was flown at half-mast. Further research disclosed that this was in memory of sailors of the Cruiser HMS *Suffolk*.

As noted above, the *Kertosono* incident took place in the Atlantic, relatively close to the Bay of Biscay which is famous for its treacherous waters, no lives were lost on that night despite terrible weather conditions yet the collision between HMS *Suffolk* and SS *Misirah* in the protected waters of the Firth of Clyde estuary (Scotland, UK) cost 12 Lives. The two ships, *Suffolk* and *Misirah*, came onto a collision course whilst manoeuvring in the confined waters of the estuary. Once again the *Suffolk's* Log is brutally candid and to the point; for Sunday 11th February 1940 the log records [10];

> 12:20 Hours "*hands to de-ammunitioning*", then at 1400 hours, "*4 ratings discharged dead.*"

1940 Feb 21st   Log records *Malaya* re-loading ammunition.
1940 Feb 27th   *Malaya* weighs anchor to leave Greenock

Having returned from one such escort run from Halifax, in February 1940, the *Malaya* arrived and anchored offshore in Greenock. As it was en-route to the UK when the *Malaya* passed the Cunard Liner *Aquatania*, one of many cruise liners "commandeered" into troop-carrying duties. Whilst the *Aquatania* survived both wars, her sister ship SS *Lusitania* was infamously sunk by a German submarine in 1915. It should however be remembered that this was at time when the Royal Navy was still learning, relearning, the lessons of anti-submarine warfare, in particular maintaining as high a speed as the groups of ships can attain; taking zig-zagging courses and moving in convoy and of course, keeping your planned route secret.

1940 Mar 1st   *Malaya* arrives at Halifax
1940 Apl 6th   Scuttle in CPO flat stove-in and was shored up".
1940 Apl 13th   *Malaya* sights *HMS Vanquisher*, a Destroyer.
1940 Apl 15th   *Malaya* sights Eddistone Lighthouse at 0449 hrs. Anchors at Devonport.
1940 Apl 21st   CPO Powell joins *HMS Malaya* [11].

And now it is time for Chief Petty Officer Powell to enter into the *Malaya's* life. CPO Powell was based at this point at HMS *Excellent*, the gunnery training establishment in Portsmouth, he joined ship on 21st April 1940 as a Petty Officer Gunner. A few weeks later, on 20th May 1940 a new Captain also joins the *Malaya* for his one year tour of duty, he is Captain A.F.E. Palliser DSC. The Navigation Officer is still Gerald Cobb, the Officer mentioned in the *Kertosono* incident, and so at least we know Mr Cobb survived whatever punished was meted out in the High Court.

1940 Apl 22nd   *Malaya* slips anchor at 0938 hrs.

During WW2 the *Malaya* was variously deployed in support of Britain's several Fleets, Home, Far East, Mediterranean, Atlantic and so forth. For a while, in 1940, it was with one of two the Mediterranean Fleets. One of which was based at Alexandria, Egypt and the other, "Force H", based in Gibraltar. The Alexandria fleet was led by Admiral Cunningham and the Gibraltar Fleet by Admiral Somerville. Malaya was based in Alexandria in the company of other famous battleships such as HM ships Warspite, Royal Sovereign, and the Eagle an Aircraft carrier [12,13].

1940 Apl 26th   *Malaya* passes Trafalgar Light at 03:50 hours
1940 Apl 29th   *Malaya* sights 3 French Battleships, 3 Destroyers to Starboard
1940 Apl 30th   *Malaya* sights 3 French Cruisers and 2 Destroyers
1940 Apl 26th   *Malaya* arrives at Gibraltar 0810
1940 Apl 28th   *Malaya* "to sea"; "took on 8 boys from HMS *Cormorant*"
1940 Apl   USA approve refitting of British ships in the US Dockyards.

1940 Dec 4th Tue *Hyperion* providing Destroyer screen for *Malaya*

1940 May Med Force reinforced including the *Malaya* from the Atlantic [14]

1940 Jul 8th "during a bombing attack on *Malaya* on Monday 8th July a bomb splinter cut out a multi-core cable – broke telephone circuits" signed Capt AFE Passiler".

1940 Jul 9th Mediterranean Fleet too slow (23.5 kt) to catch Italian Fleet off Calabrian Coast [15]

1940 Jul Malaya in Mediterranean sees action off Calabria.

Admiral Cunningham's first brush with the Italian Naval forces was off the coast of Calabria (at the "toe" of Italy) on 9th July 1940 – by which time the French had already capitulated to the Germans. The French it will be recalled chose to have their ships sunk rather than hand them over to their supposed allies the British. Perhaps they were still smarting about Sluys and Agincourt. During this brief action the British had three capital ships present and the Italian's had two of their major warships on the scene. The British fleet then comprised the *Royal Sovereign* which was too slow to take part in the action and the *Malaya* which according to the records "never got within range"; (reminding us of her position in "Jutland" - nearby but not at the forefront of the action). The Italian fleet was superior in Cruisers and Destroyers. The Italian battleship "*Cesar*" was hit - at which point the Italian Fleet turned and fled under cover of smoke. Only one British ship, the Cruiser *Gloucester*, was struck in this brief skirmish but as with so many such exchanges the effect was to render the Italian (then enemies) unwilling to risk further encounters with British forces even when they put to sea with greater forces than the old British rust-buckets sent forth into the Mediterranean by the Admiralty [16].

1941 Jan Force H encounters Luftwaffe for the first time. Moves on to Gibraltar. Operation "Excess" underway [17].

1941 Feb 9th Sun Mediterranean Fleet inc. *Malaya* Bombard Genoa [18].

1941 C.in.C of Med force promoted to Knight Grand Cross [19]

1941 March 8th   Malaya is escorting convoy SL67 [20].
1941 Mar 8th   Malaya's aircraft spot enemy battle cruisers off
Cape Verde [21].
1941 Mar 28th Fri Battle Matapan, 1st big ship battle of WW2 [22].

The Italian battle-fleet was brought to action again, one year after the Battle of Calabria. This time it was on 28th/29th March1941 in the Battle of "Matapan" (now "Akra", Tainaron, off the Southern tip of Greece).

HMS *Malaya* took no part in this action either but this was an important fleet action, though not on the scale of Jutland. It is worth noting that the Battle of Matapan was an unusual incident for its time because this was a night action (with only primitive radar and gun-sighting equipment this was a dangerous decision). Admiral Cunningham was in command of the British Mediterranean Fleet and the Italian Fleet was commanded by Admiral Iachino. Once again the Italian Fleet realising it has lost the element of surprise turned and headed for its base but was intercepted by aircraft from HMS *Formidable.*

The Italians lost three cruisers, *Pola, Fiume* and *Zara* and a number of destroyers for the loss of just one aircraft on the British side. Once again this was not an outright defeat of the enemy but it was enough to deter them from interfering with British ship movements in the Mediterranean [23].

By 1941 HMS *Malaya* was being used for regular convoy-escort duties across the Atlantic; North America, Canada, South America, Caribbean, South Africa, and of course frequent returns to various bases in the UK.

Many of the *Malaya's* tours of duty were to escort convoys to and from Halifax - Nova Scotia, Canada. As one looks at a map of the North Atlantic this looks like a simple a dash along the Latitudes 45°/55°, between Great Britain and Canada but this does not take account of the German's presence in the form of U-boats nor the ice floes to the far North. By the way, the "U" stands for "Unterseeboot"; these 'under the water boats' were first launched by the Germans in 1906 so they were already the scourge of the Royal Navy long before the Second World War [24]. German submarines lurked ominously and barley visible, even when not submerged, waiting for an easy target. They preyed upon slow, old and poorly defended merchant ships carrying vital supplies for the UK.

Convoys, especially across the Atlantic, were seen as the best way to move merchant ships, a harsh lesson learned in the First World War. Each convoy was escorted by as large a naval force as the Admiralty could bring together. Typically this would be a larger gun-ship such as a battleship or cruiser plus destroyers. The bigger ships would take on any surface ships whilst the destroyers harried submarines. Once spotted a destroyer would spend hours "hunting" the submerged stalker, dropping patterns of depth-charges until it was sure they had sunk the enemy. A massive explosion followed by the tell-tale oil spillage and debris floating to the surface – unless of course the submarine Captain was playing games and dumping oil and rubbish to feign a fatal blow. Asdic (also known as Sonar "sound navigation and ranging") was introduced into the Royal Navy in 1918 [25]. This device would make the task of tracing and attacking submarines much easier, by "listening to their sound signature - but it would not guarantee a "kill". The battle against the U-Boat was finally won with combination of surface ships, such as the Destroyers using Asdic, and with Aircraft.

The Royal Navy also introduced the "Q-Ship" This was a merchant ship armed as heavily as a destroyer but its guns were hidden giving the impression of an un-armed merchantman, it was bait. Such ships had been used with some success against Pirates in the 18th century. Q-Ships are discussed again when we look at the brave exploits of Captain Campbell VC.

To return to convoys and escorts, it was the sombre and wretched role of a designated escort ship to pick up survivors from any Merchant (or Royal Navy) ship attacked and sunk; the main naval force would be under the strictest of orders not to stop to pick up sailors cast adrift. So the pick-up ships were relied upon both in reality for those left in the water but equally important as a moral booster for the sailors still afloat in their ship but likely to be sunk at any minute – however, the harsh reality was that there was little chance of sailors surviving more than a very few hours in the icy cold swell of the Atlantic in those latitudes. Such pick-up ships were of course an easy target for further attacks and it was not uncommon for survivors to be sunk a second time.

1941 Mar 8th Enemy Battlecruisers Scharnhorst and Gneisenau sighted by *Malaya* in South Atlantic [26].

1941 Apl 6th Sun to July '41, Malaya New York, USA for major refit [27].

Whilst in New York CPO Powell met relatives and made a contemporaneous wax-disc voice recording of his recollections of Malaya's sighting of the German raiders just a month before. A transcript of this recording is reproduced in a later chapter.

Roskill states that both *Malaya* and *Resolution* were "damaged in recent action" and were amongst the first to benefit from of USA's decision on 4th April 1941 to allow RN ships to be repaired and refitted in their yards [28].

1941 Jul 4th Thu *Scharnhorst* and *Gneisenau* Bombed in Brest. [29]

1941 Jul 8th *Malaya* and *Ramillies,* under the command of Admiral Cunningham, in the Med' (Force H); bombard Bardia and Fort Capuzzo [30]

1941 ? *Malaya* "moves West" [31]

1941 ? Aug *Malaya* refitting in Dockyard.

1941 Sep 17th Mr Powell leaves *HMS Malaya.*

1941 Sep Refit Oerlikons added

1941 Oct *Malaya* in Gibraltar with Force H [32].

1942 records not available.

1943 Jan Refit guns

1943 Jul In reserve, 3 months notice, "care & maintenance" at Faslane.

1943 Sep Refit 6" guns removed

1944 Mar Guns changed and missile defence added.

1944 Jun 6th Used for shore bombardment in the D-Day landings [33].

1945 May 23rd becomes training school Vernon II (torpedo school) [34]

1948 Jan 12th Paid-off.

1948 Feb 20th Scrapped.

After the war HMS *Malaya* was converted to carry missiles — which seemed to bring her into the modern era for warships but such big ships had had their day. Like many ships before her, it was de-commissioned and used as a training ship (Vernon) then finally paid off in 1948, the last piece of "scrap", the ships much prized bell, going 'home' to Malaya. The bell was sent to the Victoria Institute in Malaya where it was used daily as the school bell.

Thus ended HMS *Malaya*'s log and the ship....

Chapter 9: Guns and Ships
The Naval Gun and its platform

~~~~~~~~~~~

The purpose of a warship is self evidently to fight. Whatever secondary roles it may take on, it must carry a weapon system, historically simple guns, to shoot at the enemy. Before the days of aeroplanes, computer-guided weapons and missiles the Royal Navy had a distinct advantage over the land-based army in that naval ships could move big guns around the world to any theatre of war. A ship was in effect a mobile fortress; mobility and flexibility remain important factors in fighting supremacy.

In both World Wars, 1914 and 1939, the navies of the world relied almost exclusively upon ballistic weaponry. "Ballistic" refers to the natural trajectory or flight that a bullet or any similar object such as a cricket ball will take when thrown or fired. It will arc through the air then fall to earth as friction and gravity overtake the initial momentum. This is in contrast to "self-propelled" or 'guided' weapons. There were of course weapons that were not ballistic, early torpedoes, floating mines and the like.

The basics of a gun are these; essentially a gun is a tube into which is put a projectile, shell, bullet or even a human being if you work in a circus. If you are a child you will use a spring-loaded mechanism or compressed-air to eject the bullet. To be more effective at killing, gunpowder, to use the term loosely, will give more thrust. A trigger mechanism is needed to ignite the powder and get things going. In the earliest days a lighted ember was offered up to the gunpowder, an exhilarating but dangerous firing system.

Before the use of gunpowder ancient armies, the Greeks and Romans for example, used ropes in various forms to catapult their projectiles. The Chinese are credited with the discovery of gunpowder AD 1000 and a German Grey-Friar Berthold Schwarz is credited with introducing it to Europe in 1313 [1].

The guns using this new explosive powder were, not surprisingly, very small and simple devices, even those carried on board ships in the 15th/16th Century were light enough to be carried on board by soldiers. These would have been something like the 'Robinet' or the 'Serpentine' with a barrel size, a bore, of no more than about 1½ inches and firing a ball weighing little more than 5 to 8 ounces. Clearly these were intended to hurt the men rather than the ship. As Peter Kemp describes below there were at this time a great many types of gun, with an extraordinary variety of names, from 'basilisk' (this name derived from the ornate mouldings on the barrel), to the 'murderer' (a more honest and direct name for a portable gun in use for several centuries on Royal Navy ships).

Guns were restricted in size because the barrel had to be strong enough in construction to allow the gunpowder to explode (it is the sudden expansion of the gases that pushes the projectile out of the barrel) without disintegrating itself, as many did.

Much of the following detail about ships' guns are compiled with the assistance of Peter Kemp's 'Oxford Companion to Ships and the Sea':-

The early guns were either cast in bronze — a technique long known and used for making church bells — or were made of wrought iron. Wrought iron barrels were built up from bars of iron welded into crude tubes and strengthened by hoops shrunk on to the outside. A bronze cylinder might be inserted at the breech end to serve as a powder chamber. Cast iron, however, replaced wrought iron for all but the largest pieces during the 16th century, bronze being too expensive when guns were manufactured in thousands.

A great many sizes and types of gun were made in a process of continuous development during the 15th and 16th centuries, ranging from the 'whole' cannon firing a ball of more than 70 pounds weight down to the 'robinet', firing a shot of between ½ and 1 pound. A multiplicity of names which were sometimes transferred from one type of gun to another were used, such as base, basilisk, bombard, culverin, perier, drake, falcon, murderer, minion, saker, passavolante, serpentine, sling, mortar, trabucchio, and others.

The guns of the 15th and 16th centuries can be broadly grouped into four classes (NB, 'in.' refers to inches, 'ft' to feet and 'lb' refers to pounds weight):

a)   The cannon. This was of large calibre and medium length and range. Its two principal sub-types were the 'whole' cannon, of approximately
7-in. calibre, 11 ft in length, and firing a 50-lb ball; and the 'demi-cannon' of much the same length, but of 6-in. calibre and firing a 32-lb shot.

b)   The culverin. This was of smaller calibre relative to its length and therefore of greater range. It was subdivided into:
(i) the culverin, a typical example of which would be of 5-in. calibre and firing a 17-lb shot; its length might vary greatly between 13 ft for a bow chaser and 8 or 9 ft for a broadside gun.
(ii) the demi-culverin, a 9-pounder of 4-in. calibre and up to 11 ft in length.
(iii) the saker, a 5-pounder of 3-in. calibre and some 9 ft long.
(iv) the minion, a 4-pounder of 3-in. calibre and also some 9 ft in length.
(v) the falcon and falconet, which were 2- to 3-pounders and 1- to 2-pounders respectively.

c)   The perier or cannon-perier. This was a short-barrelled gun firing a medium-sized stone shot for a comparatively short distance. A typical example would have been an 8-in. gun, only 5 ft long, firing a 24-lb stone shot to a maximum range of some 1,600 yards, as compared to about 2,500 yards of the culverin and 1,700 yards of the demi-cannon.

d)   The mortar. This was an even shorter gun, the original type of which was of conical bore, resembling an apothecary's mortar. Ship-borne mortars of this date fired quantities of small pieces of iron or stone or bullets, either loose or made up in linen or leather bags, their target being would-be boarders on the enemy's deck.
     The culverin type of gun was preferred for arming ships during the 16th century rather than the heavy and comparatively unwieldy cannon and demi-cannon. The steady improvement in the quality and power of gunpowder and quicker combustion, together with increasing accuracy in the manufacture of the guns themselves, permitted smaller charges to be used and the length of the culverin to be reduced. At the same time naval guns were mounted on the low wooden carriages running on small, solid, wooden wheels or trucks which they were to retain thereafter, in place of the two or four-wheeled, higher carriages or, sometimes, timber scaffolds on which they were mounted in the early Tudor ships.
     The development in the late 16th century by the English and the Dutch of the galleon, with sides pierced for gun-ports, brought about a new form of naval warfare, relying upon com-

paratively long-range broadside fire instead of boarding. Its effectiveness was first notably demonstrated in the defeat by the English fleet of the Spanish Armada in 1588.

With further improvement in the quality of powder during the 17th century, guns were again shortened, permitting greater calibres for the same weight. Even such large pieces as the 'cannon-royal', weighing some 8,000 lbs and firing a 66-lb shot, were sometimes mounted. By the end of the period, however, the usual sizes were the 42-pounder on the lower decks and the 24-pounder on the upper gun-decks. The medieval names were now abandoned and the guns identified simply by the weight of the shot they fired.

Except for the addition of the carronade, in about 1779, naval guns changed very little from this time until the industrial revolution, though refinements were made in the arrangements for absorbing the recoil, and the flint-lock was introduced in place of the slowmatch and flintstock.

The carronade, so named after the Carron Iron Founding and Shipping Company where it was invented, was a very short, light carriage gun making use of a small propellant charge to fire a relatively heavy shot for a limited range. It commended itself to the Royal Navy during the French wars of the late 18th and early 19th centuries as an auxiliary to the main armament for use in the yard-arm to yard-arm type of fight the British always aspired to bring about. It first proved itself in Lord Rodney's victory of the Saints in 1782 and soon became a regular feature of all British men-of-war, being later copied by the French. It was known in the British Navy as a 'smasher'.

By the end of the 19th Century there was an enormous array of guns for a shipbuilder to choose from when arming the ship. But one vital matter that took several centuries to resolve was the manner in which the shot was loaded into the barrel; guns could be 'muzzle-loading' or 'breech-loading'. This describes the way the projectile is put into the gun; through the open end (muzzle) or by opening the closed end, the breech. The second method, via the breech, is more complex and it took several centuries to devise a safe and quick system of opening, loading and securely closing the breech. Despite many experiments the final solution to the safe and quick loading breech was the 'interrupted screw'. This device was not finally made safe until 1880. The interrupted screw allowed the breech end of the barrel to be opened (to insert a shell) and then the breech-block shut and with just a quarter turn making the end gas tight and secure against the blast. The rate of fire could be considerably increased once this type of breech-block was accepted as reliable [2].

The projectile itself, the shell, has evolved from a carved, spherical stones, to metal balls and thence to the familiar bullet shape, cylindrical with a pointed front end. The rifling, curved grooves along the inside of the barrel, forced the shell to spin and this improved accuracy considerably. Discovered in the 1850s, at about the same time the French also introduced the elongated bullet; these developments were key to improving gunnery range and accuracy. [3].

In 1858 Sir William Armstrong brought these improvements together and refined them into what was then the modern naval gun. Firstly, an elongated shell with ratio of about 3:1 circumference to length, with flat base and rounded (ogival) head. Secondly, the multiple spiral ('the poly-groove') rifling, a great improvement on the oval shaped barrel but both ideas were intended to spin the shell as it left the barrel. Thirdly a composite barrel, not cast but built up in layers of steel and wire bindings. Finally, it was breech-loading, although Armstrong did not use the interrupted screw, this vital mechanism was not perfected until around 1880 [4].

The use of guns on warships began with small boats, powered by oars or sails and with small guns carried by soldiers. They would have carried muskets, which had an effective range of about one hundred yards and this was the usual measure for opening an engagement with enemy ships under sail. So for many centuries the "warship" was merely a form of transport to carry soldiers across a stretch of water in order that they might get nearer to their enemy; at which point a traditional hand-to-hand fight would take place using the latest land-based weaponry of the day – swords, spears, bows and arrows, catapult, fire, musket-shot and so forth.

Initially guns were mounted on merchant sailing vessels. Until the time of Samuel Pepys and the Commonwealth in the 17th Century most Naval battles were fought using ships hired or commandeered from merchant fleets – much like their crews, who were often "press ganged" into joining the Navy.

Soldiers needed a platform upon which to fight and so came specialised ships with "castles" as fighting platforms. Castles were built onto the fore and after end of cargo-carrying merchant ships and into these castles were fitted small naval cannon. The front end of a warship's upper deck remains the fo'csle as a remnant of that old arrangement.

Eventually these ships became purpose-built "men-of-war", no longer converted private ships. These formed the basis of the navy so when they were not in use they were laid up "in ordinary"; kept in reserve, afloat but otherwise left unattended. The after-castle and the fore-castle as well as being a fighting platform also provided better accommodation for the Captain and Officers. These parts of the ship became very elaborate palaces, with fine wood panelling inboard and very creative mouldings and carvings outboard.

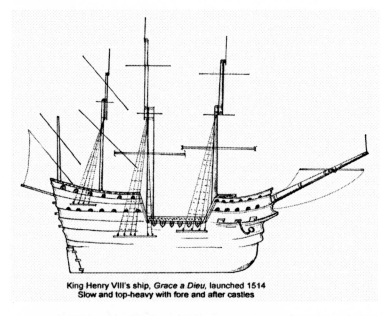

King Henry VIII's ship, *Grace a Dieu*, launched 1514
Slow and top-heavy with fore and after castles

At the height of the soldier-at-sea era in the 17th Century a magnificent pair of ships were built, for Charles I, by the Pett family father Phineas and son Peter. They first built the *Prince Royal* then the mighty *Sovereign of the Seas*. These were quite outlandish, very large and very ornate, but nevertheless they proved to be very successful warships.

The *Sovereign* had 104 bronze guns – 20 cannon firing 60lb shot; 8 Demi-cannon 30lb shot; 32 Culverins 18lb shot and 44 demi-culverines. The ship also carried an assortment of smaller artillery, musket and "stern-chasers" and "bow-chasers" – these were small guns for firing directly ahead or astern. By comparison, and 150 years later, HMS *Victory*, now in Portsmouth Naval Dockyard, had about 100 x 32 pounders. A 42-pounder cannon was rarer but for the purposes of comparison a 42 pounder had a barrel size, or calibre, of 7 inches, 7" being the diameter of a 42 pound cannon ball. Having 100 cannon of this size made a "First Class" and so a "Ship of the Line". It was therefore a leading battleship of her day [5].

You will notice if you have seen the HMS *Victory* or pictures old men-of-war that the guns, the cannon, point out through gun-ports on each side of the ship. It was a British shipwright James Baker who, in 1514, had the novel idea of moving the guns below deck. He suggested cutting holes (ports) in the side of the ship so cannon could protrude from the lower gun decks and fire as needed. It is to be noted however that another source attributes the idea to a Frenchman but as this is a book about the British Navy credit will go to the Englishman in this case – c'èst la vie [6].

Unhappily it was the misuse of this clever device (the gunport) that caused the sinking of the *Mary Rose* in the Solent off Portsmouth as noted in an earlier chapter. The details are that on the 19th July 1545 the elderly, and soon to be surprised, King Henry VIII was present. Henry, possibly with his sixth wife Catherine Parr in attendance (but more likely on his own and looking for a new girl – as any sailor might), was on the beech at Southsea watching his new ship gliding out of Portsmouth harbour into the Solent. But the *Mary Rose* was fatally overloaded with guns and soldiers in heavy armour. The Captain (Carew), claimed to have an unruly crew who had failed to close the lower gun ports. So at the first puff of wind it leaned over, took in water and tilted and tilted and tilted. Finally, and inexorably, it keeled over, sank and then waited on the seabed for rescue some 400 years later. Her skeleton can be seen on display in Portsmouth Dockyard. This should have been a lesson for all ship builders – make sure there is sufficient freeboard, that is height at the side of the ship above the waterline. Sadly a good few more ships were to go down

over the ensuing years, HMS *Captain* being one terrible example
[7].

If the *Sovereign* was the culmination of the traditional sailing ship with high fighting castles fore and aft then the "*Revenge*" was the forerunner of the lean fighting machine – still a sailing ship but now it had now taken on racing lines. 'Racing' in this case does not refer to a high speed vessel but one in which the castles had been "razed" or removed. This was upon the advice of Sir John Hawkins as Treasurer to Queen Elizabeth's ships, and in timely anticipation of a Spanish invasion in the form of the "Spanish Armada" in 1588. The *Revenge*, and others of her class, were smaller lighter vessels but much more manoeuvrable. The outcome of that sea skirmish in the English Channel is well known but if you have forgotten it was... England 1 : Spain 0.

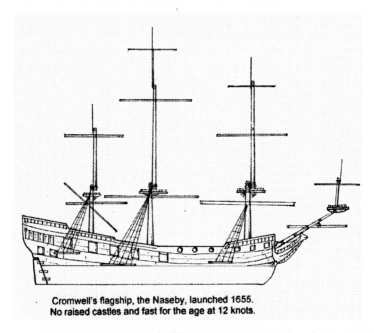

Cromwell's flagship, the Naseby, launched 1655.
No raised castles and fast for the age at 12 knots.

The *Revenge* was followed by the *Naseby*. Launched in 1655 at the direction of Oliver Cromwell during his time in charge of the "Commonwealth", the *Naseby* was the prototype for fighting ships for the next 200 years. A beautiful ship with clean lines, no fore-castle, no after-castle and a wide beam at the waterline to give her stability. An excellent compromise between size, speed, armaments and protection. The same elements that still have to be balanced by a shipbuilder of any warship. The "fighting sailor" had come of age [8].

Look at any of these old warships, such as the *Victory* at Portsmouth, and it is soon evident that it has a number of disadvantages. Almost all the guns all stick out of the sides and are in fixed positions. There is very little flexibility – the whole ship has to be manoeuvred to be in a position to fire a broadside at an opposing vessel. Manoeuvrability of the ship itself is another inhibiting factor – sailing ships by definition relies upon the wind. No wind, no movement and no fighting. The Captain with the better sailing Master has the clear advantage and should win the day. It was not unheard of for Captains to put out their rowing boats and have their ships towed into a better position and such manoeuvring could take a day or two. This tactic was used with success in the defeat of the Spanish Armada.

Not a lot was to change for several centuries. The sailing man-o'-war was a well-honed fighting machine and it was not until the age of steam and the use of iron and steel that dramatic changes came in ship design. But the Royal Navy was hampered by its own success. The Navy ruled the waves and had done so for at least two hundred years – with much the same old ships, guns, men, and systems. The Royal Navy provided the 'wooden walls of England' and this was seen as an impregnable defence. So the Admiralty was not keen to change things. Improvements to warships were often slow and incremental. This was mainly because of the very conservative nature of the Admiralty which was slow to adapt to new ideas; this was sometimes the wisest approach — to ensure a new system was indeed better than a tried and tested old system. As we know from the previous chapter, the Admiralty did not readily accept the new breech loading system for guns, nor were they persuaded by the French version of the 'interrupted screw'. Nevertheless, progress continues and from time to time a clever person comes along with an idea to improve things.

Captain Cowper-Cole was one such soul, his enterprising contribution to naval gunnery, in 1855, was to mount a cannon on a raft and, using oars, guide this primitive gun-raft towards the enemy [9]. This would of course have been for a coastal action, such a contraption would not have survived a sea voyage. It did however lead to his development of the gun-turret – a rotating metal housing in which to place, and manoeuvre, a gun.

From the middle of the 19th Century ships changed dramatically as metal hulls replaced the 'Wooden walls of England'. A combination-hull design, combining wood and iron cladding, was being developed. With the age of steam came 'combination-ships', ships that were capable of using either sail or steam. Guns were being fixed into a variety of housings, but essentially either barbettes or turrets. Barbettes were fixed emplacements, rather as one would find in a fortress, with the gun mounted on rails so that it could be moved to left or right. Muzzle-loaded cannon were giving way to breech-loaded guns with very high velocities. The final solution to mounting most guns, big or small, was for them to be housed in a turret so that the whole turret moved with the gun. This allowed the gun to be reloaded from any position and gave some protection to the gunners.

Guns were also moved from the traditional arrangement of two parallel rows – one row on each side of the ship — to gun-turrets placed on the centre line. At first this arrangement of guns was hampered by the sail's rigging, which reduced the arc of fire for each turret, but with the demise of sails that problem soon passed.

If HMS *Naseby* brought together the best of fighting sail then the whole process of designing ships had to be rethought with the introduction of iron/steel and steam-power, a whole new set of compromises as to size, shape, weight and guns was necessary.

Guns, as stated earlier, are now usually described by the diameter of the shell they fire. A ship's gun ranged from four inch to fifteen inch calibre. Small shells were still being described by the weight of the shell, such as the "3lb", a three-pounder, guns as carried on the *Malaya*. The reference to the weight of the shell harks back to the time when sailing ships listed the size of their cannons by the weight of the cannon projectile rather than the "calibre" or diameter of the barrel required to fire the projectile [10].

Returning to 20th century guns, a '15-inch gun' meant that each shell was fifteen inches in diameter, about the size of a car wheel. A 15" gun weighed about 100 tons and a single shell weighed as much as 1,920 pounds, over one ton in weight and again compares to the weight of modern car. A shell of this size was capable of being hurled in excess of 30,000 yards or about 17 miles. We know that 'ballistics' is about lobbing something into the air with as much force as you think is necessary and then watch it lose momentum and fall to earth, or better still fall onto your target. Most ball games are ballistic in nature given that the ball is usually thrown, or struck, and without further assistance goes on its way. Depending upon your choice of game, you may want distance, as in golf, or accuracy, as in cricket, or position as in football. Inevitably you usually need a combination of speed, accuracy and position.

The following notes are taken from Peter Hodges' "The Big Gun" whose contribution to my understanding of ballistics is hereby acknowledged [11].

The three major factors affecting the theoretical range of a gun are:

Firstly, and fairly clearly, the size of the propellant charge in relation to the weight of the shell;

Secondly, the length of the barrel; and

Thirdly, the elevation of the gun in its trunnions (pivots).

In order to achieve stability in flight, the ratio of projectile length to diameter is approximately the same for any size — and the limits of cartridge mass are dictated by the practical dimensions and structural strength of the breech block and chamber.

Because cordite is, by definition, a 'low' explosive which, upon ignition, takes a measurable time to expand into gaseous form (as distinct from a 'high' explosive the expansion rate of which on detonation is virtually instantaneous), it will continue to expand behind the shell for about half the barrel's length. In simple terms this means that the longer the barrel is made, the greater will be the muzzle velocity (MV) of the emerging projectile, with a consequent increase in range.

Barrel length is limited by its stiffness as a tube structure. If too great, 'droop' will occur, and thus, for heavy ordnance, a barrel the total bore length of which falls between 40 and 50 calibres (note, calibre in this sense means the ratio of the diameter of the barrel to its length, a 42 calibre gun 42 times as long as its barrel size) becomes an optimum size. The smaller the calibre the easier it is to increase the proportionate barrel length: a rifle, for example, may be very long-barrelled indeed and out-range a pistol firing identical ammunition by many hundreds of yards.

Quite apart from the structural problems of building a long-barrelled gun, an attendant consideration is that of barrel life. A high MV creates greater wear - and relining a big gun may be a protracted and expensive exercise. In peacetime, expense is usually the deciding factor; in war, time is all-important.

Country of origin	Gun	Bore as a multiple of the Calibre	Nominal MVf/s (feet/second)
GB	15 inch, Mark I	42	2450
GB	13.5 inch, Mark V	45	2582
USA	14 inch, Mark IV	50	2800
USA	14 inch, Mark I	45	2600
Comparison of battleship guns; their bore length, calibre, and muzzle-velocity.			

Peter Hodges goes on to explain in extraordinary detail the complex science of external ballistics at this point in order, he says, to understand the real significance of a surface weapon's maximum elevation. He states that the theoretical range of any missile — be it shell from a gun or stone from a catapult (though not, of course, a powered rocket) — is governed by a formula which is finally multiplied by the trigonometrical term 'sine of twice the angle of elevation'. At this point we leave Peter Hodge's very clear and erudite exposition of gun theory... far too detailed for this book but worth tracking down if the reader wants more detail about shell trajectories.

Given this complex trigonometry plus the unpredictable forces of nature (wind, rain and gravity) it will come as no surprise that the chances of being hit by another ship's gun-fire were actually quite small – all navies wasted an enormous amount of ammunition failing to hit the intended targets — so all the more unfortunate if your ship was quickly "bracketed". That is, shells falling short then just over your head, the next salvo of shells were sure to hit unless your captain could move the ship rather quickly in a new and unpredictable direction!

'Range and director' devices helped to improve fire control. Three people should be remembered for their contribution to usable systems for gauging range, speed and predicted position, namely, Arthur Pollen, 1905, Lieutenant Dumaresq and Lieutenant (later Admiral) Frederick Dreyer 1911. The German versions were much better at Jutland and consequently they found their targets rather quicker than the British [12].

Many paintings of fighting ships will show just how many shells, or cannon-balls, are seen to be falling into the water, it helps to give a sense of action in the picture, but it also reflects quite accurately how many shells fell short of their intended target. Not forgetting of course that the English sailing man-o-war chose to fire a little downwards and so bounce their cannon ball at the waterline; this gave more chance of holing the ship at the water line and so sinking the opposition. It was also the inspiration for Barnes-Wallace's bouncing bomb in WW2.

We now have a better idea how guns and ships evolved so it's time to meet the sailors.

Chapter 10: The Sailors

~~~~~~~~~~~

The Royal Navy is about warships — but sailors are needed to sail them and the better the sailor the more efficient will be the ship. So this chapter is about the people who have made the Royal Navy a success. Nelson will get first mention because he is *so* famous.

Horatio Nelson is probably the first name to come to mind if asked to name a legendary sailor. Provide a clue by removing one arm, either arm, from its sleeve and cover one eye, left or right, and it is certain people will to know to whom you refer. In fact his surgeon removed his right arm but the eye-patch is another myth. He lost the sight of his right eye but not the eye itself; the closest he got to an eye-patch was an occasional use of a shade over his good eye [1].

Although he *is* famous, his birthday on 29th September 1758 is not a national holiday; nor is Trafalgar Day – indeed most people would be hard pressed to remember it is on 21st October. His monument, Nelson's Column, stands in the middle of Trafalgar Square in London but few of the tourists paddling in the pools of water just below him could name his Battle honours, St Vincent, Nile, Copenhagen and Trafalgar. He is famous because he wanted to be famous.

From the outset Nelson had a few things in his favour; not least he had connections in an age when patronage was the key to success. His Uncle, Maurice Suckling, was Comptroller of the Navy and would provide introductions for the young Nelson. He also had luck on his side; he could have lost his head and not just an eye. In his own words he records, "...it (the splinter) was within a hair's breadth of taking off my head...", but to his wife he writes less dramatically, "... it was a slight scratch, a blemish unseen".

In fact Nelson was lucky to live long enough to see any action at sea because he was a sickly child and illness plagued him all his life. He was a charismatic person, and according to the history books he was a good leader and brave sailor; a combination which earned him respect and affection throughout the Fleet.

His "battle honours" are as follows;

Born 29th September 1758 in Burnham Thorpe, Norfolk;
Midshipman, aged 12 years, 1st January 1771;
Acting Lieutenant 1776 at 17 years of age;
Married Francis Nesbit 11th March 1787;
Promoted Captain of the Agamemnon, 30th January 1793.
Meets Lady Hamilton, (maintaining the tradition of 'a girl in every port').
Battle of St Vincent; receives the sword from Spanish, 14th February 1797.
Honoured as "Knight of the Bath", 20th March 1797.
Promoted Rear-Admiral of the Blue.
Right arm amputated after leading an attack on Santa Cruz, 24th July 1797.
Honoured, "Order of the Bath", 27th September 1797.
Battle of Nile, 1st August 1798.
Entertained by Lady Hamilton (with Sir William Hamilton her husband).
Honoured as "Baron of the Nile and Burnham Thorpe". September 1798.

Nelson and his supporters were disappointed that this honour was not to a higher social position but as he was not commander in chief, (Admiral Jervis, Lord St Vincent was) it was not yet appropriate — but he could take comfort from the Sultan of Turkey who awarded him the "Plume of Triumph" – how quaint sound other nation's honours and titles.

Promoted to Rear Admiral of the Red 14th February 1799
Honoured as "Duke of Brontë" 13th August 1799.
Promoted Vice-Admiral of the Blue 1st January 1801
Separated from his wife Francis 13th January 1801.
Daughter "Horatia" born to Nelson and Lady Hamilton 30th January 1801.
Battle of Copenhagen, 2nd April 1801.
Honoured "Viscount Nelson of Nile etc...."
Promoted Commander in Chief Mediterranean (Fleet), 16th May 1803.
Battle of Trafalgar, 21st October 1805.
Died on board HMS Victory, 21st October 1805
Buried at St Paul's Cathedral, London.

It was during the Battle of Copenhagen that Nelson 'failed' to observe Sir Hyde Parker's signal to withdraw. In fact Parker was well aware that Nelson might be in a better position than himself to continue with the battle and was tacitly giving Nelson the option to fight or withdraw whilst taking responsibility for the withdrawal – Parker was described as a wise but not resolute commander but his faith in Nelson was well founded.

What the records tell us about this minor incident, of apparent blindness, is as follows; upon receiving knowledge that Parker had raised a signal of withdrawal Nelson decided he would continue in the certain knowledge that capitulation at this juncture would bring annihilation of the British fleet, he therefore remarked,

"... I only have one eye, I have a right to be blind sometimes...
I really do not see the Signal...".

The action against the Danes continued and the British won the day.

The battles and honours listed above indicate that Nelson was a courageous man. He was an inspirational leader of men, quite happy to lead a boarding party onto the enemy's ship or to stand prominently on deck in the heat of battle. He was apparently assertive but not a tyrant. Nelson preferred to share his plans with his Captains, they would then know his general strategy and only the minimum of orders were required as battle ensued.

As a tactician he could take advantage of the relaxation of the rules of engagement, in particular the sacrosanct 'line of battle'. Too rigid adherence to this battle plan led to Admiral Byngs' undoing – in fact his execution. Nelson was a more flexible thinker. Such flexibility in the face of rigid rules is known as the "Nelson touch". Nelson also benefited from improved flag signalling so that by 1803 he could use Popham's alpha/numeric codes to send very detailed, coded messages to his Fleet. His well known signal "England expects every man to do his duty" was transformed into a flag signal in moments – the unfortunate Admirals Byng and Graves might have had better results if their signalling had been as clear to understand.

Nelson also benefited from a "professional" fighting force, his sailors had spent many months at sea honing their skills in sailing and at gunnery whereas Napoleon's naval forces were at their worst. The French Revolution had killed off the corps of senior naval commanders, the experienced officers; the ships were worn out and the sailors were ill-prepared. It was Admiral Pierre de Villeneuve's ill-luck to be compelled by Napoleon to put to sea and de Villeneuve knew exactly how Nelson would deal with his motley crew. The details of Nelson's campaigns need not be explained in detail in this brief biography but essentially he was willing to use unexpected tactics by sailing close in-shore or cutting through the enemy's lines to cause mayhem in what should have been an orderly exchange of fire in two neat parallel lines of ships.

Nelson was not however without his failings, which he tended to pass over in his own notes 'Sketch of my Life'. Two incidents were less than auspicious. His attack on Fort St Juan in 1780 and, even more disastrous, his attempt to take Turk Island (in the Bahamas) in 1783. James Trevenen, an officer present at the Turk Island action was less circumspect about Nelson's efforts

".... the ridiculous expedition against Turk Island, undertaken by a young man merely from the hope of seeing his name in the papers, ill depicted at first, carried on without a plan afterwards, attempted to be carried into execution rashly, because without intelligence, and hastily abandoned for the same reason that it ought not to have been undertaken at all..." ;

In summary, he was ill-prepared for this adventure whilst the French were ready and waiting for him. Later successes allowed Nelson's early failings to fade in the memory so has his extraordinary time in Naples, meeting the Hamiltons and the Royal Court including the Queen of Naples. At the time England thought this all an ill-judged intervention by Nelson. His affair with Lady Hamilton was too openly displayed for England's sensibilities and the rescue of the Royal Family was not part of Britain's plans for Nelson or indeed Italy. As with all enduring heroes, history paints a glorious and immortal picture [2].

~

John Jervis, 1st Earl St Vincent, 1735 to 1823. This man might well have stood on the column in Trafalgar Square making it Jervis's

Column for without Jervis's support and confidence Nelson wouldn't be there; in fact Jervis was the more senior officer. Like Nelson he began life as a Midshipman and rose to the rank of First Sea Lord in 1800 and was Commander in Chief of a number of operations. A brilliant tactician against the French, who were supporting the Americans in their fight for independence, he had for example, a spectacular success when in command of the *Foudroyant* in 1782 capturing the French ship *Pégase*.

Not one man on his own ship was killed and he suffered no more than two black eyes and his reward for this adventure was a Baronetcy. Jervis was also Commander in Chief at the Cape St Vincent engagement against the Spanish. Nelson took the decision to break from his line and attack the enemy directly; he made the decision, as the records show, at precisely 12:50 hours on 14th February 1797 and Jervis (as the Commander in Chief) made the same decision to signal his ships giving permission for them to leave their stations and attack their opposite number and he made his signal at 12:51, just one minute later. Nelson had anticipated his thoughts and risked Court Martial, instead he has takes centre-stage in Trafalgar Square.

~

Next in line is Sir Francis Drake, 1543 to 1596, he was a short, stocky red-haired man born in Tavistock, Devon. From the outset he was in conflict with the Spanish ships and Drake's name is always associated with the defeat of their Armada (1588) and the game of bowls he is reputed to have played on Plymouth Hoe whilst Spaniards were sailing up the English Channel.

Drake's first command in 1567 was as Captain of the 50 ton ship *Judith* which he used for a slave trading voyage whereupon he was attacked by the Spanish off the coast of Mexico. At that time Drake was a Privateer, meaning he was acting privately, not actually commissioned by the Navy or the Monarch (Queen Elizabeth I), but acted in the knowledge it had given her tacit approval to do mischief against Britain's enemies.

Although it is Drake who is remembered for saving England from the Spaniards Lord Howard of Effingham was actually Commander-in-Chief and Drake his Vice Admiral. But Drake was the better self-publicist. As for the game of bowls, this was first recorded in 1736, 150 years after the Armada, and may be another apocryphal story about the Navy. It is however true that the Spanish took many months organising their fleet, the Armada. It is also true that the English had several days' warning of their approach up the Channel and it should be noted that the wind was against the English, who could not have easily sailed out of Plymouth Sound to meet the Armada anyway. So there would have been ample to finish a game if one was underway.

The Spanish were first spotted on 19th July (1588) off the Lizard (Cornwall), a point on the extreme South-West Coast of England. Their fleet of 130 ships was arrayed in a huge crescent formation, which was first engaged by the British off Eddystone Lighthouse, to the South of Plymouth, on the 21st two days after first being sighted. But the more decisive part to this running battle took place off the coast of France at Calais and an area called Gravelines. The Spanish fleet was split into several smaller groups and a number of ships burned; defeated they fled North around Britain and so severe were weather conditions that they arrived back in Spain with only 67 ships intact — from an original force 130.

Drake is also reputed to be the first Captain to take his ship around the world in the *Golden Hind* 1577-80 and was knighted by Queen Elizabeth I. Despite his gallantry he lost favour when he failed to destroy the remnants of the Spanish fleet in 1589. However, he did succeed in becoming Mayor of Plymouth but failed in a further attack on the Spanish in 1596. He died on 28th January 1596 of Yellow Fever in the attempt. He was fittingly buried in the Caribbean Sea.

~

Three years after Drake's death Robert Blake was born, in Bridgewater, Somerset. As a General-at-Sea, later the title was changed to 'Admiral', he is famous for his actions in the three Dutch Wars. Initially he suffered several defeats at sea by the more experienced Dutch Navy which was under the command of the very experienced and professional sailor, Admiral Tromp.

The British and Dutch fought sporadically over 21 years before the newly titled 'Royal Navy' finally took command of the North Sea and the English Channel as "Sovereign of the Seas". Legend has it that Tromp tied a broom or brush to his masthead as a defiant gesture signalling he had swept the North Sea free of the British; Blake answered by tying a whip to his masthead when he thought he had finally whipped the Dutch. In reality a broom tied to the mast was a signal that the ship was for sale; it seems unlikely that Blake would mistake a for-sale sign for such a gesture but the story is a good one.

Blake also had some success in 1654 against the notorious Barbary Coast Pirates. Like Drake, he also had to face the Spanish and managed to capture enough of their treasures to make himself a very rich man. His contribution to the development of the Royal Navy was also considerable. He introduced the Article of Wars and Fighting Instructions, precursors to Queens Regulations and the Naval Discipline Acts. In his time the Navy developed long-range gunnery; ship to ship rather than close-quarter fighting, and the line-ahead formation for broadside battles. Clearer signalling helped to improve manoeuvring the fleet without frequent conferences on the Admiral's ship. In Blake's time pay, rank and the organisation of ships' ratings all helped to lay the foundations for Nelson's successes a hundred years later. He died, on 7th August 1657, on his way back to Plymouth and was buried in Westminster Abbey – but he didn't lay there for very long because upon his restoration King Charles II had him exhumed and thrown into the River Thames – so in the end he had a rather unusual, unplanned and definitely unexpected burial at sea — as befits a seaman [3].

~

There are two sailors named 'Cook' to be mentioned here. The first was Fred' Cook, 1865 to 1940, an American who claimed to have explored the Arctic and North Pole but was proved to be a fraud. The more famous James Cook, 1728 to 1779, was a Captain in the Royal Navy and was born in Yorkshire. Famed for his skills as a navigator he began his sea life in the Merchant Navy but preferred the excitement offered by the Royal Navy. His surveying of the St Lawrence River paved the way for Britain's successful recapture of Quebec and the conquest of Canada.

Leaving the cool Northern Latitudes he was sent to explore and map the Southern Oceans in search of the fabled 'Terra Australis Incognito', a supposed continent where we now know Antarctica lies. He is rightly remembered for providing a diet sufficiently well planned that his crew suffered no Scurvy – something of a miracle for the time.

Cook surveyed in detail many of the Islands of the Pacific including New Zealand and he was able to prove, in 1773, that Terra Australis Incognito did not exist. He returned to Portsmouth on 29th July 1775 – where he should have stayed – for was killed by Polynesians whose approbation had turned to obloquy when he returned [4].

~

Samuel Pepys, 1633 -1703, was not a sailor but his contribution to the Royal Navy was fundamental. Pepys was an extraordinarily resourceful man; he had to be to survive in England in the 17th Century. He had to tread a wary path between shifting religious bigotry, catholic and protestant in turns and between monarchy and commonwealth. These were revolutionary times indeed but he not only survived, he was very successful. He showed remarkable resilience to change and he had good connections, in particular a cousin Edward Montague, later the Earl of Sandwich.

Pepys had the rather lengthy job title 'Clerk of the Acts of the Kings Ships'. Money, for Pepys personally and for the Navy, was always a problem but he was determined to improve things. He was particularly keen to improve work in the Royal Dockyards, which were rife with fraud, dishonesty and corruption. To him goes credit for the better administration of the Navy. Samuel Plimsoll is another man who never went to sea but to him goes credit for the Plimsoll Line, by defining the load limit for ships. The Plimsoll line can be seen on any large vessel. Mr John Harrison (1693 to 1776) the carpenter is to be remembered for his Chronometer. This remarkably accurate timepiece enabled navigators to calculate their Latitudinal position as well as their Longitude making long sea voyages that much safer and predictable.

~

Returning to real sailors, William Bligh rose to the rank of Vice-Admiral, his dates are 1754 to 1817. He was a most skilful navigator but apparently an abysmal manager of men. His claim to fame, or infamy, arises from his command of HMS *Bounty*. His crew mutinied on 28th April 1789. The cause for this unusual turn of events in the Royal Navy, which has had very few mutinies, was probably a combination of circumstances; Bligh's incompetence, not as a technician but in his leadership, and the attractions of the South Sea folk, the women were particularly attractive and kind spirited.

Life back on the high seas held no attractions once the crew had settled into the idyll on the Pacific island of Tahiti. It is well known that after the mutiny Bligh gave an outstanding example of his technical and navigational skills by rescuing himself and eighteen of the more loyal members of his crew. He sailed some 3,600 miles across the Pacific Ocean in an open boat sailing from Friendly Island to Timor (near Java) without losing a soul and presumably managing to maintain discipline without causing too much aggravation.

Upon his return to England he was appointed Governor of New South Wales. The Admiralty probably couldn't stand his irritating ways in England any more than his crew and, as if to confirm his woeful lack of management skills, he also managed to quarrel with his Deputy to the extent that he got himself arrested and sent back to England. However incompetent he was he nevertheless rose inexorably through the ranks of the Navy List to the position of Vice-Admiral [5]. As for the mutineers, most were caught and hung or died prematurely.

~

Until this point our naval heroes have been long dead but this triumvirate are a little more modern.

Fisher, Jellicoe and Beatty were key players in the First World War (at Sea).

The first is John Arbuthnot Fisher, 1st Baron of Kilverstone, 1841 to 1920. Peter Kemp helpfully summarises his contribution to the Royal Navy [6].

1. His name will always be associated with his introduction of the all-big-gun battleship, the first being HMS *Dreadnought*.
2. He also introduced the nucleus crew system, whereby two-fifths of a ship's complement would be permanent.
3. He reduced the sea-going fleet by scrapping older ships.
4. He redistributed naval forces, concentrating the main elements in home waters rather than the Mediterranean.

He is credited with improvements to gunnery and gunnery training and amongst other innovations the introduction of oil fuel in preference to coal.

Despite his long struggle to introduce the *Dreadnought* type battleship he could already see the submarine would bring about their demise. He was clearly a radical thinker and like many leaders he engendered great loyalty in some but was loathed by others; this was very destructive for the Navy as it brought the pro- and anti-Fisher lobbies into constant conflict. Whatever his strengths and weaknesses he did bring some preparedness to the

Royal Navy in time for the 'Great War'. Although even this praise is tinged with a certain doubt, for his wholesale destruction of the Fleet in favour of the Dreadnought Battleship gave Germany, amongst several other seafaring nations, a chance to catch up, it produced a level playing field so it was just a matter of time, who could afford to build the biggest and best ships most efficiently and quickly – Britain lost its clear lead as the pre-eminent sea power.

The next two men in this triumvirate, John Jellicoe and David Beatty, had to work with the Navy Fisher had given them. In brief Jellicoe was the more senior officer but Beatty was a self-publicist, like Nelson and Fisher. Jellicoe by contrast was the quiet but masterful tactician. They each had their own followers.

Jellicoe, 1st Earl John Rushworth Jellicoe, 1859 –1935, was appointed by Fisher, as Director of Ordnance and served on the committee developing the *Dreadnought*. His early years are marked by an unfortunate misadventure, more accurately a naval blunder of magnificent proportions as befits battleships.

Vice-Admiral Tyron was the Commander in Chief in this debacle, he was organising training manoeuvres in the Mediterranean, so he was the mastermind behind this epic disaster — no enemy were involved — this was 22nd June 1893 and Britain ruled the waves and all eyes were upon this well-disciplined force, supposedly about to demonstrate its elite qualities in ship-handling. Tyron was giving a practical demonstration as to how he might manage his fleet in times of war.

It all comes back to the matter of naval discipline; an order is an order and must be obeyed, no matter how foolish, or risk Court Marshall. Tyron was giving the order and Markham was his unlucky second in command, whose duty it was to follow orders and ensure Tyron's signals were complied with. When Tyron ordered his ships to go about, by turning inwards towards each other, Markham was quite unable to convince Tyron that there was not enough room for the two ships to do so safely. Inevitably, at least for everyone except Tyron, Tyron's ship HMS *Victoria* was struck by Markham's ship HMS *Camperdown*. Unfortunately Victoria was a terribly designed ship and soon went down. Tyron chose to stay aboard and go down with his ship. Having insisted, as all commanders do, that his orders be followed without question his last words were an unavoidable admission *'it is all my fault'*. Fortunately Markham survived the ramming, indeed it proved the *Camperdown* was strong enough to ram another capital ship and survive. Amongst the survivors from HMS *Victoria* was Jellicoe [7]. In fairness to Tyron, the German Fleet had practiced similar manoeuvring of the fleet and it was just such a sudden and tight change of direction that allowed the German Fleet to escape at Jutland.

Jellicoe is not remembered for this debacle in the Mediterranean but of course for his part in the 'defeat' of the German High Sea Fleet in the First World War. There is little doubt that his preparations and training of the Grand Fleet for the Jutland encounter were sound and that Britain maintained control of the North Sea and therefore Germany's routes into the Atlantic, but it remains a controversial battle. The High Seas Fleet remained cornered with little room for manoeuvre, but Jellicoe's tactics have been discussed, debated and argued over ever since. His intention was to engage the enemy in the traditional battle-line formation and this he did. He hoped to "cross their T" and this he did, twice.

But he failed to follow up his early attack and bring about their annihilation for fear of mine fields and torpedo attacks on his own ships. When the High Seas Fleet retreated he didn't give chase immediately and waiting for morning to try and relocate them and failed to do so [8].

1st Earl David Beatty, 1871 – 1936 was in contrast to Jellicoe a flamboyant character, a charismatic socialite. He enjoyed, hunting fishing and shooting, he had a strong personality with exceptional dash and courage - a Boy's Own hero. One example will serve. When Executive Officer on the Battleship HMS *Barfleur* in the China station, despite his injuries he led a naval detachment of sailors to extricate Admiral Seymour from Hsiku; this earned him early promotion to Captain.

Like Jellicoe, Beatty is remembered for his opening moves in the Battle of Jutland. To be brief, he did lead his Battle-Cruisers in the attack upon the German Fleet but did so before forming his own ships into a workable Squadron, he left four slow battleships to catch him up. More surprisingly he then delayed the order to open fire, in fact his Captain did so, and this delay lost him any advantage of surprise and distance; he was also working with ships that were not well protected and with ammunition that was quite inadequate to deal with German armour-plating [9].

~

From the Second World War two, amongst very many, heroes of the Navy deserve mention here. Admirals Ramsay and Cunningham.

First, Admiral Sir Bertram Ramsay, who spearheaded the evacuation of Dunkirk in 1940 (Operation Dynamo). This was one of the most successful evacuations of World War Two, a withdrawal but in spectacular fashion. As it was a retreat and not an advance it should count as 'blunder' in this chapter but since the Royal Navy was coming to the rescue of the Army in this instance it's not a blunder by the Navy. Bertram Ramsay was born in 1883 and went to sea at the age of 16 as a midshipman. For two years he served on HMS *Dreadnought* — a ship that we know changed warship designs thereafter. Ramsey qualified as a signals officer and then attended the new Naval War College.

In World War One Ramsay had served in the Grand Fleet and the Dover Patrol. Between the wars, he lectured at the Imperial Defence College and in 1935, he was promoted to Rear-Admiral when he became Chief-of-Staff to the Commander-in-Chief of the Home Fleet, Admiral Sir Roger Backhouse. Both men clashed over who had responsibilities for what, and in 1938, Ramsay resigned and was put onto the retired list. In 1939, he was recalled to take over the Dover command. With the collapse of the British and French armies in 1940 under the onslaught of Blitzkrieg, Ramsay was put in charge of 'Operation Dynamo' - the evacuation of British and French troops from the beaches of Dunkirk. Based in Dover, Ramsay oversaw a successful plan that brought back to Britain more than 300,000 men who might otherwise have perished if the German army had pressed on with its high speed advance through France.

After Operation Dynamo Ramsay studied the problems of an invasion of occupied France. When it was clear that this was some time off, Ramsay assisted in the planning for the invasion of Sicily.

In 1944, he was put in charge of the Allied Naval Expeditionary Force for the invasion of France. As a result he played a major part in the planning for D-Day.

Ramsay's last operation was the Allied attack on Walcheren, which allowed the port of Antwerp to be used by the Allies.

On January 2nd, 1945, Ramsay was killed in a plane crash on the way to attending a conference in Brussels [10].   ~

Andrew Browne Cunningham, 1st Viscount Cunningham of Hyndhope (1883-1963), British admiral of the fleet, known throughout the Royal Navy as 'A.B.C.', was the foremost British naval commander of the Second World War. He entered the Navy by way of H.M.S. *Britannia*, and first saw active service with the Naval Brigade during the South African War of 1899-1902. He was given his first independent command in 1908 while still a lieutenant when he was appointed to H.M. Torpedo Boat No. 14. For most of the next ten years he was first and foremost a Destroyer man. A succession of commands included that of H.M.S. *Scorpion*, a coal-burner in which he served for seven years, including a large part of the First World War (1914-18).

In 1914 Cunningham took part in shadowing the German Battle-Cruiser *Goeben* and Light Cruiser *Breslau* and was later sent to the Dardanelles. While serving there he was promoted to Commander and awarded the D.S.O. Later he joined the Dover Patrol and was present in support of Admiral Keyes's raid on Zeebrugge in April 1918. He was given a bar to his D.S.O. in 1919 and a second bar the following year for his services when his ship, then H.M.S. *Seafire*, was in the Baltic with a squadron under Admiral Sir Walter Cowan. He was promoted Captain in 1920.

Between the wars Cunningham held various destroyer commands. He was flag-captain to Cowan on the America and West Indies Station 1926-8 and later commanded the Battleship *Rodney*. Shortly before the opening of the Second World War he was for some months at the Admiralty, a Vice Admiral and Deputy Chief of the Naval Staff. When war broke out he was in command of the Mediterranean Fleet.

After Italy entered the conflict in 1940, just before the collapse of France, the Mediterranean became an area of increasing tension. Cunningham, always with inferior numbers, dominated the Mediterranean, winning spectacular successes in a naval air attack on Taranto in November 1940 and by his destruction of a cruiser squadron in the battle of Cape Matapan in March 1941. German intervention in the Middle East, and their successes in Greece and Crete from which British expeditionary forces had to be withdrawn in the face of overwhelming air superiority, caused Cunningham such loss in ships and men as might have broken the spirit of a less buoyant leader.

Misfortune continued well beyond the entry of the U.S.A. into the war in December 1941. In 1942 Cunningham was sent to Washington as head of the British Admiralty Delegation. He returned to the Mediterranean in November as commander-in-chief of all naval forces, under the supreme direction of General Dwight D. Eisenhower, during the landings in French North Africa and in the later invasions of Sicily and the Italian mainland. In July 1943 he had the satisfaction of accepting the surrender of the Italian fleet, and in October of the same year he succeeded Admiral of the Fleet Sir Dudley Pound as First Sea Lord, thus becoming professional head of the Navy and a member of the Chiefs of Staff committee, responsible, under the guidance of Winston Churchill, for British maritime strategy.

Cunningham was present at summit meetings of the allied heads of state at Quebec, Yalta, and Potsdam, and he continued as First Sea Lord until after the conclusion of peace with Japan, when he retired. In 1945 he had been created a Knight of the Thistle, the only man to be thus honoured for services at sea, and in the following year he became a viscount.

Cunningham, like Lord Nelson, was a prince among delegators. Having once proved a subordinate, he trusted him thenceforward, and the response he received from this trust was magnificent. He was valiant in action and in facing adversity. He was staunchly loyal to his superiors and generous to his equals. It is fitting that, although Cunningham was buried at sea, he should be commemorated, with other great commanders, in the crypt of St. Paul's, and that his bust should be seen in Trafalgar Square. The author acknowledges Peter Kemp's 'Companion to Ships & the Sea' for details of Cunningham's illustrious career [11].

~

Woodward is the last in this parade of Admirals. Admiral Sir John F Woodward GBC KCB born 1933, joined the Royal Navy in 1946 at age thirteen. He became a submariner, and received his first command, the Valiant-class nuclear hunter-killer submarine HMS *Warspite*, in 1969. In 1978 he was appointed to the Ministry of Defence.

Woodward was promoted to Rear Admiral and in 1981 appointed Flag Officer First Flotilla. In 1982 he commanded the South Atlantic Task Groups in the Falklands War under the Commander-in-Chief Lord Fieldhouse. For his efforts during the war Woodward was knighted.

In 1983 Woodward was appointed Flag Officer Submarines and NATO Commander Submarines Eastern Atlantic. In 1984 he was promoted to Vice Admiral, and in 1985 he was a Deputy Chief of Defence Staff. Before retirement in 1989 he also served as Commander of the Naval Home Command and Flag Aide-de-Camp to the Queen.

The following notes outline Woodward's contribution to the retaking of the Falklands and how he has earned a place in this book alongside Nelson and Jellicoe. Because of the long distance between the Falklands and United Kingdom, the British were reliant on a naval task force. This task force would have to be self-reliant and able to project its force across the littoral area of the Islands. The taskforce centred on the two small aircraft carriers, commanded by Rear Admiral J. F. Woodward RN (commonly known as Sandy Woodward). A second component was the amphibious assault shipping, commanded by Commodore M. C. Clapp RN. Contrary to common belief, Admiral Woodward did not command Commodore Clapp's ships. The embarked force comprised 3 Commando Brigade Royal Marines, with attached units from the Parachute Regiment under the command of Brigadier J. Thompson RM. Most of this force was aboard the hastily commandeered cruise liner Canberra. Both Clapp and Woodward reported directly to the Commander in Chief Fleet (CINCFLEET), Admiral Sir John Fieldhouse, in Britain, who was the overall commander of the operation. In order to keep neutral shipping out of the way during the war, the UK declared a 'war exclusion zone' of 200 nautical miles (370 km) around the Falklands before commencing operations.

The final moments; retaking the Falklands: On the night of 11th June, after several days of painstaking reconnaissance and logistic build-up, British forces launched a brigade-sized night attack against the heavily defended ring of high ground surrounding Port Stanley. Units of 3 Commando Brigade, supported by naval gunfire from several Royal Navy ships, simultaneously assaulted Mount Harriet, Two Sisters, and Mount Longdon. During this battle thirteen were killed when HMS *Glamorgan*, which was providing naval gunfire support, was struck by an Exocet missile — fired from the back of a truck on the mainland — further displaying the vulnerability of ships to anti-ship missiles.

On this day Sergeant Ian McKay of 4 Platoon, B Company 3 PARA died in a grenade attack on an Argentine Bunker which was to later earn him a posthumous Victoria Cross. After a night of fierce fighting all objectives were secured.

On the night of June 13 the second phase of attacks started in which the momentum of the initial assault was maintained. 2 Para captured Wireless Ridge and the 2nd Scots Guards captured Mount Tumbledown.

On June 14 the commander of the Argentine garrison in Port Stanley, Mario Menendez, surrendered to Major General JJ Moore Royal Marines. 9800 Argentine troops were made POWs and were repatriated to Argentina on the liner Canberra. On June 20 the British retook the South Sandwich Islands and declared the hostilities were at an end. The war lasted 72 days, with 236 British and around 700 Argentinean soldiers, sailors, and airmen, killed.

Militarily the Falklands War was important for a number of reasons. It was one of the few major naval battles so far to have occurred after the end of World War II. As such this conflict illustrated the vulnerability of surface ships to anti-ship missiles and reaffirmed the effectiveness of aircraft in naval warfare. It also vindicated Britain's decision to develop the 'VTOL' (Vertical Take or Landing) Harrier aircraft, which showed its very desirable flexibility and operational capabilities in being able to fly from forward bases with no runways. At sea it demonstrated the domination of airpower in major engagements and the usefulness of carriers as part of a modern fleet.

The logistic capability of the UK armed forces was stretched to the absolute limit in order to mount an amphibious operation so far from a home-base, onto mountainous islands which have few roads. After the war much work was done to improve both the logistic and amphibious capability of the Royal Navy.

The roles of special force units, which destroyed many Argentinean aircraft, and carried out intelligence gathering operations, were reaffirmed. The usefulness of helicopters in combat, logistic, and casualty evacuation, operations was reaffirmed.

At sea, some shortcomings of warship design were apparent — the danger of using aluminium in ships, because in some instances it actually caught fire after being struck by incoming missiles, and the use of nylon in uniforms, as it can melt to the skin and catch fire resulting in needless deaths and injuries compared to cotton clothing.

On land, questions were subsequently raised about the quality of personal equipment. The issue boots were criticised and also the lamentable radios.

Politically the Falklands War illustrated the role of political miscalculation and miscommunication in creating war. Both sides seriously underestimated the importance of the Falklands to the other. The Falklands War also illustrated the role of chance in determining what happens in a war. The war might have ended in an Argentinean victory if one of their Exocets had hit an aircraft carrier, or if Argentina had waited a year or two before seizing the islands. By which time several carriers would have been decommissioned by the Government's fleet restructuring. Equally, if the Argentine had made better preparations to hold the islands, they might have been able to do so, but they did not expect that the British would attempt to retake the islands from a base 6,000 miles away. Either way, an Argentine victory would have been an unacceptable show of weakness on the part of the UK during the Cold War.

Not for the first time, a 'decent' war boosted morale in Britain. It was said by diplomats that following the British victory there was an increase in international respect for Britain, formerly regarded as a fading colonial power. With acknowledgements to the various World Wide Web sites for these notes on

Admiral Woodward and the Falklands Islands, we now move onto the sailors who actually work the ship.

Chapter 11: The Sailor
About a gunner and his ships.

~~~~~~~~~~~

The personal choices for our next individual when planning his career were a) corset-making or b) join the Royal Navy; the Navy won. But of passing interest the reader may wish to know that Pompey was once as famous for its foundation garments, whalebone-corsets and the like, as the eponymous towns, Cheddar for Cheese, Axminster Carpets and Eccles for its very tasty Cakes. At its height the corset industry in Portsmouth employed some 4,000 local women. There are two possible reasons for this unusual industrial success in Portsmouth. In the first instance, the bulk of heavy industry was concentrated in the Royal Dockyard and so inevitably employed most of the male population of Portsmouth (leaving the women to find lighter employment and factory work); secondly and improbably, it was a coastal town so whalebones were easily delivered here. The tradition remains in so far as more risqué forms of undergarment are still manufactured in at least one factory in Portsmouth [1].

This chapter is not about Admirals or men of high station, it is about other ranks and in particular Peter J. Powell, a Chief Petty Officer Gunnery Instructor, to whom this book is dedicated.

 It is also about the ships and bases he served in. Peter Powell is not his real name but the details of his service are. Peter represents the many thousands of matelots, like those in this picture, who serve the Royal Navy with distinction but whose contribution receives little recognition in history books. Mr. Powell, known to friends and family as 'Pete' was born in Portsmouth on 29th September 1909 and benefited from the steadily improving education provision and, more importantly for a growing lad, the 1906 School Meals Act which meant he didn't go hungry at school.

We know that as a result of these educational improvements Master Powell was educated to the age of fifteen, a lot longer than his forbears. It had of course been a most dramatic fifteen years for Master Powell. The Great War started (for Britain) on 4th August 1914 when he was just five years old — so he wouldn't have known much about that except perhaps to be woken with the persistent sound of gun fire and bombs to which he must have become quite inured.

At that age he would have had scant regard for the sinking of the Titanic 14th April 1912, despite the loss of 2,206 souls that night; Scott and Edmundsen were racing for the South Pole and this might have captured his attention in the classroom, despite Scott's disappointment to find, on 17th January 1912, that Edmundsen had beaten him. Not a British success, but Scott's team showed typical naval discipline, comradeship and self-sacrifice. Captain Oates you will recall left the tent and went to his certain death in the hope that his fellow explorers would make it back to base camp – he left the tent with what are now immortal words "I am going out now - I may be some time". All the more poignant when you consider the team was beaten by disastrous and unexpectedly severe weather just eleven miles from a base camp and safety. None of them survived. It's the tragic stuff of legends [2, 3].

In 1926, at the age of fifteen Master Powell travelled to Suffolk, on the East coast of England, to join the naval training ship/base HMS *Ganges*. In fact by then *Ganges* was a shore base but by tradition kept a ship's name.

As his introduction to naval life and discipline *Ganges* is worth explanation; training ships were introduced as a means of preparing young men for life at sea and in particular life in the Royal Navy. The name '*Ganges*' came into Royal Navy service in 1779 when 3 vessels were presented to the Navy by the Honourable East India Company. One of them was the 'Bengal', built on the Thames at Blackwall, this was later re-named H.M.S. '*Ganges*'.

The first *Ganges* was broken up in 1816; it was her successor that became the famous or infamous boys' training ship. It was a vessel of 2,285 tons with 3,594 tons displacement. It was built in Bombay, made of teak and laid down in May 1819; it was launched on 10th November 1821 - arriving at Portsmouth in October 1822 where it was fitted out as a Guard-ship for service in Jamaica.

After a spell in the West Indies it returned to Portsmouth to be re-fitted as the Flagship of Rear Admiral Sir R.H. Otway then based in Rio de Janeiro from 1826 to1829. Between 1830 and 1855 it led an undistinguished career spending most of her time as Guard-ship at Portsmouth and Sheerness with short trips to the Mediterranean. On June 25th 1857 it was commissioned as the Flag-ship of another Admiral, this time, Rear Admiral R. L. Baynes in the Pacific station and left in September 1857 — paying off in 1861 and so distinguishes herself as the last sailing ship to be a sea going Flag-ship.

In 1866 it became a boys' training ship in Falmouth harbour where it remained until August 1899. It was then towed to Devonport and later arrived in Harwich Harbour in November 1899. The townspeople of Falmouth unsuccessfully petitioned against the ship's removal having become very fond of the old hulk. HMS *Ganges* remained in Harwich harbour as a boys' training ship until July 1906. For seven years the old wooden '*Ganges*' served her purpose but a particularly severe winter proved that better conditions were necessary to ensure the well-being of the boys. The sick quarters was the first permanent building to be moved ashore, using land that previously had served for land-based recreation purposes only. This move was soon followed by the transfer of most of the training facilities despite fierce opposition from those who could not envisage sailors being trained on dry land.

The '*Ganges*' (ship) was towed away early one day in July 1906 to Chatham, renamed the '*Tenedos III*' it acted as tender to H.M.S. *Pembroke* and finally becoming '*Impregnable III*' in 1922. Details about HMS *Ganges's* history were provided by the Ganges Association, whose contribution is acknowledged [4].

This long and illustrious history of this famous ship would have been of little interest to the new recruits, "Ganges Nozzers" as they were called; their lives were filled with the dreaded, tough, hard discipline overseen by Instructors turning boys to men. Like poor Sisyphus before them, the Ganges Nozzers had to run up and down Laundry Hill in an equally fruitless and enduring punishment. It's as well that the Instructors of Ganges were not familiar with other punishments meted out by Greek legend or one or two more nasty ones might have been introduced – like Ixion who was fastened to the circumference of a wheel ceaselessly revolving or Tantalus, stood up to his chin in water but unable to drink. On further reflection, perhaps even these punishments may bring back memories! [5].

Having survived Ganges, Master Powell, now aged 17 years, was very proud to step aboard the *Iron Duke* on the 26th June 1926, as 'Boy 1st Class'. Proud as he might have been, it is difficult to envisage a lesser mortal than a new Boy, even if he was "1st Class"; even the dhoby-wallers (laundry staff) would have had higher status. Inevitably, he would have been totally overawed by one of the biggest ships afloat. It had a ship's complement in excess of a thousand men, all a good deal more important than him. But he would have been especially proud because this was one of Britain's more famous ships — it had been the flag-ship of Jellicoe in the Battle of Jutland.

The *Iron Duke* was, by the mid-1920s, an old ship. Other mighty vessels like the *Hood* (launched in 1926) had superseded but *Hood* was itself eight years old but it established itself in the nation's heart as the finest ship afloat – beautiful lines and an impressive sight – intended to maintain Britain as the "sovereign of the seas". *Hood* was therefore a more up-to-date battleship and very beautiful to behold but *Iron Duke* had earned a place in the affections of the nation as Admiral Earl Jellicoe's flag-ship at Jutland in *The Great War*. The *Hood* had yet to prove itself.

HMS *Iron Duke* was built in Portsmouth and launched in 1912 when Master Powell was just 3 years old, he would have followed its career over the years and at seven years of age he would have heard about the daily news-stories of Jellicoe's momentous battle off Jutland – the stuff of heroes in an age of heroes.

By the time Mr Powell stepped aboard HMS *Iron Duke* it was elderly, a venerable warship now being used as a gunnery training ship equipped as it was with 8 x 15 inch guns as her main armament. *Iron Duke* had been demilitarised, reduced to a non-fighting role in the various treaties that followed The Great War. These treaties were aimed at limiting another build up of armaments. These included the Paris Treaty of 1919, the Washington Naval Treaty 1922 and the London Treaty 1930-36 all of which were supposed to regulate the size of ships, and their armaments, of the major forces in Europe; Germany, Britain, France and so forth [6].

Boy Seaman Powell spent seven months on this ship – probably spent learning the ropes (literally) and keeping out of trouble. His chosen path was gunnery so the *Iron Duke* was excellent proving ground for him and a ship to which he returned some ten years later, with a little more status, as a Petty Officer.

Between ships Boy Seaman Powell was allocated a shore base, usually in Portsmouth as his home town. On this occasion he spent a week in HMS *Victory* – now renamed *Nelson* to avoid confusion with the man-o'-war, which is still in commission and flying the white ensign as proof of this.

As his record of service shows, see appendix 1, our nominated sailor served on the following ships after HMS *Iron Duke*:- HMS *Tiger*, HMS *Suffolk*, HMS Revenge, and *LE Macha* a patrol vessel.

After his initial stint in Iron Duke he returned to barracks for 8 days in HMS Victory and just a short walk from his family home in Buckland and later his "married quarters" in Tipner, a suburb of Portsmouth and very near the old Naval small-arms rifle range. His next posting was to HMS *Tiger*, still as a Boy 1st Class, but during this period he formally signed up for 12 years as "Able Seaman Powell" and was then specialising in Gunnery.

Shakespeare rather unexpectedly can help us with information about an early "*Tiger*". The first lines of Macbeth were inspired by an intrepid merchant seaman, called Ralph Fitch, who set off for Syria and thence to Aleppo in search of spices. In Macbeth this is translated into the lines "... *her husband's to Aleppo, master o' the* Tiger...", Macbeth, Act 1 Scene 3 [7].

So with that slightly obtuse introduction to ships named Tiger we return to HMS *Tiger,* an altogether different ship. According to Admiral Viscount Jellicoe, whose job it was to deploy such ships in his Fleet at Jutland, he tells us that the *Tiger* was a Battle-Cruiser of 28,500 tons, with a speed of 29 knots with main guns 8 x 13.5 inch and 12, 6 inch plus secondary armament and torpedo tubes. Like the *Iron Duke*, HMS *Tiger* was being used as a gunnery training ship for the newly promoted Ordinary Seaman Powell. Here he learned about small arms and a ship's main armament, in particular how to operate 6-inch guns.

Powell's transfer to HMS *Tiger,* which stationed in Portsmouth, coincided with the arrival of her new captain, Captain Campbell VC, DSO. The abbreviations after his name give a hint this man's career. If Jellicoe was a hero by reputation and leadership then Campbell was a hero because of his personal actions, "for valour" in the face of the enemy as required to earn the initials V.C.

The Victoria Cross medal needs no explanation but the specific reasons for Captain Campbell earning it do. The details very briefly are these; On 17 February 1917 in the North Atlantic Commander Campbell, commanding HMS Q.5 (one of the Royal Navy's 'mystery' ships) sighted a torpedo track. He altered course and allowed the torpedo to hit Q.5 aft by the engine-room bulkhead. The 'panic party' got away convincingly, followed by the U-boat. When the submarine had fully surfaced and was within 100 yards of Q.5 - badly damaged and now lying very low in the water - the commander gave the order to fire. Almost all of the 45 shells fired hit the U-boat which sank.

A "Q ship" may also need further explanation. Such vessels were disguised a 'Trojan horses'; in this case Q5 was a merchant ship converted to a warship with heavy guns secreted behind removal bulwarks with the obvious aim of luring German submarines into the open. Captain's Campbell's exploits vividly portrays the danger of manning such vessels, a torpedo was capable of sinking far bigger ships than converted cargo carrier. For this and similar acts of heroism he was awarded a Victoria Cross, one of very few awarded to sailors, indeed to few people at all. Thus on 2lst April, 1917 the London Gazette announced with the usual brevity of military communications:-

"The King has been graciously pleased to approve of the grant of the Victoria Cross to Commander Gordon Campbell, D.S.O., R.N. In recognition of his conspicuous gallantry, consummate coolness, and skill in command of one of H.M. ships in action."

Returning to Ordinary Seaman Powell, he served two and half years on Tiger and was further promoted to Able Seaman. He was discharged to shore leave, and more training, on 16th May 1929 and after a few days in *Victory* (the base) waiting for redeployment went to HMS *Excellent* (a Gunnery Training establishment). If *Ganges* made men of boys then *Excellent* made sailors of men with a great deal of marching, drilling and running – everything was done at the double on Whale Island – with Gunnery Instructors inviting the wretched matelots to do it again, and again and again; louder and louder and louder; smarter and smarter and smarter still. The Senior Service in the making.

Many old sailors will remember the gravel parade ground, which produced a unique sound of precision marching [8]. After several months learning small drill including the use of the Lewis Machine Gun Able Seaman Powell served aboard HMS *Suffolk*, from 1930 to 1933.

HMS *Suffolk's* place in this brief history is a little sad for it lost twelve sailors in a tragic accident in the Clyde; all the more tragic because no enemy ships were involved, this event took place in peace-time. As we learned in an earlier chapter, the collision between HMS *Suffolk* and the merchant ship S.S. *Misirah* was in the protected waters of the Firth of Clyde. HMS *Suffolk* was built in Portsmouth, and it was commissioned in the very same week Boy First Class Powell joined the Navy.

Another twelve months ashore and then AB Powell is off to join HMS *Revenge*. By now he was getting used to big ships and their big guns. In the *Revenge* he learned about the biggest of naval guns, the 15 inch ship-killing monsters.

HMS *Revenge* was a Royal Sovereign class Battleship armed with eight 15-inch guns. In 1930 it was based in Portland and like the *Malaya* served at Jutland in the 1st World War and in WW 2 it was used to escort the Halifax convoys, sailing back and forth across the Atlantic offering a protective shield to the much needed troops and goods sent from America and Canada.

Time on board was obviously well spent because AB Powell was discharged from HMS *Revenge* on July 1936 and was later promoted to Petty Officer, so he came out of his 'square rig' (the rating uniform) and into a 'fore and aft rig' (collar, tie and jacket, officer-style uniform) [9].

Petty Officer Powell had another tour of duty on HMS *Iron Duke*, during which time the 2nd World War was declared. PO Powell returns briefly to Excellent in 1940 and then joins HMS *Malaya* to put his fifteen years of training and practice in effect. HMS *Malaya's* story has been told in another chapter and won't be repeated here suffice to say the *Malaya* survived the war.

In the previous chapter we learned a little about the routine of the ship HMS *Malaya*, at this point we can get a glimpse of life on board a battleship from a sailor's perspective.

When joining ship sailors are allocated a station card and his mess, dormitory style, where a group men, about of 15 to 20 per mess, would spend their lives at sea; eating, sleeping, and passing their day in the company of their mates when official duties were finished. In addition to their duties allocated day-by-day and organised into "watches" or shifts the crew had allotted positions for "Cruising Stations", requiring one-third of the crew to be on duty; Defence Watches, one-half", or "Action Stations", requiring the entire crew. At these times, 'battle stations', the whole crew would move to their appointed positions. A great many men were required to fire the big guns, as many as 80 people might be needed for each turret and *Malaya* had eight 15-inch guns. The bigger guns were controlled centrally and this required observers perched high in the superstructure of the ship, here for example would be the Spotting Top crew. Information passed via the Director Positions to the Transmission Station deep inside the ship. Two pieces of equipment became vital for calculating the range and position of enemy ships, remembering that both the ships were moving at high speed and at varying directions to confuse each other. To assist in the very complex calculations required for gun control Admiral Sir Frederick Dreyer, then a Lieutenant, gave his name to an early form of fire (gunnery) control system and Arthur Pollen refined this and was rewarded handsomely for his contribution.

Lieutenant Dumaresq also brought improvements to gunnery control with what might be thought of as an early electromechanical computer. Of particular importance was the *rate of change* (of a ship's position) so that the relative positions of enemy ships could be calculated, not just at the point of firing but more importantly the positions of the ships by the time the shell had been fired, passed through the air and arrived near, or better still, on target. Spotters were required to record fall of shell and this task sometimes fell to aircraft, when available. Given sufficiently accurate estimates of the enemy's position, course and speed the process of calculating the direction of fire was automated. Despite great advances, British rangefinders were not as good as the Germans' [10,11].

When not at Action Stations or on routine Watches sailors passed their time in a variety of hobbies and leisure pursuits, drawing, painting, model-making, knitting & embroidery, knot tying, letter writing and board games especially the Navy's very own special form of Ludo known as "Uckers". As in any enclosed institution, food was also an important part of the daily routine. By the 20th Century the Royal Navy was providing a quite a palatable cuisine and sailors acknowledged that their diets were often better than their folk back home – who were restricted to "rationed" food supplies.

There is one important ritual which hasn't been mentioned so far – "Up Spirits", the daily issue of a tot of rum to all ratings. The issuing of rum was for perfectly sensible and practical reasons. In the 16th/17th Century ships were quite unable to keep fresh drinking water palatable for more than a few days so a weak beer was provided. The Navy even set up its own breweries in the Portsmouth and Gosport area to ensure adequate and consistent supplies. When abroad local wines and spirits were substituted and so when Jamaica was captured by the British in 1655 ship's Captains made use of the local beverage — rum. Until 1740 each man was issued with a neat half pint of rum each day. It is now a familiar story that in 1740 Admiral Vernon ordered the dilution of the rum with up to three parts water. This thinned version was known as "grog" from Vernon's nickname "old grog" (a reference to his boat-cloak made of a cloth known as grogram). Along with cigarettes, rum was the currency for bartering, paying debts or recognising a special day, a birthday for example. A sip of rum, "sippers" might be offered for a small favour whilst a more substantive debt might warrant "gulpers" – the equivalent to two sippers.

The entire process of storing, guarding, diluting, issuing and finally drinking the rum was a very strictly controlled and ritualised affair and so it was not surprising that when the when the fleet drew the last tot of rum on 31st July 1970 this day was referred to as the "Black Day". In reality the demise of "Up Spirits" was recognised as a necessary and healthy step for all concerned in a modern navy where technical skills are more important that a sailor's brute strength dulled by an alcoholic haze [12,13]. By the way, the solution to carrying fresh water was to use clean metal tanks and not wooden casks and the metal tank was made compulsory throughout the fleet by 1815. On a similar note of preservation, food storage problems were solved by the invention of the tin can in 1810 by the Frenchman Nicolas Appert [14].

And so with this brief glimpse of life at sea HMS *Malaya* continues her various commissions and deployments. It was used frequently as an escort to the North Atlantic convoys. Ideally a convoy required the protection of larger Royal Navy warships such as HMS *Malaya*, which was big enough to repel attacks by German raiding battle-cruisers. Destroyers were needed to deal with Submarine attacks and aircraft to provide protect from enemy aircraft and to act as observers. Aircraft could provide much better sighting of and protection against submarine attack. Rather poignantly convoys also required smaller ships to act as "pick-up" vessels. Sailing to the rear of the convoy their sad duty was to pick up survivors from ships sent to the bottom. The convoy itself was not to be delayed by rescue attempts and the Royal Navy warships were too busy hunting the enemy.

One such convoy, code number S.L.67, was memorable for Petty Officer Powell when serving on the *Malaya*. The ship's log provides the facts, it reminds that HMS *Malaya* is a battleship of 31,100 tons with eight 15" guns plus sundry secondary armament. In charge was Captain Palliser. On Saturday 8th March 1941 at midday the Malaya's log records her position as 21°-11' North & 19° - 21' West, putting her to the West of the Cape Verde Islands (North West Africa) [15,16].

From this point P.O. Powell provides the details; what follows is a transcript of a wax disk voice recording by Petty Officer Powell. He made this unusual recording on a very early quite primitive voice-recording machine whilst visiting relatives in Providence (Rhode Island, New Jersey) in April 1941. His ship, HMS Malaya, was docked then in New York and one of the first to benefit from America's agreement to refit and repair British warships. This recording gives his account of a brief contact with both German and Italian battleships:-

"... we were taking a convoy from British West Africa towards England and it was all very, very slow ships. All these were the old crocks from the English Merchant Navy and all the allied merchant navies and any other countries who had ships that wished protection; we were willing to take them.

We left Freetown and had been at sea about ten days and owing to so many troubles with these old merchant ships we hadn't got very far.

We had a couple of convoy vessels; there was one a British destroyer. It did a lot of work besides rounding up the old crocks that had fallen behind. We used to send her out to the horizon to have a

*look around for any suspicious looking vessels
and one day it reported smoke on the horizon and
the captain told her to go along and investigate.*

*Off it went, steaming away. It wasn't long before
it reported that the whiff of smoke was the German pocket battleships the* Gneisenau *and*
Scharnhorst.

*Now we had a very clever captain on board our
ship and he just told the destroyer to shadow them
and report to our ship. The captain made all the
necessary arrangements for our ship to give battle.*

*Of course we were outgunned by these Germans
and in theory we should have had a good hiding,
obviously we would. But still, our captain, he was
a very clever man. He figured it out that if we
waited until the sun was low, that we could get
very, very close to these battleships without them
spotting us. This would be to our advantage because they were much newer ships than the* Malaya *and they had a greater range. They could engage us with their more modern guns and with
our old guns we wouldn't even be able to reach
them with our shells. So we had to do something
very tricky.*

*Anyway, we had the reports coming through from
the destroyer - and apparently the German pocket
battleships hadn't sighted us – and it gave us their
course. So we veered away from the convoy, so
they wouldn't get into any trouble with any shells
going over or short.*

*This course, that we went on, would bring us right
in range of the sun.*

*[Whether or not the enemy can see you] depends
entirely on the type of day that it is. If it is a very
sunny day, clear blue sky, when the sun is low,
when it's setting, it is almost impossible to look
into the rays of the sun. As practically all sailors
will tell you, it is very hard. If you gaze into these
rays for more than a few seconds your eyes water
and it gets even worse.*

*Well, as it happened we knew we could only en-
gage at 27,000 yards but the German ships' range
was over that, 30,000.*

*They came within sight and we got our ranges and
we knew they hadn't seen us, otherwise they would
have opened fire on us. Our ranges were showing
30,000, then we got closer, at 29,000. We were
just waiting for 27, that's when we could fire.*

*We got down to 28,000, just below. Then the cap-
tain said strict silence was to be observed right
throughout the ship. Everything was deathly
quiet.*

*Then just as we got to 28,000, or just below
28,000 yards, the Germans must have sighted us
– for they turned about and then huge columns of
smoke came from their funnels and they raced
away. Then of course the range, instead of decreasing began to increase so we could not engage
them.*

*(Well why would they run away?..... Why didn't
they want to fight?)*

*It was not because they were afraid; it's mainly
because they've only got two of these pocket battleships, not really pocket battleships, they're battle
cruisers. They cannot afford to get damaged. With
this British ship we could get damaged and we
have got so many Navy yards we can go to, we*

can soon be repaired. With the German raiders damaged they've got nowhere to get repaired except back to Germany and being damaged and going very, very slowly it is almost certain the British fleet would sink them before they reach port.

Did you sink a battleship?

No, no, we didn't sink a battle ship, they managed to get away.

The Italian fleet had 19 ships; we engaged a battleship off the Port of Italy. We engaged the Italian fleet there and damaged one of their biggest and fastest ships but it managed to get into port while we engaged or chased some cruisers to another part of Italy.

How did you get to Providence?

My ship, the Malaya, *is docking at New York, we're in there for repairs and of course having some relations in Providence, New Jersey......."*

Transcript ends.

Both Captain Palliser and Petty Officer Powell leave HMS *Malaya* later in 1941 whilst the ship undergoes repair and refit.

This did not mark the end of PO Powell's naval career although it was his last big ship. He spent the remainder of the war in land-based gunnery training establishments (see appendix 1). He was promoted once more, in 1944, to Chief Petty Officer and served his time in Excellent.

He then spent eighteen months doing time for his pension (21 years service required for a pension) with a patrol vessel "*Le Macha*", this was a Royal Navy Vessel sold to the Northern Ireland Navy as a mine hunter.

Thus ended the career of this C.P.O., he stepped ashore on the 7th October 1948 for the last time as a sailor and so ended his 24 years service (including time at Ganges) with the RN.

This chapter has been about the 'ordinary' sailors of the Royal Navy and one extraordinary 'sailor' should be mentioned since his role was something of a mystery, indeed his very existence was mysterious.

On 30 April 1943, as part of Operation "*Mincemeat*", a body dressed as a fictitious Royal Marine was given the name and rank "Major Martin". This supposed victim of an air crash was placed into the sea from the submarine, HMS Seraph, off the Spanish port of Huelva. As anticipated, the Spanish authorities showed their find to the Germans. The papers with the body deceived the Germans into believing that the imminent Allied invasion would come in Greece and not Sicily. This rather bizarre subterfuge became the subject of the book and a film, 'The Man Who Never Was'. As a diversionary plan it was clearly most successful, in that Sicily was not reinforced for the impending Operation Husky and when the Allies stormed ashore on Sicily they caught the German and Italian defenders almost completely flatfooted. The man who devised the scheme was Lt. Cdr. Ewen Montagu, a Royal Naval Reservist who represented naval intelligence on the 'Inter-service XX Committee' (XX for double cross) [17].

This chapter will end with Chief Petty Officer Powell's retirement from the Royal Navy, which was on 26th October 1949. After twenty years service he was discharged with a character reference 'very good' and rewarded with a service pension – he was also awarded a long service award (3rd January 1943; three good conduct badges in 1930, 1935 and 1940. CPO Powell was also awarded four war service medals. They were the '1939-45 Star; the Africa Star; the Atlantic Star & rosette and the Italy Star. To be awarded the 1939-45 Star; the Atlantic Star and the Italy Star required a Royal Navy Sailor to have served six months in 'areas of active operation' during the relevant periods whilst the Africa Star was awarded for one day or more in any service at sea in the Mediterranean during the relevant periods in 1943 [18].

Chapter 12: Women and the Royal Navy
~~~~~~~~~~

'Britannia rules the waves' or at leas used to and so it is with Britannia we begin this chapter in recognition of the many women who have played a part in the life of the Royal Navy. Reflecting Britain's social order, men dominated the armed forces, the 'front line', with women playing an ancillary role and they did so until well into the 20th century. In the 21st century the share they same rights, and risks, as men to take up arms.

The title Britannia was the Roman, Latin, name for the British Isles, at least the English and Welsh parts of those islands. The title was happily accepted by the British and came to refer to the spirit of strength and militarism of Britain. In 1664 King Charles II chose to personify Britannia in the form of a woman, typically wearing a helmet, carrying a shield and trident. This form was an adaptation of a Roman coin, a sestertius from the reign of Emperor Antoninus Pius (138 to 161 AD), better known for his 'Antonine Wall' than his depiction of a Britannia-like figure on his coinage [1].

King Charles chose a favourite courtier, Frances Teresa Stuart, as the model and her image was depicted on English coinage right up to 1971 when decimal currency was introduced but it is still occasionally used. In 2004 the Royal Mint issued a £5 Crown coin depicting both Britain's Britannia and France's Marianne to celebrate 100 years of *entente cordiale*. This may have little to do with the Royal Navy except that Charles chose to strike a medal with this new image in recognition of his Navy's successes against the Dutch. It was of course Charles who gave the British Navy its Royal status. Presumably he was very proud of 'his' Navy and in Britannia he certainly left us an enduring icon. Such iconic woman were frequently used as the subject of figureheads on the stem of sailing ships and the drawing at the start of this chapter features Britannia in the form of a wooden figure now on display in Britannia RN College.

Before we move to our next heroine we have the good fortune to know Samuel Pepys' opinion of this new image, thus:- "...*Did observe the King's new medal, where, in little, there is Mrs Stuart's face as well done as ever I saw anything in my whole life, I think; and a pretty thing it is, that he should choose her face to represent Britannia...*". We know from his diaries that he thought Frances the most beautiful courtier and dreamt of 'sporting' with her [2,3].

Queen Elizabeth I has a reputation and a place in Britain's history at least equal to Britannia. Her contribution to the development of an ocean-going, 'blue-water' Navy has been described in earlier chapters and will not be reiterated here; suffice to say that it was 'her' navy royal that successful repelled the 'Spanish Armada' in 1588, a crushing defeat for a much superior naval force and politically a mortal blow to Philip II of Spain [4]. The current Monarch, Queen Elizabeth II is of course head of the armed forces as the Lord High Admiral of the Royal Navy though her position is one of influence rather than direct control.

Apart from this singular massive and decisive strike against Spain the British were a constant source of irritation not least by their Privateering and open Piracy aimed at relieving the Spanish of their ill-gotten treasures. And amongst those pirates were not a few women; two examples will serve to make the point. Mary Read and Ann Bonny; clearly some women liked front-line service where the action was. They are described as "... howling like banshees, flashing their cutlasses and singeing the air with shrill oaths and curses ...". Both were ultimately caught, in 1720, convicted and sentenced to death but both avoided execution by claiming to be pregnant [5]. What is clear is that some women were not content with secondary role and some went so far as to disguise themselves as men and enlist as a sailor with the attendant duties, hardships and risks.

These two characters were clearly exceptional women but in the age of sail women on board a warship were not so unusual. Their presence was not always welcomed not least because they were not subject to Naval Discipline and were free to roam the ship and get in everyone's way. If these visitors were not officially recognised then no provision was made for their food, victualling and so they were consuming the already restricted rations of food and water intended for the seamen.

Whilst it was not intended that warships would carry women, their presence was sometimes perfectly legal and proper, if for example they were the wives of government officials, or the wives of senior officers. Admiralty Regulations at the time of Nelson, 18th/19th century, stated that

> "...no women be ever permitted to be on board but such as are really the wives of the men they come to, and the ship not too much pestered even with them...".

This does not appear to exclude married women and therefore seems a rather liberal Regulation. In truth however many women were far from married and their motives not entirely honourable – no doubt a nuisance for the Captain and Sailing Master but to the delight, and pleasure of the common sailor.

Whilst discussing the pleasures of female companionship this is a timely point to remind ourselves of the Ladies in Nelson's life. Apart from his mother, Catherine Nelson (who died when Nelson was just nine years old), there were two significant women in his life – Francis Nisbet and Lady Emma Hamilton.

Nelson met Frances 'Fanny' Nisbet on the Island of Nevis in the West Indies and ultimately married her on 11th March 1787. They returned to England and lived in Burnham Thorpe, Norfolk on the East coast. Nelson was then on half-pay, that is to say he was not required for active service. Nelson was inevitably unhappy with his enforced retirement even if it was temporary, and Mrs Nelson was not happy with her isolated existence in Norfolk, particularly in the cold snow-bound winters. By the age of thirty-five she was described, in Carola Oman's Book 'Nelson', as debilitated and neurotic and the marriage, in the formal language of the age was 'without issue'. In Nelson's own words he had inherited Frances' son from her first marriage but '...by whom I have no children...'. They gradually drifted apart until Frances Nelson, now Lady Nelson, made a public declaration on 13th January 1801, '...I am sick of hearing of dear Lady Hamilton, and am resolved that you shall give up either her or me...'. Lord and Lady Nelson never lived together after this public declaration. They did however remain on good terms and continued to write affectionately to each other.

The cause of this outburst was of course Nelson's preoccupation with Lady Amy 'Emma' Hamilton. Nelson first met Emma, in 1793, in Naples. She was the wife of the British Ambassador, Sir William Hamilton. Nelson's reputation (as a hero) was increasing with every encounter with the enemy; he had successes in the Battles of St Vincent (1797) and the Nile (1798) and by 1797 was promoted to Rear Admiral. He met Emma in Naples where he was given a particularly warm welcome and treated as a hero, the same adulation did not follow him on his return to Britain. By 1799 Nelson had fallen under the spell of Lady Hamilton's blandishments and 'relationships began' – resulting in the birth of their child Horatia on 5th February 1801. One extraordinary aspect of this relationship was the continued support Nelson received from the cuckolded Sir William Hamilton who remained loyal and friendly to Nelson until his death; in his Will he bequeathed a portrait (by Madame le Brun) of his wife to Emma '...his dearest friend, Lord Nelson'.

So far we have dealt with those women who had no genuine role in the Royal Navy so it is time to introduce the Women's Royal Naval Service, the 'Wrens'. The Military Service Act of 1916 was intended to provide an adequate stream of sailors but despite the introduction of the Royal Naval Volunteer Reserve and later conscription (compulsory military service for all young men) there were never enough men to man the ships and the front line so women were introduced into the service.

The Wrens evolved in several stages. The first phase was the development of an entirely new shore based women's service. This new organisation was headed by Dame Katherine Furse. This ancillary service had its own recruitment, training, terms of service, its own style of uniform and ranks, from 'Wren' equivalent to Ordinary Seaman, to Chief Commandant equivalent to Rear Admiral.

Their duties were many and varied, including cook, steward/waitress, portering, telephonist, telegraphist, coders, drivers, dispatch riders and more practical engineering skills such as mechanics, fitters and turners — but 'Never at Sea'! as their motto informs us. Taking on these roles released many thousands of men for sea-going duties. Whilst their presence was sometimes viewed with some ambivalence it was acknowledged that their contribution was invaluable and the Wrens were acknowledged to be the best of the women's services [6,7]. The Wrens were disbanded after the war on 1st October 1919.

The second phase was their reintroduction in 1939, this time headed by Dame Vera Laughton-Mathews. At first these Wrens were 'immobile' that is, they served only in their home base but eventually a more flexible approach was taken, indeed it became compulsory for Wrens to move from base to base as the service required. From the outset the term 'auxiliary' was avoided as they were seen to be an integral part of the Royal Navy, although in reality their duties were still almost exclusively shore based and not sea-going. A few Wrens did serve on boats, usually harbour and coastal duties on liberty boats, tenders and survey craft. At its peak, in 1944 there were 74,000 Wrens.

All this was excellent preparation for the third phase of the Wrens, its full integration into the Royal Navy. This was a slow and evolutionary process beginning with their establishment as a permanent service in 1947. By 1977 the service was brought under the purview of the Naval Discipline Act, this was not because the Wrens were in need of greater disciplinary control, the effect of this move was to more fully integrate the male and female divisions of the Navy and open up a great many more opportunities for the Wren service.

Paradoxically their full integration came in 1993 with the disbandment of the entire service. Women could now join *the* Royal Navy and not just the female branch. Equality had arrived; hereafter their recruitment, training, terms and conditions, ranks and even the uniforms were unified. The first women to serve on HM ships came in 1994. The final branch to be opened to women is the Submarine service because of practical reasons of space and accommodation.

Whilst the W.R.N.S. no longer exists as a separate service for women, nursing is still provided by a parallel service, the QARNNS, the Queen Alexandra's Royal Naval Nursing Service. It seems a curious anomaly that men were not allowed to serve in the QARNNS until 1982 – the time of the Falklands war – this is despite the fact their patients were mostly male.

The origins of this nursing service owe much to the somewhat disreputable women who found themselves on board men-o'-war and who tended the seamen's wounds in battle. Regrettably they were as famous for their drunkenness and debauchery as they were for their helpfulness. Nevertheless the need for Nursing and Medical assistance on board warships became apparent. Florence Nightingale is famous for her pioneering contribution to the Nursing of sick soldiers in the Crimean War but less well known is Mrs Eliza Mackenzie who provided a similar service in the Naval Hospital in Therapia (Constantinople) in 1854.

Nurses were first officially employed by the Admiralty in 1883 and by 1884 a certified 'Naval Nursing Service' was established at Haslar Hospital, in the Portsmouth Naval base (more precisely in Gosport just across the harbour). Queen Alexandra took a personal interest in this nursing service and invited the Admiralty to have the service come under Patronage, thus the Queen Alexandra Royal Naval Nursing Service was founded.

Although this chapter is about women and the Royal Navy several (male) Doctors are worthy of mention for their contribution to the improved health of the Navy. Dr James Lind is known as the 'father of nautical medicine' for his understanding and methodical studies of diseases and in particular the effect lemon juice had in controlling scurvy. Sir Thomas Spencer-Wells also worked at Haslar Hospital in the mid-nineteenth century and his name has come down in (medical) history for his invention of the haemostatic forceps — anyone who has worked in a hospital will be familiar with "Spencer-Wells Forceps". So far as the Navy was concerned he used his influence to improve conditions for the Naval Medical Officer.

Dr., Sir Gilbert Blane, a student of Dr Lind, is the author of *Diseases of Seamen* (1785). He was Physician to the Fleet and later Commissioner of the Sick & Wounded Board. One of his many important contributions to the health of seamen was the introduction of lemon juice to all ships to prevent scurvy.

Returning to the QARNNS, their role like that of the Wrens, was firmly established during the Great War. However their duties required them to work much closer to the front line than Wrens; they were deployed in hospital ships and land-based hospital bases all over the world. These Nurses faced much the same dangers as the sailors they tended. For example, those Nurses based in the Hong Kong station suffered most cruelly when captured by the Japanese.

The arrangements for providing the Navy with a nursing service appear to have been quite pragmatic; the Nurses work in civilian hospitals until required by the Royal Navy. This useful arrangement still exists for Nursing and Medical staff, who continue to work in civilian hospitals in peacetime but have a liability for Sea Service at times of conflict.

Like the WRN the QARNN Services were brought under the direct control of the Royal Navy through the 1977 Naval Discipline Act and the Ministry of Defence reminds recruits that "... QARNNS Officers are part of the Royal Navy and you will be expected to maintain the same standards of behaviour and appearance as any other holder of the Queen's Commission..." [8].

So far we have dealt with several groups of women; those who are more myth than real, Britannia; we have heard about women in the age of sail who provided services that must be left to the imagination, they weren't all wives and they certainly weren't there to do the cooking and cleaning! We know the Wrens provided technical and administrative support and the QARNNS a much valued nursing service. The last woman, who stands in a group on her own, is Mrs Agnes Weston, more familiarly known as 'Aggie Weston' the name given to her many sailors' Rests (hostels). Mrs Weston, later Dame Agnes Weston, did much to improve life for the sailor and equally importantly for the sailor's family. The following details about Dame Agnes Weston are provided by the Royal Sailors' Rest web site [9].

In 1873, at the age of 33, Agnes was invited to Plymouth by sailors returning to their home port. There she met Sophia Wintz who became her partner in her life's work. They started small — with Sunday afternoon tea and biscuits in open house at Sophia's parents' home in Plymouth. They quickly outgrew this and moved to a store outside the dockyard gate. They converted it to a meeting place similar to the one 'Aggie' had run in Bath.

In 1876 they converted the store into a hostel, serving meals, providing cheap accommodation and places to be quiet and to relax. The idea was always to give the sailors a 'Home from Home', where they could unwind, enjoy home cooking and — in their single cabins — have some privacy. The majority in the Navy of the time were living in crowded mess-decks and sleeping in hammocks. The Home, or Rest, was also very cheap, run on a not-for-profit basis.

The Rests always consisted of both Hall and Hostel areas. The Hall was used for Bible classes, services, temperance meetings and social gatherings to which sailors were encouraged to bring their families. There was always a full social programme.

The Hostel consisted of the restaurant, recreation rooms and cabins. Rests were never just hostels - they were always concerned with activities for the whole sailor and his family.

During this time Agnes started a savings club for sailors who wanted her to keep their pay so they weren't tempted to spend it. This prompted her to persuade the Admiralty to pay sailors pay into bank accounts - and also to pay allotments to their families - a system that was still in place until the early 1970's.

The first Rest in Portsmouth started as a result of a national tragedy in 1878 — the loss of the frigate HMS *Eurydice* with most of her crew of 320. Agnes immediately went to Portsmouth to try to see what suffering she could relieve and made a nationwide tour to raise money, both for the Rest and for the bereaved. She worked tirelessly for naval wives and families and was instrumental in getting widows pensions introduced in 1894.

The Royal Warrant bestowing 'Royal' on the Sailors Rests was awarded after the Royal Naval Exhibition at the Chelsea Hospital in 1892. In 1898 Agnes was summoned to Windsor to meet the Queen. In 1901 she received an honorary degree from Glasgow University, amongst the first ever awarded to a woman.

Agnes died in 1918, aged 78, and was buried with full naval honours, the first time such an honour had been given to a woman. Her gravestone gives her name, dates and the simple epitaph, 'The Sailor's Friend'.

Chapter 13: Ghosts and the Royal Navy

~~~~~~~~~~~

So far we have dealt with real, ships, real men and real women but now we turn our attention to the less real world of ghosts, apparitions and superstitions associated with the Royal Navy. There are no photographs or pictures in this chapter because the author was unable to locate any authenticated reproductions of any occult sightings. Superstitious people might note the entirely coincidental but apposite numbering of this chapter 13, regarded by many as an unlucky number. This short chapter describes some of the mysteries associated with the sea and the Royal Navy – none of which is verified!

The information for this chapter is drawn mainly from Raymond Brown's unusual work; 'Phantoms, Legends, Customs and Superstitions of the Sea' and his contribution is acknowledged. A number of World Wide Web sites also provided many weird, bizarre and often inexplicable stories. The stories and legends will be given without further comment from the author as to their veracity [1].

So far as mariners are concerned the occult or the mysterious tends to fall into several categories; namely, ghostly sightings of ships and people; ships that disappear in mysterious circumstances and then there are the many beliefs and legends about what is lucky and unlucky for the well being and safety of the ship and its crew. Well known amongst the first category is the *Mary Celeste*. Whilst definitely a ship, in so far as the actual ship was found by the *dei Gratia* in December 1872, it became a mystery ship of legendary status because it was found drifting — without any crew or passengers — off the coast of Portugal. But the ship was nevertheless real enough, the *Mary Celeste* was a three-masted barque built in Nova Scotia, it left New York in November 1872 and was later found drifting. No satisfactory explanation has been agreed and the name of this unfortunate ships is still used to describe any ship found floating in similar circumstances.

A rather less tangible ship but equally famous and the subject of many story books and even operas, is the *Flying Dutchman*. The name 'Flying Dutchman' originally referred to the Captain rather than his ship but ghostly sailing ships seen drifting by in ethereal form are universally referred to as the *Flying Dutchman*. Like the *Mary Celeste,* it is reputed to have been a real ship a Dutch one lost at sea sometime in the 16ᵗʰ century. Years later ghostly images of the ship were sighted in the vicinity of the Cape of Good Hope. The Royal Navy lends some credence to these stories for in the ship's log of HMS *Bacchante* (as Raymond Brown cites) no less than thirteen members of the crew claim to have seen this vision and their observations are recorded thus:

> *'July 11 1881. During the middle watch the so-called Flying Dutchman crossed our bows. She first appeared as a strange red light, as a ship all aglow, in the midst of which light her masts, spars and sails...stood out in strong relief... '* [2].

Another ship to mysteriously disappear then re-appear unexpectedly and in vaporous fashion was one of the Royal Navy's own vessels HMS *Barracouta*. On this occasion, in 1821, a small squadron of HM Ships were surveying the coastline around Africa when the lead ship, HMS *Severn*, sighted the *Barracouta* some two miles to leeward, apparently it came close enough for the *Severn's* crew to distinguish familiar faces — only for the ships to disappear. The mysterious part of is that the *Barracouta* was known to be three hundred miles away at the time of the sighting.

Remaining with the disappearance of ships the Bermuda Triangle and its associated tales stands alone in the chronicles of sea mysteries in so far as the 'mysteries' are confined a specific area of the ocean, about 1,500,000 square miles bounded by Bermuda, Miami, Florida, San Juan and Perto Rico. Many ships and aircraft disappear if they venture into, or over, this area. Giam Quasar has compiled a web site (Bermuda-triangle.org) in which he lists more than eighty ships lost in the Bermuda Triangle. Inevitably there are many explanations for this seemingly occult phenomenon. One plausible but disputed idea is that methane gas is being released from the ocean bed and this gas reduces the buoyancy of the surface water; any ships unlucky enough to be in the vicinity of this less dense water will lose all buoyancy and plummet to the depths below – without a trace being left behind, as one might expect if a ships is damaged before going down.

Whilst a sudden loss of buoyancy would explain the loss of ships of any size and of normal buoyancy it doesn't explain the loss of aircraft nor does it seem to deal with the electro-magnetic disturbances associated with this notoriously dangerous area. Both ship and aircraft compasses are said to be affected by such disturbances – this might explain why some aircraft are misdirected by their equipment and head out over the Atlantic Ocean and into oblivion. Once again this could explain why aircraft are 'lost' but not the ships, they can be misrouted by faulty compasses but they can nevertheless remain afloat until found and this was not the case with the eighty ships listed by Giam Quasar if his studies are correct [3].

The Bermuda Triangle is included in this chapter because at least one Royal Naval vessel came to grief in this peculiar zone. HMS *Atalanta* was at the time of its disappearance a training ship with 290 cadets aboard her. Previously known as HMS *Juno* it was re-commissioned at Devonport in September 1878 and subsequently arrived at Bermuda on 29th January 1880. Her Captain, Cpt. Francis Stirling, put to sea two days later and that was the last to be heard of HMS *Atalanta*. A Board of Enquiry disclosed that nine Royal Naval Ships had sunk without trace since 1840 (not all in the Bermuda Triangle). The three hundred lost souls are remembered in a memorial in St Ann's Church Portsmouth and their names listed in an electronic memorial web site [4].

Amongst the earliest of apparitions, or the sound equivalent, is 'Drake's Drum'. This is a real artefact, a drum said to have been carried by Drake in the 16th century and now in the Plymouth City Museum (UK). It is claimed that it will sound when England is in danger and did so on board HMS *Royal Oak* in 1918. It is said to have continued beating, or at least the sound of a beating drum was heard on board the ship from an unknown source, until the German Fleet surrendered. This particular phantom phenomenon is therefore regarded as auspicious and most welcome. A less welcome sound emanated from the woman haunting HMS *Asp* in 1850. Her peculiar noises, and later her regular appearances, were quite naturally very disturbing experiences for the Captain (Cpt. Alldridge) and his crew.

A number of individuals have made themselves known in very curious ways; the visitor to HMS *Asp* above and next the limping sailor of Chatham who is amongst the more humble beings to be sighted. The Royal Naval Barrack records, with the usual brevity of log books, '*ghost reported seen during the middle watch*'. The apparition was said to be a sailor in 18th century garb and with a wooden leg, he was seen hobbling around Cumberland block in 1947 and again in 1949. As is often the case, this 'man' was said to have died an untimely death, murdered by escaping

French prisoners during the Napoleonic wars [5]. The author also has in his library a reference to a photograph purporting to show a ghostly thief stealing rum rations from the pusser's store; the image has all the hallmarks of a hoax and one wonders if the cameraman wasn't viewing the Pusser (Purser), collecting the rum ration, through a rum-induced miasma.

A more substantive character, in rank at least, was Admiral Tyron. In another chapter we learned about his disastrous manoeuvring of two columns of battle ships. He had them turn inwards; they were far too close and the first two ships collided. Tyron as Admiral of the fleet was on board HMS *Victoria* at the time. Like many Captains before and since he stayed aboard the ship as it went down and was inevitably drowned – but here is the ghostly part of this tale — he appeared in the drawing room of his London home in front of his wife, Lady Tyron and her guests.

Less corporeal, if ghosts can be corporeal, are jinxes; typically sailors come to regard some ships, or people serving on the ships, as jinxed. One such ship was HMS *Hampshire* which sank with Field Marshall Kitchener on board. This ship's fate was thought by many to have been influenced by the curse of an Egyptian mummy, which had floated away from the *Empress of Ireland* (which itself sank whilst the mummy was on board). The sinking of the *Titanic* was also blamed on this artefact and added to the absurdity of the belief.

The Scharnhorst, a German Battleship, was thought to be jinxed. Even as it was being built it rolled over and killed 61 workmen. Once ready for launching it again gave sailors justification for their scepticism by breaking her moorings and sliding prematurely into the water, crashing into two barges as it went. And so her troubles continued; during a raid one of her guns exploded killing 12 men; on a homeward bound journey her radar failed and it struck another ship; this ill-fated ship was finally sunk by British forces off the coast of Norway.

The German submarine U65 was equally 'unlucky'; twelve men died before it saw any action and it was frequently haunted by a ghost. Accidents continued unabated for the poor submarine until sighted (on 10th July 1918) by an American submarine who found the German sub' drifting and unmanned – possibly the first submarine form of a '*Mary Celeste*'. It mysteriously exploded and sank before the Americans could torpedo her [6].

There are plenty of opportunities for the real to be misrepresented as occult, giant squids for example have been described as monster of the deep but more picturesque and sometimes more welcome are mermaids.

Mermaids have appeared in folklore for centuries — they were said to have the head and body of a human and the tail of a large fish. Zennor in Cornwall was the scene of one of the most famous sightings of a mermaid. A local man was enticed to live with the mermaid underwater — to this day they say you can hear a mermaid singing on moonlit nights.

Some saw mermaids as frightening creatures, bringing death and destruction. Sailors dreaded seeing one at sea as they thought it was a sure sign they would be shipwrecked. Others liked to have mermaids around - and even married them. It's said that men would trap the mermaid by hiding one of her possessions, like a mirror or comb. The mermaid would live with the man until it found her belongings — then she'd return to the sea forever.

The general belief in Mermaids made some people very rich — just over a hundred years ago mermaid 'skeletons' were put on show around the world. Experts soon realised they were fakes, made using a monkey's body and the tail of a fish. Not surprisingly, many doubted mermaids ever existed at all and believe large seals have been mistaken for them. Whether loved or feared, or just a chance to make some money, mermaids remain one of the more intriguing and fanciful legends of the sea [7].

It is not surprising that sailors become very superstitious spending many months at sea in hazardous conditions anything tending to foreshadow disaster would be attributed with magical and unwelcome powers. Nelson was as superstitious as any other sailor; he insisted a horseshoe be nailed to the main mast of all the ships he served in. For similar hopes of good luck a coin was set below the main mast of sailing ships before the mast was stepped in place. Two other traditions intended to ward off ill-fortune and bring good luck are continued; the time-honoured tradition of asking a woman to launch ships by breaking a bottle of wine on the side of the ship and the ceremony of 'crossing the line'.

The ceremonial launching of ships, using a bottle of wine, is familiar to anyone who has seen even the smallest of vessels set afloat, but the rituals associated with crossing the equator may be less well known. The ceremony of crossing the Equator for the first time involves much ritual in the imaginary 'Court of his Oceanic Majesty, King Neptune'. This informal event celebrated by officers and ratings on equal terms and usually results in the novitiates getting very wet. A certificate is sometimes issued and these can be very elaborate and finely crafted documents.

Chapter 14: Rats, Cats and Weevils
~~~~~~~~~~~

Royal Navy ships have been host to a great many unusual creatures in its long history. Perhaps this was because ships were so big they could easily accommodate the odd animal without difficulty. Some animals were most welcome – either as pets or as fresh meat whilst other creatures were a scourge; rats and weevils have been the unwelcome passengers on board His Majesty's ships for hundreds of years. So this chapter is about the strange variety of creatures associated with the Navy.

Let us deal with the unwelcome ones first – Weevils. Most people will know that in the days of sailing ships, and well into the 20th Century, hard-tack biscuits were a staple part of a sailor's diet and that after months in storage they were infested with weevils. It is a traditional story that ill-fed sailors used to tap their biscuits on the mess table before trying to eat them; however, given the minute size of a weevil at just 1 or 2 mm long, and therefore barely noticeable, this might well be another apocryphal yarn, in reality the food provided for sailors was often better in quality and quality than they might get at home. [1]. Nevertheless the Grain Weevil does not become any more desirable even with its Latin name "*Sitophilus granaries*". It is a beetle and one of 500 British species. Another equally unwelcome beetle is the Death Watch Beetle, *Xestobium Rufovillosum*, which has a penchant for the oak timbers of ships and churches alike. More disastrous still is the Teredo worm, Latin name *Teredo Navalis* giving it its common name, Ship Worm. It is in fact a mollusc, famous for tunnelling into the hulls of ships in such profusions as to render the ships unseaworthy. This brought about the necessity to sheath wooden hulls with copper plates [2].

Rats, as familiar on land as sea, remain a nuisance amounting to a plague even in the 21st Century. Rats are a problem in every possible way – the physical damage they do, the consequential damage they cause, for example to electrical cables and the diseases they carry plus the sheer nuisance of their presence make these the most repellent of ships' passengers. Rats are rodents, and there are two British species, the brown and the black. The black rat, also known as the 'ship rat', "*Rattus rattus*", emanated from Asia and, with their fleas, are reputed to have brought the bubonic plague, the Black Death, to Europe in the middle ages.

To try and stop ships bringing disease into port an Act of Parliament in 1825 required, still requires, the use of a yellow flag, signal letter "Q", as a signal flag to be flown when entering harbour to indicate "My vessel is healthy and I request free pratique (entry to port)"[3].

On to more welcome creatures associated with the Royal Navy's ships and sailors. Historically, animals were not at all uncommon on board ships, especially on board ships going on a long sea voyages. Animals that could supply fresh meat were kept in mangers, for example one Royal Navy ship sailed to the East Indies in 1764 with a goat, a pig, six dozen fowl and thirteen ducks on board [4]. For many years thereafter pets would also have a place on board a large ship although there is little room for a pet in a modern warship and the Admiralty finally banned animals on board HM Ships in 1975.

The list of animals and creatures, real and mythical, associated with the Navy is strange indeed. Some were pets living on board the ship, these were usually cats, dogs and caged birds; some were official like 'PO(Dog) Flloyd' who is based in Gibraltar [5]. Some pets were unofficial, like the Budgie rescued by HM Submarine *Trenchant* — which was given sanctuary in the place in sick bay having been rescued from certain death in Devonport harbour [6]. Many animals were mascots and quite a few were exotic gifts and of course many merely an association by name, Lion and Tiger for example.

For many ratings the Navy starts with the training ship, HMS *Ganges*, which provides us with our first example of an animal mascot – the badge of *Ganges* depicts an Elephant. Presumably an Indian one (the one with smaller ears) reflecting the ship's early historical connections with India. HMS *Ganges*, the ship, was provided by the Honourable East India Company in 1779. It was therefore apposite that Captain Murray Dunlop marked his 100th Passing Out parade, as the last Commanding Officer of Ganges, astride elephant "Maureen" (a 12 years old beast that weighed two tons).

HMS *Excellent*, the naval training base on Whale Island in Portsmouth Harbour, also provides some unusual animal associations. Indeed such was the range of animals kept on Whale Island this base actually had a Zoo – until the outbreak of the 1st World War when the Zoo was dispersed for the protection of the animals. The Island also had stables and it was not unusual at that time for the Commanding Officer HMS *Excellent* to be on parade on horseback. Horses were rather less common than other animals on board ships but the future King Edward VII did have his stabled on board HMS *Serapis* in 1875.

None of the examples so far have had an official war time role but the next creature had a very important role – the humble pigeon was used as an important method of communicating both on land and at sea. Pigeons won more Dickin Medals than any other creature.

The Dickin Medal was instituted by Mrs Maria Dickin in recognition of animals doing their bit to aid the war effort. She had already founded the People's Dispensary for Sick Animals (PDSA) in Whitechapel, London in 1917 (to provide care for animals whose owners couldn't afford vets' fees). She also established an award for animals, quickly dubbed the Dickin Medal "the animals' VC" awarded to those animals who displayed *"conspicuous gallantry and devotion to duty associated with, or under the control of, any branch of the Armed Forces or Civil Defence units"*.

Of the fifty-four recipients, three were London police horses, which had performed their duties bravely during the Blitz. Five dogs were also decorated for helping to find people trapped in buildings by bomb damage, often braving fire, smoke, noise and collapsing masonry. One dog got the medal for rescuing other animals. This was Beauty, a wire-haired terrier belonging to Bill Barnet, who led a PDSA animal rescue squad in London. By the war's end Beauty had found 63 animals that would probably otherwise have died, trapped in bombed buildings. As well as the Dickin medal, Beauty was festooned with civic honours including *"the freedom of Holland Park and all the trees therein."*

Perhaps the most remarkable dog to be decorated was Judy, an English Pointer who was a mascot on a number of Royal Navy gunboats in the Far East. When her ship was torpedoed, she saved her marooned crew from thirst by finding fresh water. When the crew was captured, Judy spent two years as a Prisoner of War in Sumatra, where prisoners were kept in conditions of appalling brutality. Judy saved the lives of several men by threatening and distracting Japanese guards when they tried to beat prisoners. She survived several attempts by the Japanese to shoot or bayonet her and was liberated in 1945.

The only Royal Navy cat to win the Dickin Medal was Simon, the ship's cat on HMS *Amethyst*. In April 1949, Amethyst was heading along the Yangtse River to Nanking to evacuate British citizens caught between warring Chinese Communist and Nationalist forces. She came under fire from Communist artillery and suffered 17 dead and 25 wounded from her crew of 170. During the famous 'Yangtse Incident', HMS *Amethyst* spent more than three months trapped on the river, starved of medical supplies, fuel and food. Despite injuries from the shelling, 'Able Seacat Simon' waged war on the rats that were raiding the ship's food supplies, starting with 'Mao Tze Tung', the name the sailors gave to the leader of the rat band.

When he wasn't ratting, Simon and Peggy, the ship's terrier dog, comforted their wounded shipmates who had to endure stifling heat and swarms of mosquitoes, and sometimes even rats nibbling at their fingers and toes. When the *Amethyst* finally escaped, her Commanding Officer, Lt-Cdr John Simon Kerans, contacted the PDSA to recommend Simon for a medal. Aside from his conspicuous gallantry in dealing with the rats, wrote Kerans, 'His presence on the ship, together with Peggy the dog, was a decided factor in maintaining the high level of morale of the ship's company.

They gave the ship an air of domesticity and normality in a situation which in other aspects was very trying'. Simon became a huge celebrity, but never fully recovered from his wounds and sadly died a few months later.

The animal species that won the largest number of Dickin Medals was the pigeon. Thousands were employed by all the armed services. Pigeons vary enormously in their endurance, stamina and determination to get through and those who won a medal had persevered against all the odds (usually hostile weather rather than enemy fire), to deliver vital messages. Paddy the pigeon, who brought back the first word of the D-Day landings from across the Channel, was stuffed after he died. This may offend the sensibilities of some but it does demonstrate the high regard in which he was held [7].

The British Army's Royal Signals Museum at Blandford displays the body of pigeon 2709 of IX Corps, which died of wounds on 4 October 1917. The pigeon was despatched with a message from Divisional Head Quarters on 3 October at 1.30 p.m. It was hit by a bullet, which broke both legs, but the bird struggled home to its loft miles away and the message was retrieved at 10.35 am on 4 October. The bird died soon afterwards [8].

Like the Army and the Air Force the Navy also had its pigeons, overseen by the 'Naval Pigeon Service'. Devonport for example had in its magnificent clock tower a pigeon loft for housing sixty homing pigeons. Fifty-two birds were recruited for intense training, first off the end of the pier, then out in the harbour and finally from torpedo boats out in the Channel. The French Navy tried similar experiments but the system proved unreliable; too many birds were lost in fog and bad weather [9]. Despite these setbacks pigeons were used frequently by the Navy and were most certainly used at the Battle of Jutland (1916) as a quick, reasonably reliable and a secret means of communicating — so long as they were not shot down by the enemy.

Naval Air crews also took pigeons on their missions, in case they had to ditch in the sea and before the days of automatic radio signals. Coming down at sea was a serious risk for Naval pilots, not least because of the unreliability of the engines, and each aircraft trailed a long copper wire to act as a radio aerial - and two carrier/homing pigeons as a back-up in calling for assistance.

As the Captain of HMS *Amethyst* pointed out, cats and dogs bring comfort, amusement and diversion from the realities of life at sea and at war. Cats however tend to maintain their independence and aloofness and were rarely 'enlisted' by the crew and if they were enlisted the feline defaulter might find themselves at Captain's table deserting the ship. Dogs by contrast tend to remain loyal to a ship or person and were frequently listed as part of the crew, issued with papers, uniform and hammock — the Admiralty actually encouraged this in the war years, through the Allied Forces Mascot Club, recognising the important role they played in the life of servicemen [10]. 'PO(Dog) Flloyd', who is based in Gibraltar, is probably one of the few remaining enlisted dogs, other than those with specific RN roles such as security dogs and 'sniffer' dogs used to find drugs and explosives.

A dog at least as famous as Flloyd if not more so was "Just Nuisance" who was also enlisted, as 'Able Seaman', and was based at HMS *Afrikander* (a South African base) as a "bone crusher" with religious designation "Scrounger" — like many a matelot you might think [11]. The Navy News November 2002, shows the Great Dane on his death bed with a Nurse to provide comfort; he was sadly missed by many.

More of a mascot than a pet, a young bear cub was to be found on HMS *Royal Oak* [12] and in 1921 another bear, named Trotsky, (captured during the mission to support the White Russians) was brought aboard HMS *Ajax*.

HM ships are given their title by the Ship & Badge Committee of the Admiralty and they have often chosen creatures - mythical, ancient or real and here we have a few; *Antelope; Blackbird; Centaur; Dolphin; Elephant* – yes there was an HMS *Elephant*, (owned by the Spanish until we took it in 1805); *Fly; Griffin; Hare*, and so on through the alphabet.

Some of these creatures featured as figureheads on the stems of old sailing ships and many of those beautifully carved images are preserved. Richard Hunter has catalogued many and his details are listed in the bibliography.

Chapter 15: Battles and Blunders

~~~~~~~~~~~

Having traced the development of Britain's navy we can now reflect on lessons learned. Jaques Mordal lists 128 significant sea battles, world wide, not just those involving Britain, since 480 BC beginning with the Battle of Salamis whilst David Thomas has trawled the Admiralty's records and lists more than 180 battles in which Royal Navy ships were involved and subsequently awarded 'battle honours'. These dates are mainly after 1660, and therefore the restoration of monarchy, but there are notable exceptions such as the Spanish Armada in 1588. Warren Tute adds a further eighteen notable trouble spots in which the Royal Navy has been actively involved from Palestine 1946 to Falklands 1982, and the list grows each year. We therefore have a great deal of material to draw upon [1,2,3]. Many of the fleets taking part in these action set sail from the principle ports of Britain, namely Chatham, Portsmouth and Plymouth (Devonport).

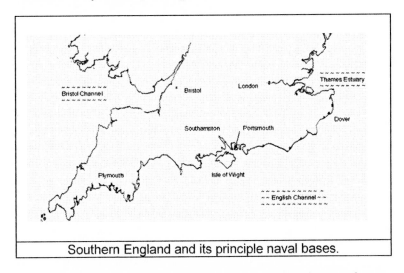

Southern England and its principle naval bases.

In this chapter we look at the way in which the Royal Navy and other Navies of the world are used; their successes and failures as they try to translate political ambition into nautical success. To bring some order to the chaos of sea warfare in this chapter we shall follow the action according the intended method of engagement, fleet action, bombardment, blockade, combined-forces operations and so forth. As we shall see the Royal Navy's role was not confined to sea battles — it is expected to undertake a multiplicity of jobs not specifically related to warfare, such as surveying, civilian rescue, diplomacy, joint training exercises with other branches of the armed forces or with other nations — all of which add to the Navy's efficiency and flexibility.

To begin with one of Britain's, or more specifically England's, early battles, the Spanish Armada. The Armada was defeated as everyone knows but this was not a battle of equal forces. Indeed the Spanish fleet was far bigger the English squadrons and the Spaniard managed to maintain their enormous fleet in a well disciplined and tight formation as they sailed down the English Channel. This an early example of a fleet action, as most men-o-war engagements were, fleet against fleet, whereas the sea wars of the 20th Century were rarely large fleet affairs (Jutland being one of the few exceptions). In the case of the Armada, the Navy's role was to defend Britain against an invading force. The Spanish intended to sweep the Navy from the Channel then bring over a large army, supposedly waiting at Calais.

Having entered the channel after months of preparation the Spanish chose not to enter Plymouth Harbour and engage Howard and Drake while they were still at anchor; they might have had greater success if they had. Instead they drifted down the Channel and the English had to work hard over the following days to get the 'weather gauge' and whilst hoping so picked off small elements of the Spaniard's fleet. When the Armada arrived at Gravelines, off Calais, it was still a formidable force barley dented by the English ships but the English fleet now sent in fireships to disperse the Spaniards and again set about picking off individual Spanish ships at their leisure and by splitting the Spanish forces and began to gradually decimate their numbers. The English tactics, far from a full scale fleet action, were nevertheless very damaging to the enemy who were in the following days unable or unwilling to retrace their route along the Channel. So the bedraggled Spanish fleet made its way Northward around the coast of Britain and suffered considerable storm damage, this further decimated what was left of the fleet and gave England a clear victory. The Spanish set out with 130 ships and 29,000 men, mostly soldiers not sailors; they lost sixty four ships and 10,000 men failed to return to Spain [4].

Whilst the defeat of the Armada demonstrated Britain's sailing and fighting skills there was no formalised system for engaging the enemy. The organisation of sea battles came with the several battles fought against the Dutch in the 17th Century. The Three Dutch Wars were conducted in the North Sea and were a straightforward conflict between two nations asserting their power and their intent to control the seaways.

The Dutch had a well practiced and professional Navy and defeated Britain's forces several times. England gradually began to get the better of the Dutch navy and mastering the art of sea warfare was therefore in a position to sign the Treaty of Breda (1667) on equal terms. Charles II was sufficiently impressed to grant the Navy 'Royal' status; henceforth it is the Royal Navy. A number of elements of sea warfare were developed in this time including the use of heavy guns — so ships fought at a greater distance and therefore were less reliant on close quarter, hand-to-hand fighting. This required improvements in signalling. Long range fighting also required the fleets to be better organised and the line-ahead formation was adopted with some enthusiasm.

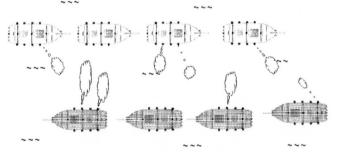

Line ahead formation:
Two fleets attacking with maximum fire power.

Fighting Instructions were promulgated requiring Admirals, also a new concept from this time, to form into a single column in order to sail past an enemy fleet firing broadsides en route [5].

The line ahead formation became something of a dogma; Commanders disregarded these Fighting Instructions on pain of death. Line ahead had clear advantages in that the whole fleet action could be conducted in an orderly fashion and with big enough guns firing at the correct range it could be devastating for the enemy. But it also stifled initiative, it could take hours, even days to bring the fleet into position and individual captains could not respond to the action as it unfolded, this was often compounded by imprecise signalling between ships.

The innumerable actions against the French, when Napoleon was attempting to rule Europe, helped to improve the Royal Navy's techniques for sea warfare; as noted in previous chapters, guns, signalling and fighting instructions were being refined to the point that Britain could claim dominion over the seas and "Pax Britannia", a hundred year's of relative peace for Britain.

Amongst the 'innumerable' battles fought against Napoleon and his allies were those in which Nelson played a part and they were central to Britain's continued sovereignty of the seas Cape St Vincent –in 1797; Jervis was commander in chief but Nelson made his name by breaking the sacrosanct 'line of battle' to engage the enemy closer, as was his wont. In 1798 Nelson smashed Napoleon's Egyptian ambitions in the battle of the Nile, from which only two of thirteen French ships escaped.

It was in the battle of Copenhagen that Nelson put a telescope to his blind eye and declared he could see not see Parker's signal to disengage the enemy and claimed he was entitled to be blind sometimes (often misquoted as "I see no ships"); he continued the battle to a conclusion (a British victory against the Danish). The most famous of all Nelson's battles was that at Trafalgar in October 1805, in which the Royal Navy sank or seized some eighteen Franco-Spanish ships.

The battle of Jutland is generally accepted to be a unique sea battle. A number of factors came into play at a moment in history to make this so. It was of course a battle during World War 1 between Britain's Grand Fleet verses Germany's High Seas Fleet. It was the culmination of an arms race over several decades between these two belligerent states. It was also the zenith of battleship actions; hereafter sea warfare would involve more wide ranging ship types, aircraft carriers, destroyers and submarines, using far more sophisticated weaponry, radar, guided missiles and torpedoes. At the time of Jutland, 31st May 1916, these were all on the horizon but not yet in regular use. This battle relied upon the new, all steel and big gun, dreadnought type battleship and would be a test of planning and design. Jutland was the last great sea battle where the light and weather conditions would be critical. With limited radar and only minimal aircraft surveillance this was a game of hide-and-seek on a very grand scale. There was every possibility two entire fleets could hide in the vastness of the ocean and never meet at all. The main protagonists Jellicoe, Beatty, Hipper and Scheer each relied upon the knowledge of the other.

The action takes place in the North Sea and involves two fleet actions – a preliminary cruiser action in which Vice Admiral Beatty led the battle-cruiser force from Eastern coast of Britain confronted a German force led by Admiral Hipper. Beatty is criticised for failing to gather his force into a single massed squadron before taking on the German Ships; it was during this encounter Beatty made now famous observation that there is '*something wrong with our bloody ships*' (in so far as the armoured protection for his ships was inadequate). Nevertheless Beatty did what was expected of him, which was to led the Greman fleet into a trap – the full might of the British Grand Fleet off Jutland peninsular. This was the seond phase.

The two great fleets met at about 6 o'clock in the evening and it was over by nightfall. Admiral of the Fleet Jellicoe successfully anticipated the direction of his enemy and twice succeeded in 'crossing the T' of the German fleet, giving the Grand Fleet the advantage of firing broadsides at the enemy.

A number of blunders arose during the course of this battle. Beatty's actions have been noted; the Admiralty's radio intercepts of German signals were not passed efficiently to Jellicoe; signalling between ships during the action was at times faulty; British range-finding and gunnery, and even the shells themselves, was not as good as the Germans; British ships were not as well protected as Germany's. Finally, towards the end of the day Jellicoe was not informed of various sightings of the German fleet – including HMS *Malaya* which at the end of the main battle was straggling at the rear of the retiring Grand Fleet when it passed within range of the tail end of the High Seas Fleet but failed to inform Jellicoe. For detailed discussions of this action see for example 'The Grand Fleet' by Admiral Viscount Jellicoe for a contemporaneous account and 'Castles of Steel' by Robert Massie for a more distant and pragmatic view.

History judges Jellicoe the winner but in fact it was something of a draw. The British lost more ships and men but the

German High Seas Fleet never confronted the Grand Fleet again and so Britain won the day.

Although the Navy was engaged in a great many sea battles it spent a lot longer just blockading its enemies. Several methods were used for blocking a harbour. If the entrance to the harbour or estuary was narrow, Portsmouth Harbour for example, then the entrance can be physically blocked by sinking ships. It would be a temporary inconvenience but could be effective whilst in place. The Allies used this technique in World War 2 to block the Belgium ports of Zeebrugge and Ostend in order the restrict German U-Boat activity. No less than 140 warships were engaged in this operation and such were the risks that eight Victoria Crosses were awarded.

More typically in the days of sail an anchorage would be blockaded by a squadron of warships patrolling some distance outside the base, acting as a permanent threat to any commander minded to take his ships to sea. Such blockading could be close. For example in 1803/4 the Spanish Fleet was trapped in Cadiz by the British "Spanish Squadron" whilst Nelson maintained a more distant blockade of Toulon, in this case it was not intended to restrict movement of ships but to observe their movements and act accordingly.   Blockading by these methods could last for many months so it was a soul, and ship, destroying commission with no guarantee that the enemy would be effectively confined. This form of sea-going blockade did have one benefit – it meant seamen were well practised at station-keeping, gunnery and sailing and this would give them a distinct advantage when battle was joined, referred to as 'combat supremacy' [6].

Like many activities at sea, blockading was subject to regulation. One such principle, indeed a maritime law, is that neutral states recognise a belligerent force's declaration of blockade. The mere 'declaration' became a paper exercise so Britain in 1908 promulgated a set of rules including the rule that a blockade would not be recognised unless there were forces present capable of maintaining an effective blockade – if a ship then breaks the blockade it can be seized at any point in its voyage [7].

Blockading was of course intended to stop the movement of shipping, in or out of harbour and if successful could seriously affect a nation's fighting ability or more generally its very survival if supplies routes were interrupted.

But blockading was not always successful and the 'Channel Dash' by the Germans in 1942 was one notable failure. Several of the German Battleships including Scharnhorst and Gneisenau, with surface ships and aircraft as escort, made their ways safely up the Channel from Brest to their home bases in Germany. Britain's failure to block the Channel was a propaganda coup for the Germans but in effect relieved some of the pressure on the Atlantic convoys. For Britain the failure was caused by unreliable equipment, notably airborne radar. It was also a failure of communication in so far as the Admiralty wasn't told surveillance of the Battleships was lost. As we shall see in other examples, there was a failure of intelligence, of information gathering — the Germans were sweeping the Channel in advance of their dash but this information was not used to good effect by the British [8].

Blockading was a tacit threat but bombardment was a more immediate and destructive threat and very frightening for the civilian population in coastal towns. Towns along the East coast of Britain were frequently attacked in this manner and it must have severely tested the morale of these people, in just the same way as the aerial bombardment of London, and many other cities, wreaked havoc and distress in the whole population. It may seem a simple matter for a squadron to sail up to a lightly defended town, shell it and take flight before an effective counter attack can be launched but success relies on the usual elements of good planning, having the right equipment, good information about the target and secrecy. If secrecy is maintained the element of surprise will be in your favour. Operation Menace was fine example of failure on all these points.

Whilst the French had often been our enemy, in this debacle they were supposed to be allies, albeit rather reluctant ones. The events unfolded in the summer of 1940 shortly after France fell to the Germans in June 1940. The French, unwilling to allow their supposed allies the British to take command of their war ships, scuttled them or at least some ships but those in the French Territories of West Africa and in particular in the port Dakar still had to be dealt with — either they passed to British control or the Germans would have the benefit of them.

Charles de Gaulle, as Leader of the Free French Movement, had an idea, which the British Government accepted in the forlorn hope that success would save them from the ignominy of having to fire on ships that in a sensible world should have joined their own fleet. De Gaulle overestimated his assumed position as a leader and presumed he would be welcomed as a hero in Dakar. He managed to persuade the British that this was the case but this was a drastic failure of intelligence gathering. Other failures followed quickly enough. Operation Menace was intended to support de Gaulle who would 'hoist the Free French Flag in the French Territories of West Africa'. The British Commanders, Vice-Admiral Cunningham and Major-General Noel Irwin were required to support de Gaulle covertly so that he would not appear to be a puppet of Britain. The operation was to look as if French led. It was further expected that surprise rather than force would win the day. Far from remaining a secret the whole operation was widely known by friend and foe with the exception of one key player – Admiral Sir Dudley North who was commander at Gibraltar.

The Vichy Government of France were amongst those who came to hear of the plan well in advance of its execution and arranged for Admiral Bourragué to take three Cruisers and three large Destroyers from Toulon to reinforce Dakar. Had Admiral North been apprised of Operation Menace he would have intercepted this squadron; instead he signalled them '*bon voyage*' quite unaware of their destination or purpose. Admiral Bourragué must have been amused if not bemused by this reaction. And so the farce continued.

Almost nothing seemed to go as planned – indeed it was the planning that was at fault. The troops enjoyed a luxury cruise on liners that had been taken from civilian service so quickly they had not been cleared for troop carrying. Troops enjoyed morning tea in their cabins and five course meals. Meanwhile the commanders and their staff were crammed into HMS *Devonshire* – in an office seven foot square and with just three typewriters, two of which were broken and with little else to support the commanders of this exercise – when things go wrong they do tend to go wrong in every detail. This motley fleet was code named Force M.

Eventually, on 23rd September 1940, the French sloops entered Dakar Harbour with the British squadron out at sea, over the horizon. The Vichy, well aware of the British presence, would not accept de Gaulle's emissary and he fled the scene. When the British over flew Dakar, distributing thousands of leaflets explaining de Gaulle's intention, the aircraft were fired upon; this rather confirmed the Vichy's opinion of the adventure.

Admiral Cunningham had to decide his next move. Anticipating only limited resistance, poor intelligence and the use of
out-dated maps misled him, he decided it was time for action.
Once again things did not go as he might have wished, a fog descended and so he was firing blind. At this point readers should
be reminded that bombardment of shore batteries by ships is
rarely successful and poses higher risks for the ships than the
land based positions; the dictum of the day was 'ships are hopeless against forts'. So it was on this occasion, the British Battleships, *Barham*, *Resolution* and the *Cumberland* fired over a hundred rounds of 15" shell and hit nothing whilst a shell from a
coastal battery hit the *Cumberland*, which then had to withdraw
for repairs. Admiral Cunningham tried aerial bombing but once
again he was ill-equipped. The 250-pound bombs were quite inef-
fective against the armoured decks of the French battleships. A
torpedo attack met with the same resounding failure and did not
score a single hit.

Conversely, Lieutenant-Commander Lancelot was in command of the sole Vichy submarine in Dakar. By now it seems inevitable that luck should be against Cunningham; Lancelot had
trained with the Royal Navy so he was able to read their flag signal for turning his ships. Anticipating their move Lancelot pretty
well inevitably scored a direct hit on the *Resolution*.

Admiral Cunningham finally accepted defeat and withdrew
Force M, HMS *Cumberland* had already limped away from the
battle field and Cunningham was obliged to tow HMS *Resolution*
back to Freetown, Sierra Leone for urgent repairs. He was later
teased by a French commander, 'why did you keep shelling my
vegetable garden' [9,10].

It would be quite unfair to leave the reader with the impression that this was Admiral Cunningham's finest hour. He was
a reluctant participant in this misjudged and lamentable adventure but he went on to command some very successful actions in
the Mediterranean including the domination of the Italian Fleet.
The Dakar affair does however teach, or at least remind, us many
lessons about sea warfare – planning, preparation, good information, the right men and equipment, an achievable objective and
above all secrecy where needed.

Admiral Cunningham provided us with a fine example of
poor planning - we can blame Charles de Gaulle for that - but also
he provides many examples of excellent use of the Royal Navy

including ship to ship actions, combined operations, air and submarine action, evacuations and so on. The Mediterranean was a very lively place in World War Two.

Operation Judgement (11th November 1940) serves as an example of the Navy's use of its Fleet Air Arm. Operation Judgement is more commonly referred to as the air raids on Taranto and off Cape Matapan. The first was an aerial attack on the Italian Fleet moored in Taranto harbour. In summary, three Battleships were torpedoed, one Cruiser hit, the dockyard severely damaged and half the Italian Fleet was put out of action. It is presumed by some observers that this successful attack was copied by the Japanese in their air raid on Pearl Harbour but Bernard Ireland advises us that the Japanese attack was already in an advanced stage of planning and Taranto merely confirmed the feasibility of such an attack on a fleet anchorage [11].

The Taranto air raid was a seaborne (air) attack of a land base, led by the Fleet Aircraft carrier *Illustrious*, in contrast the Matapan action was between opposing fleets but again the use of air strikes was critical to its success. On this occasion, 28th March 1941, Admiral Cunningham was again flying his flag in HMS *Warspite* and his squadron was accompanied by the fleet (aircraft) carrier HMS *Formidable*. They intercepted an Italian force, which included their battleship *Vittorio Veneto* plus their escorting cruisers and destroyers. The *Formidable* flew several sorties and succeeded in hitting the *Pola*. Ultimately the Royal Navy sank three heavy Cruisers, *Pola, Fiume and Zara* and several smaller warships. This was a very good example of the use of air cover and similar tactics were used to deal with the German battleship *Bismarck* two months later. It that action it was the aircraft carrier Ark Royal's Swordfish aircraft that managed to hit Bismarck. It was struck right aft, damaging her propeller and jamming her rudder – in many ways a lucky strike after so many torpedoes had failed to hit but this one was enough to slow Bismarck and allow the Cruiser HMS *Dorsetshire* send her to the bottom — after her guns had been disabled by the Battleships HMS *Rodney* and HMS *King George V*. The *Dorsetshire*, with HMS *Maori* then proceeded to rescue 110 men (of the ship's complement of 2,400 souls).

During the course of World War 2 there were a great many combined operations. Combined operations in this sense referred both to the combination of armed forces, naval, army and air-force, and also refers to the collaboration of British and other nationals, notably the Americans. WW2 operations of this sort include 'Operation Torch' (North Africa, 1942); Operation 'Husky' (Sicily, 1943); Operation 'Avalanche' (Salerno, 1943); Operation 'Shingle' (Anzio, 1944); Operation Dragoon (Marseilles & Toulon, 1944), but the most complex must be the D-Day landings, codenamed Operation 'Overlord' (landing on the Northern coast of France 6th June 1944). The naval contribution was codenamed Operation Neptune.

Overlord has been, repeatedly, described as 'the most massive and complicated operation in naval history, executed by the largest fleet that had ever been put to sea for any purpose at any time in any part of the world'. The Royal Navy's contribution included escort duties, anti-aircraft and anti-submarine cover and shore bombardment. Naval forces were divided into Eastern and Western Forces. Each comprised about 350 warships including 3 battleships, 13 Cruisers and 44 Destroyers. It is common knowledge that the landings met with variable resistance but were not repelled by the Germans and Overlord can therefore be judged as a success [12,13].

So far in this chapter we have dealt with the Royal Navy in combat but it does have other roles. Almost as familiar as Overlord is Operation Dynamo, not a landing, quite the reverse it was a withdrawal, in fact a complex evacuation of troops from Dunkirk (on the Channel Coast of France, May/June 1940). Kemp describes it as 'a heroic epic of sea warfare and of patient, disciplined courage by an army in adversity'. For the records, 308,888 men were rescued during nine days of constant harassment by German bombers, submarines, surface ships and mines. A total of 45 allied ships, destroyers and personnel carriers were sunk or severely damaged in this action [14].

Operation 'Demon', the evacuation of Crete in April 1941 was in some respects even more hazardous than Dunkirk in so far as the German air strikes by their Luffwaffe were virtually unopposed and the lifting of troops had to take place at night. Nevertheless the Navy had learned lessons about evacuating large numbers of troops and 51,000 troops, representing 80% of those involved, were rescued. Bernard Ireland describes a small piece of the action:

"...HMS Hotspur was deeply involved. As her First Lieutenant recalled, Dunkirk had given us good experience of this... the gun crews had been splicing special slings with which to hoist army stretchers from a rocking boat, and noosed recovery lines for hauling men out of the water, cook had been baking a double load of bread and making giant sandwiches and fannies full of cocoa... some of the upper mess deck was roped off for operations, if a leg had to come off then a mess table was the best place to do it'. The commentary continues; 'This Destroyer was escorting a pair of passenger ships and loading went very slowly....daylight brought the (German) Stukas and Ju 88.... two Destroyers and one of the passenger ships were sunk and only fifty men survived from the three ships' [15].

This brief description of one minor incident hints at why such actions are described as 'brave', 'heroic', 'courageous', epic; it clearly takes well trained and disciplined men with these attributes to repeatedly confront the enemy in this manner. In this rescue operation 2,261 men were killed or 'missing in action' and in all three Cruisers and eight Destroyers were sunk; and no less than twenty other ships were significantly damaged. Clearly such evacuations are 'blunders', the result of a failure at some point but nevertheless recovering from such disasters is courageous and heroic and as we have seen with Dunkirk they can be on an epic scale.

Some may judge the Iraq war, 2003 as a blunder. A blunder by the Americans for 'invading' Iraq and Britain for aiding them. Interestingly the decision-making may have been based on faulty intelligence (about the supposedly imminent use of weapons-of-mass-destruction), which, as we have seen throughout history, can lead to some disastrous engagements. Blunder or not, Iraq saw the Royal Navy at work again, code named Operation Telic the usual support was provided, minesweeping in The Gulf, troop-carrying, Aircraft Carrier support, shore bombardment and coastal patrols and communications.

This concluding chapter is reflecting on the many roles of the Royal Navy and up to this point we have concentrated on big ship actions, but there is a branches of the Royal Navy that operate more covertly and secretly, the Royal Marines, Commandos and Special Boat Service ('SBS').

Royal Marines, essentially soldiers at sea, are an elite corps specialising in amphibious warfare. Wherever there is military action, the Royal Marines are likely to be involved. They were prominent, for example, in the Falklands campaign, and they could be found wherever the British armed services are actively involved including locations as diverse as Sierra Leone, Afghanistan, Iraq and Northern Ireland.

The Royal Marines number approximately 500 officers and 5,400 men and, especially since the end of the Cold War, the Corps appears to have reverted to its traditional role of being ready for operations anywhere in the world. All Royal Marines, except those in the Royal Marines Band Service (who take on ancillary and medical roles), are first and foremost, commando soldiers. They are required to undergo what is recognised as one of the longest and most demanding infantry training courses in the world. Like the Army's Special Air Service, more familiarly known as the SAS, the SBS would be expected to operate behind enemy lines, to reconnoitre, to provide information, to disable key installations such radar and communications and to act as spotters for bombardments or missile launching. The SBS specialises in mounting clandestine operations against targets at sea, in rivers or harbours and against occupied coastlines [16].

Not all the Royal Navy's roles are combative, ships and men don't sit in harbour waiting for a war, although war is their purpose the gaps between wars are used for their many other roles and now is the time to see what else the Navy does. Training is of course vital and having mentioned the Iraq conflict the Navy's role there has shifted from enforcement to training; the RN Basra River Service provided training for the Iraqi's own 'Iraqi Riverine Patrol Service' [17].

The monthly newspaper "Navy News" publicises an extraordinary range of activities from patrol duties; training exercises; fund raising and charity work; parades and 'guards of honour'; surveying; joint exercises with other branches of the British armed services and with foreign navies; bomb disposal; civilian rescue and so on. The Royal Navy's own web-site reported the contribution made by the RN ships in December 2004 when the Indian Ocean was hit a 'tsunami', (a massive surging tidal wave, caused on this occasion by an undersea tectonic plate movement as the earth itself shuddered). HMS *Chatham* and Royal Fleet Auxiliary vessel *Diligence* assisted in rescue and recovery operations. Much less significant, but just as vital to the participant, the round-the-world yachtswoman Ellen McArthur rendezvoused with HM ships *Gloucester* and *Iron Duke* in the same month.

A number of events reported in 2003 are noteworthy, not least the underwater disposal, by a Royal Navy Diving Unit (SDU2) of two 1,000lb and a 1,600lb German parachute mine, one presumes these were dropped in World War Two and not more recently. The Second Sea Lord, Vice Admiral James Burnell-Nugent continues to maintain a positive public profile and to show his versatility, taking a steel-drum lesson as part of the Navy's (cultural) Diversity Action Team. On a similar note of diversity the RN Chaplaincy Services has published a directory of local advisors to ensure support is available to service personnel of all faiths.

Several towns honoured ships' crews with the Freedom of the City, entitling those honoured to march through the city with fixed bayonets. HMS *Superb* was so honoured by Stafford and 40 Cdo. Royal Marines by Taunton.

Fund raising and charity works features regularly and is clearly appreciated by the recipients, usually worthy causes such as schools, nurseries, hospitals, city farms and the like. Sports and competitions have always played an important part in the lives of service men and women, to keep them fit and well occupied. Not surprisingly sailing features high on the agenda and the Royal Navy did well in the 2003 Fastnet Race, in their new Challenger 67 yacht 'Adventure', which took two trophies, the Culdrose and Inter-Regimental Cups. The list of sporting events is long and varied including shooting, climbing, cricket, football, cycling, marathons and swimming – the Royal Navy is not always top of the league but usually puts on a good show.

Like many other large organisations, governmental and otherwise, the Royal Navy seems to be subject to constant change and reorganisation, largely because of Defence Reviews and the greater integration of the armed services and of course changes on the international scene. The Royal Navy no longer stands alone as it did in the 18th/19th Century; it frequently operates jointly with other forces from the European Union (EU), the

North Atlantic Treaty Organisation (Nato), the United Nations (UN) and of course other naval forces of the Commonwealth.

As we come to end of this final chapter we can reflect on the Royal Navy's position in the opening years of the 21st century.

Does Britain still need a navy? Jellicoe thought there were four good reasons for a powerful naval force:- firstly, to ensure British ships have unimpeded use of the sea; secondly, in the event of war, to bring steady economic pressure on our adversary by denying him use of the sea; thirdly, in the event of war, to cover passage and assist any army sent over seas to protect its communications and supplies; fourthly, to prevent invasion of this country, and its Dominions, by enemy forces. These have been replaced by the Ministry of Defence's the 'Missions of the Armed Forces' which is to provide peacetime security; security for overseas territories; defence diplomacy; to promote British interests; to promote peace and humanitarian operations; to contribute forces for foreign conflicts that may affect British interests; to respond to conflicts involving NATO allies; to counter strategic attacks against NATO [18].

We can safely conclude that Britain did once need, or chose to have, a mighty naval force, one that was equal to any two other naval powers, in order to maintain the position espoused by Jellicoe. It is equally clear that Britain can no longer afford such an extensive naval force, nor does Britain need such huge naval forces as she did when she stood alone against several European nations. In July 2004 the Defence Secretary had the unpleasant task of telling Parliament, the nation and the armed forces that there would be cutbacks in military spending. With his announcements came the inevitable debate about whether British armed forces could meet their objectives. Given the propensity for the British Government to engage its military resources world wide it seems they will be stretched if not overstretched in their commitments.

Perhaps there should be fewer commitments. Britain no longer stands alone against other nations - and would be quite incapable of doing so. The answer now is 'joint'; joint training, joint procurement; joint exercises; joint operations; joint command (and joint, shared costs one hopes).

Whilst it seems apparent to the author that defence costs must be within the nation's ability to pay there are presumably benefits to be had in maintaining standards of excellence and in-

novation in military development. There are, one assumes, benefits of military procurement to industry and therefore to the
economy. With defence comes a defence industry [19,20].

Britain's navy is no longer 'Sovereign of the Seas' and
hasn't been for a very long time. The Royal Navy is no longer the
Senior Service; it is in partnership with other services. It does
have a long and proud history and still maintains the highest
standards of professionalism.

The epilogue: Remembrance

The final words should be about those many thousands of sailors 'lost at sea', a euphemism for killed in action, more accurately died in the service of the Royal Navy and the nation. Many sailors died other than in battle, in Tudor and Stuart times disease was far more dangerous than the enemy's gunfire, and not a few were executed for a wide variety of misdemeanours.

Accidents also account for many losses, to cite just one fatal example, HMS *Bulwark*, a Battleship of the 1st World War, was accidentally blown up whilst loading shells, 138 men were killed when faulty cordite exploded prematurely. But, of course, many thousands die in the heat of battle. From the Battle of Sluys in 1340 when 25,000 French sailors and 4,000 Englishmen were killed to the sinking of a single ship, HMS *Hood* 1941, when only three men from a crew of 1,419 survived. That's six hundred years of sea battles. Each year, on 11th November, at the 11th hour, Britain undertakes to remember those who sacrificed their lives; words cannot effectively convey the impact of so many deaths, so an anonymous Indian poem will serve the purpose:-

When I am dead
Cry for me a little
Think of me sometimes
But not too much
Think of me now and again
As I was in life
At some moments it's pleasant to recall
But not for long
Leave me in peace
And I shall leave you in peace
And while you live
Let your thoughts be with the living.

anon

The glossary that follows explains some of the more obscure nautical references in this book plus a few phrases and sayings which have 'gone shore'.

Glossary and Etymology

Albion: Myth has it that Albion was the fourth son of Neptune and his name is given to England. Although rarely heard now it was used frequently by the military to describe their homeland and the place they were defending during First and Second World Wars.

Andrew: An alternate name for the Royal Navy after Lieutenant Andrew Miller a well known press-gang officer of the Navy's Impress Service in the 18th Century.

Balloon: Balloons had various uses before the days of aircraft, radar and satellites. They could be manned as observation points to oversee the enemy (on land or at sea) and the fall of shot or they could be floated up in their hundreds to deter in-coming aircraft. From this use the term 'the balloon has gone up' has passed into common usage referring to the onset of trouble. Even more obscurely, and probably apocryphal, there were two types of barrage balloon; the first, 'A' type, was rigid and the 'B' type was inflated without a frame, that is, limp. Colonel Blimp was a well known but fictitious war-time cartoon character devised by Lieutenant A.D. Conningham R.N. and drawn by the cartoonist Sir David Low. Col. Blimp's name was self-evidently (but doubtfully) derived from type-B limp balloons.

Barrel, to have someone 'over a barrel' is to have them at your mercy. It comes from the practice of placing a drowning person over a barrel to try and clear his lungs; at this point the poor wretch was at the mercy of those ministering to him.

Beam: the maximum width of the ship.

Biscuits: biscuits were an important part of the Navy's food provisions, see 'hard tack'. The Makaton (sign language) sign for a biscuit is to imitate breaking a biscuit with your elbow and is a reference to sailors breaking hard tack biscuits.

Bite the bullet: a phrase suggesting someone is about to do something they would prefer not to do. It has its origins in the Indian Mutiny (in the days of Empire) when it was erroneously claimed (probably by the media) that British military leaders ordered soldiers to bite the ends of

222

cartridge-cases greased with pig or cow fat. Believing this to be the case, and against their devout beliefs, the soldiers mutinied.

Bitter end: the very end of a rope was tied to a post or bitt so that end of the rope is the 'bitter end' and now more commonly refers to the end of an activity; to keep going to the bitter end of a difficult situation.

Board, 'to go by the board': anything lost overboard was said to have gone by the board (the boards from which the ship is constructed) and thus it refers to something cast aside.

Boat, 'all in the same boat' has the obvious meaning that everyone is in the same position, more specifically in the same lifeboat. That is, they are all on equal terms when the ship is sinking.

Boatswain's whistle: a small high pitched whistle originally used to signal orders it was also carried as a badge of office but is now confined to ceremonial duties such as 'piping the side' for honoured guests arriving on board ships. Its origins are said to derive from the days when Greek, Roman, and presumably British, galley oarsmen kept time with a pipe or flute. The title 'Boatswain' is now shortened to Bo'sun.

Bow: front end of a ship.

Bottom: The ships itself was once referred to as the bottom (now more commonly called the hull) and 'bottomry' was an early form of mortgage; money raised by the Captain, based upon the value of the ship and its cargo, and used to pay the costs of the voyage itself. Along similar lines, 'general average' was a precursor to Insurance wherein each of the interested parties paid a contribution towards any losses during the voyage. From these early beginnings Edward Lloyd went on to develop, circa 1688, 'Lloyd's Register' of ships and their insurance [1].

Brass Monkeys: A term used when it is very cold. In full, the phrase is 'cold enough to freeze the balls off a brass monkey'. This has nothing to do with the gonads of primates. There are two divergent explanations for this phrase. The first and generally accepted version is that it refers to a brass cradle holding a pyramid of cannonballs ready for use. In cold weather the brass contracts and the cannon balls are upset. The second explanation refutes the first version on the grounds that cannon balls were kept in 'garlands' - wooden frames on the side of the ship and not in brass trays, which would have been too unstable. No definite alternate explanation is offered other than a reference to a model of a brass monkey. Such an inert object would only be affected by the most extreme of temperatures; this seems a rather vague and unlikely etymology [2,3,4].

Broadside: to fire a broadside is to fire all guns in one direction. In the days of sailing ships that meant firing all the cannon on one side of the ship towards the enemy; in more modern battleships it meant pointing all the main guns (which were on the centre line of the ship and so capable of firing to Port or Starboard) to one side and firing one massive salvo.

Builders Old Measurement: a formula for calculating the tonnage of a (wooden) ship adopted by Britain in 1773 so as to be able to fix harbour dues. The formula was $((L - 3/_5B) \times B \times \frac{1}{2}B) / 94$, where L is length of ship and B its Beam.

Bulkhead: the walls or vertical surfaces in a ship, the horizontal surfaces below your feet being decks and above your head, the 'ceiling', is the deck head.

Burn your bridges; this phrase had its nautical counter-part 'to burn your boats'. In both cases it refers to burning boats or bridges so that there was no retreat. This was a device used by Roman military leaders to ensure their soldiers/sailors didn't leave the battle prematurely.

By and large now has the meaning 'broadly speaking' but historically and nautically speaking 'by' refers to sailing close to(wards) the wind and 'large' refers to sailing with the wind on the ship's quarter (near the stern). It was simpler to sail 'large' but the course was less precise. When building/buying a ship it was always worth checking how it sailed 'by and large'.

Captain's Table: Refers to the arrangements for dealing with day-to-day defaulters and offenders of minor transgressions. Defaulters stood before the Captain or a Senior Officer to have the offence read out and a suitable punishment recorded. More serious offences required a Court Martial.

Cat: see 'swing the cat'.

Chip on the shoulder: refers to the custom and practice of taking small pieces of wood from the Royal Dockyards, if the wood was small enough to go under the arm it was acceptable but if it was so big as to be carried on the shoulder – this would lead to arguments with gatekeeper. Hence a an argumentative person has a 'chip on his shoulder'.

Chock-a-block: full or at its limit; in nautical terms it to refers to a block-and-tackle or pulley when the two blocks are brought together so there is no more room for manoeuvre.

Conscription: compulsory national, military service, requiring young men to join the armed forces, usually at times of conflict, when the conscripts are referred to as hostilities only, 'HO'. See also Impressment.

Colours: Flags, particularly those signifying your country, for example the Union Jack and White Ensign. Much ceremony is attached to lowering the flags at night and is known as 'colours' or 'evening colours'. The saying, when passing an examination, 'to pass with flying colours' is a reference to a multiplicity of flags flown by ships at times of celebration — when they are said to be 'dressed overall'.

Copper bottomed: refers to ships' hulls being sheathed in copper to prevent them getting fouled and infested with the teredo mollusc or ship worm which could do more harm to a ship's hull than enemy gun-fire. Such a ship was therefore first class and virtually guaranteed to complete the voyage and from which comes the term a copper-bottomed deal.

Crossing the Bar: a euphemism for death.

Crossing the Line: the ceremony of crossing the Equator for the first time and involves much ritual in the Court of his Oceanic Majesty, King Neptune. An informal event celebrated by officers and ratings on equal terms and usually resulting in the novitiates getting very wet.

Crossing the T: this manoeuvre is only relevant to battleships capable of firing a broadside. The aim of a commander was to position his line of ships across the front of the enemy's line (thus forming a 'T'), this enabled his ships to fire all their guns, a broadside, towards the enemy, who could only reply with their forward facing guns/turrets.

Cut and run; refers to the rare occasions when a ship had to cut its anchor rope, abandon the anchorage and flee (for example, if being chased). It now means to abandon an activity and rush off.

Dead in the water has that precise meaning either through a lack of wind or loss of motive power; it also has the more generalised meaning that a scheme has no chance of success.

Dhobey, or dhobi, or dhoby. The word will be common enough to most old sailors and in its various spellings refers to washing clothes. It is included here in recognition of the many Indian words that sailors and soldiers purloined from that part of the Empire. It is Hindi in origin and is frequently used in the phrase 'dhobey wallah' a laundry worker.

Displacement: The weight of a ship or its mass is usually given in tons, for example in Jane's Fighting Ships. But for the purposes of this book the weights given are only approximate because the method of calculating weight varied. In some early instances it referred to the amount each ship could carry, weight therefore defined the load not the ship. Thereafter the weight or displacement (remember Archimedes) depended on what was included, guns, stores, armaments, crew and so forth. See also Builders Old Measurement.

Doldrums: literally a belt of very calm waters in the Atlantic Ocean with virtually no wind, which means sailing ships float aimlessly for days on end; hence to be in the doldrums is be in a depressed and aimless state. See also Horse.

Dutch: the Dutch were frequently the antagonist of the Navy in the 17th century and we are left with a lot of phrases and sayings associated with the Dutch. Many of them have rather negative connotations. Here are a few; Dutch auction (from a high to an increasingly low figure), D~bargain (not a bargain); D~comfort (no comfort at all); D~treat, (each pays for him/her self); D~courage (false bravery). Finally, double-Dutch, gibberish (rather like this entry).

Flat: a term describing living quarters on one floor of a building is taken from a ship and has a similar meaning – an open area between decks where, or example, men live.

Flotsam and Jetsam. Flotsam is equipment, goods or cargo accidentally lost overboard; anyone who finds such goods has a legal interest in them as salvage; whereas jetsam are goods deliberately thrown overboard, jettisoned, (perhaps to save the ship from sinking) and such goods remain the property of the original owner.

Fiddle: although musical instruments like the fiddle were common on sailing ships (to amuse sailors and keep time by beating a regular rhythm while they worked) another sort of fiddle was the raised side of the square wooden plate to stop food sliding off in a gale. The term 'on the fiddle' (doing something illegal) arises from sailors' suspicion that if someone's plate was piled high with food right onto the fiddle it was assumed that sailor had somehow managed to take or be given more than his fair share of food, he was seen as being 'on the fiddle'.

Foc'sle: Front part of the top deck of a ship, from the days of sailing ships that had fore-castles.

Footloose and fancy free: its origins date from old sailing ships; footropes were in place to help men keep their balance whilst furling sails to the yard-arms.

Grog: Is a diluted form of rum. To avoid excessive consumption of alcohol Admiral Vernon introduced watered-down rum rations. Sailors called this 'grog', in affectionate memory of 'Old Grog', Admiral Vernon, who was already famous for his great-coat made of Grogam cloth.

Hand over fist: now refers to someone making increasing financial gains but nautically it referred to someone simply climbing up a rope — when one hand was raised over the other (which was of course held in a tight fist on the rope). Hence making money 'hand over fist' is to make progress swiftly and effectively.

Hard Tack: Those infamous biscuits said to be infested with weevils. They were made of wheat and pea flour and by being hard-baked could be stored for long periods of time.

Horse; to 'flog a dead horse' now refers to wasting time on a situation doomed to failure; it refers to the Horse Latitudes — which can be found 30 degrees either side of the Equator. In these Latitudes a sailing ship was often becalmed. As sailors were sometimes paid in advance there was no incentive for them to work hard during this quiet period, they were in fact working off their advance pay (and making very little progress through the water) which came to be known as the Dead Horse — so they were, rather obtusely, 'flogging a dead horse' [5].

High and Dry: has the literal meaning to be high and dry above the tide or to be stranded having gone aground. To be left high and dry means you are in an impossible situation without support.

Hoop, to be put through the hoop: what started as a sailors' game in idle moments was transformed by the bosun into a rather effective punishment. Three or four sailors would be tied by their left hand to a large metal hoop and each would man strike the man in front with a whip or 'nettle'. It soon became an imaginative if painful punishment when the blows became harder and harder and so arose the term 'to be put through the ordeal of the hoop' now shortened to the more common phrase 'put through the hoop'.

Impressment: An early form of conscription into the Royal Navy. Imprest or prest refers to the payment made in advance for services rendered, often referred to as 'the King's shilling'. The term was corrupted to 'press' or to force. In order to get enough men to work the ships the Quota Act of 1795 was passed and an organisation, the Impress Service' was set up to 'invite' sea-faring men to join the Navy; such invitations were sometimes quite forceful and the Impress Service had a fearsome reputation, Lt. Andrew Miller was so adept at filling His Majesty's Ships that his name has passed down in history (see Andrew above). Although abandoned in the 19th century at least one source claims impressment is still legal (in the form of national conscription) [6,7].

Jack or Jack Tar: a sailor; 'tar' makes reference to both the tar used to preserve clothing, along with everything else on board a sailing ship, it also refers to Tarpaulin, a heavy, tarred canvas used to make sailors' clothing.

Know the ropes; getting to know the ropes, literally learning about the very many cables, stays, hawsers, braces, shrouds, sheets, lines, cords, on a sailing ship. On such a ship there is just one 'rope' and that is the bell-rope.

Kye, Ky or Ki: a hot drink made with cocoa powder.

Line manager: from the person who took the lead in firing the line on whaling ships.

Littoral: Refers to the shoreline, between high and low water.

Long shot: to fire a gun at its extreme range with little likelihood of hitting the target and now meaning any course of action that is unlikely to succeed. However one long-shot, in fact the longest shot, that did succeed in hitting the enemy, is credited to HMS *Warspite*. It is believed it hit a moving target in July 1940 when it shelled the Italian ship Giulio Cesare at a range of 26,000 yards, just under 15 miles away [8].

Loose end, to be 'at a loose end' referred to the end of rope unravelling. Sailors seen to be lounging around aimlessly were given the task of whipping the ends of these rope hence the phrase, to be idle is to be 'at a loose end'.

Loose cannon: on a ship a loose canon is a very dangerous thing, more likely to kill friend than foe and likewise in a boardroom a person acting like a loose cannon will do more harm to the company than to its rivals.

Matelot: A sailor; the term is French in origin.

Money for old rope: to sell old and worn out rope that is dangerous and quite useless. The correct name for such old rope was 'junk' and this word is now in common usage with the wider meaning of any rubbish.

Monkey: powder monkeys; another apocryphal tale. It is said the small boys on board sailing ships who supposedly carried canisters of gunpowder to the cannons during engagements were so called because of their agility in moving around with their dangerous packages in the heat of battle. It is more likely that chains of crew, boys, men (and any women on board) passed the canisters hand to hand — a much safe system.

Moustaches or full set: It is a curious requirement of the Royal Navy that you are either clean shaven or have a full-set, that is a beard and moustache. The order derives from Queen Victoria and probably relates to her mourning of her beloved, and moustachioed, Prince Albert – presumably she didn't want to be reminded of his image.

Nail your colours to the mast: In military terms this meant keeping your flag flying at times of war - if necessary by nailing your flag to the mast; if you are not showing your colours it will be assumed you have 'struck' (lowered) your colours and are surrendering to the enemy. On land the term means to declare your position clearly and unequivocally, particularly as to whose side you are on.

Nave: The ecclesiastical term for the long central aisle of a church and is derived from the same Latin route for naval, *Navis,* meaning 'a ship'. It refers to the fact that church roofs were built along the same line as ships' hulls — probably by the same master craftsmen.

Nip and Tuck: of uncertain naval origin but the author suggests it derives from splicing rope; each strand is nipped (folded or twisted) and tucked so each strand in turn talks the lead as the splice progresses. Hence a close run race in which the lead alternates. In plastic surgery it is inferred that unwanted skin is similarly nipped and tucked.

Offing or off-shore: if something is 'in the offing' it refers to something about to happen and refers to the nautical term off-shore. When ships were close to the shore and about to anchor they were said to be 'in the offing'.

Ordinary: ships laid up, with masts and guns removed and held in reserve, were referred to as being 'in ordinary'.

Petard, 'to be hoisted by one's own petard': A petard was a canister of explosive; the fuses were sometimes unreliable and the engineer setting the fuse may be caught in the blast — hoisted by his own petard. There may be a similar explanation for the phrase to 'carry the can'. As before, a canister of explosives which might detonate whilst being carried — so nobody wants to carry the can or take responsibility.

Pipe: see boatswain's whistle.

Pompey: A familiar name for Portsmouth. Portsmouth is a City, and has been a city since 1926. It is on the South coast of England and might reasonably be called the home of the Royal Navy, although there are other bases that have served the Navy for at least as long as Portsmouth. The name Pompey has an uncertain history and the advice of the Portsmouth Museum on this point is acknowledged. Firstly it may refer to a guardship 'Pompee' moored prominently in the harbour at the beginning of the 19th Century.   Secondly it may refer to a number of Portsmouth based sailors who, in 1781, climbed Pompey's Pillar (near Alexandria) and thereafter became known as the 'Pompey Boys'. Thirdly and least likely a drunken sailor roused himself in the middle of a lecture about the fall of the Roman Empire and on hearing about the death of General Pompey he called out 'poor old Pompey'. Fourthly, a pompey is a Yorkshire term for a prison and may relate to Portsmouth's Naval Prison. Fifthly, the local fire brigade was known the 'Pompiers' and were a common sight practicing on Southsea Common and would have been very prominent as ships came into harbour. There may well be other explanations.

Point blank: suggests something is very close or forthright and comes from the French phrase 'point blanc' (centre or bull's-eye) and militarily refers to guns being fired at close range so there was no arcing of the shell as it travels straight to the centre of the target. It now refers to someone making a point directly and without prevarication.

Port: the left side of the ship when facing forward. Signified by the colour red, so at night if you see a red light you can work out which side of the boat you are looking at and therefore its direction of travel.

Press gang: See Impressment. Tradition has it that beer tankards were made with glass bases so that press-gang 'victims' might see if a shilling had been dropped into their beer and so, unwittingly, accept the King's Shilling as a 'volunteer'.

Pull you finger out: This advice, to act promptly, derives from the days of cannon, when a sailor (or soldier) would stick his finger into the small ignition hole after the ignition powder had been poured in (to avoid a spark igniting the powder prematurely). The gun captain would let him know when he wanted the finger removed without delay! The term 'flash in the pan' is also associated with the ignition hole of these old guns — if the trigger mechanism failed and the ignition powder failed to detonate the main charge in the barrel it was referred to as a mere 'flash in the pan'. For a slightly different reason the term 'to hang fire' also refers to these guns in so far as the delay between igniting the powder and the gun discharging was referred to as hang-fire. The term now refers to a delay. See also Petard. Apropos guns, the phrase 'lock, stock and barrel' refers to the three main elements of a rifle and therefore means all its parts in other words, 'everything'.

Purser: The paymaster and supplies officers (historic). The term pusser refers to anything vaguely associated with the purser, pusser's rum, soap, shirt and so forth.

Push the boat out; to 'push the boat out' has the obvious connection with ships and sailors and refers to the still common practice of celebrating at great expense before going off to sea.

Pusser: See purser above.

Q-Ships: Merchant ships re-equipped with heavy guns hidden behind movable bulkheads; intended to lure German submarines into surfacing and attacking an apparently easy target. A similar device was used by the Royal Navy and the American Navy to lure Pirates into the open.

Quarterdeck: the after part of the top deck of a ship.

Racing lines: 'Racing' in this case does not refer to a high speed vessel but one in which the castles had been "razed" or removed.

Rate: the term rate refers to the size and armament of the old men-of-war sailing ships; thus a large ship like HMS Victory had over a 100 guns and was a first rate ship and from this comes the common phrase 'first rate' meaning something of quality and distinction.

Salt, 'rubbing salt in the wound'; presumably referring to the practice of rubbing salt into a wound after a man had been flogged to prevent infection of the wounds; now taken to mean adding insult to injury.

Salvage: correctly used the term means compensation paid to someone who has recovered goods, or indeed saved a whole ship, lost at sea. In a more general sense it refers to the goods and materials recovered after being lost at sea. Such recovery is usually by finding goods washed ashore but it also refers to things recovered from the depths. Isolated, coastal communities took advantage of this salvage right by luring ships, using false lights, onto rocky shores - where they inevitably sank close enough to the shore for salvaging.

Scuttle: the correct term for a circular porthole (window) in the side of a ship.

Shake a leg or 'show a leg': it now has the meaning to get on with your duties but its origins owe something to the hairiness of sailors' legs and the smoothness of their female companions' — to prove you were not a sailor the bo'sun would call out 'show a leg' at which point you were obliged to prove to him you were a female visitor and therefore excused duties.

Shipshape or 'all shipshape and Bristol fashion': refers to the fact that Bristol was once a premier sea port and its ships had a reputation for high standards and seaworthiness. Hence the phrase implies everything is neat and tidy and in good order.

Ships that pass in the night: an obvious reference to a brief encounter.

Ship types and classes: sailing men-o'-war were readily classed according to their size and the number of heavy guns they carried, a hundred or more for first rate, a ship of the line, to small sixth rate vessels carrying about thirty guns – not a fighting ship but an escort. This classification changed with the coming of steel. Ships then ranged from Battleship, Battle-Cruiser, Cruiser, Destroyer, Frigate, Sloop, Corvette, Coastal Patrol Vessels and Launches. Other ships joined the fleet and don't fit this orderly nomenclature such as the Monitor (with a large single gun), the Submarine, the Aircraft Carrier and Amphibious craft. There are of course numerous ancillary vessels such as mine-sweepers, hospital ships, supply ships and so forth.

Skyscraper: the top-most sail of a square-rigged ship. Now more familiar as a description of very tall buildings (which may comprise a number of 'flats' also naval in origin, q.v.).

Sling your hook, amongst other contenders for this saying it is suggested that this refers to the ship's anchor (the hook) being placed in its sling (the cradle for the anchor) just before a ships sets sail; the modern meaning therefore, if someone is told to 'sling their hook', is an invitation to leave.

Son of a gun: an illegitimate child born on board a ship. If the father is not identified then the child is said to be a 'son of a gun' and makes reference to the usual place for giving birth, behind a screen on the gun-deck. The term was once rather dismissive and contemptuous but now has a less disparaging meaning of shock and surprise.

Spick and span: something that is bright and new or as good as new. A 'spick' was once a nail or tack and a 'span' a wood-chip or wood shaving. Thus a recently launched ship would still have bright spicks and left-over span and so it was 'all spick and span'!

Spike his gun: has the literal meaning of spiking a gun to stop it being fired and now suggests action taken to stop someone causing harm.

Splice the main brace: literally, to splice the large rope holding up a mast - for which the riggers were rewarded with an extra tot of rum; therefore a celebratory drink after completing a difficult job.

Square Rig: refers to a style of uniform as worn by ratings (i.e. not the Officers). Several elements of the Uniform are square including the white shirt and the collar but the term square rig is said to derive from the fact that when bell-bottom trousers were folded for storage the resulting creases gave the impression of square rigged sailing ship. (Officers wear a 'fore-&-aft rig', that is, a jacket, collar and tie).

Square meal: refers to the square, wooden plate or tray on which meals were served and came to mean in modern parlance a substantive and wholesome meal — though they were far from this in the early years of Royal Navy cooking. Plain and simple as this explanation is the etymology of this phrase is disputed; Michael Quinnion suggest the term is American in origin and was first used by Mark Twain in 'The Innocents Abroad' 1869). However square plates and trays for food were in use by the English for centuries, so this alternate explanation is to be doubted [9].

Starboard: the right side of the ship when facing forward. The term derives from the early days when the rudder was mounted on the side of a boat. The boat was steered from that position so this was the 'steer-board' side of the boat. Signified by the colour green, so at night if you see a green light you can work out which side of the ship you are looking at and therefore its direction of travel.

Stern: rear or after end of a ship.

Sweet Fanny Adams: at least one explanation is naval in origin. Fanny Adams, a young girl was murdered and her body dissected for disposal by the villain. At about the same time the Royal Navy was changing rations from salt-beef to tinned chopped mutton (presumably early in the 19th century when tin cans for preserving food was discovered). With a rather macabre sense of humour this unpalatable mess was referred to as 'Sweet Fanny Adams'. It now suggests something worth nothing.

Swinging the lead: swinging the lead was a very important job so its current term of abuse for someone wasting time is surprising. To ascertain the depth of water a heavy (lead) weight is dropped into the water (by the way, the weight had a hollow base to capture some of the material off the bottom, giving the Captain useful information about the location, sandy or rocky – not least to help him decide what sort of anchor to use). This was considered an easy job for the sick or wounded so the lucky (albeit sick or maimed) sailor was seen to be 'swinging the lead' and not undertaking his full duties.

Swing a cat: or 'not enough room to swing cat' might (but doubt-fully) refer to the cat-o'-nine tails, a whip with nine tails, used to flog sailors. To be effective a large arc was required swing the whip and lash the victim and draw blood — so a small place wouldn't be any good, it would be 'too small to swing a cat'. The phrase has another equally improbable reference; that of shooting as a sport when cats were swung in the air as the targets. As before, there was sometimes insufficient room to swing the poor cat [10].

T: Crossing the T, see 'Crossing the T' above.

Taken aback: to be taken aback is to be surprised and its origins stem from sails being taken aback by a sudden change of wind direction which would cause the ship to stall.

Three sheets to the wind; a fairly common saying suggesting a person is drunk and incapable of any useful activity. Sheets are ropes and so three sheets to the wind refers to a fourth sheet going adrift leaving the other three ropes, and the sails to which they are attached, flapping uselessly in the wind.

Toe the line: in the Royal Navy it referred to sailors stepping up to a white line to receive their pay; the white line kept them at a safe distance from the Paymaster's table. It now has a more generalised meaning - to conform. There are other, American, explanations about parading on board ships with toes in line with the wooden planking but the British version will suffice, it has the same meaning.

Tonnage: see displacement but note that the term 'ton' as used to describe the weight or displacement of ship derived from the tuns or barrels wine stored ready to be carried by ships. A tun held about 250 gallons of wine. The ship was then described as carrying so many tuns or tons [11].

Touch rock bottom: as the term infers a ship is in serious trouble if it is so low in the water it touches a rock strewn seafloor. And this might happen if a ship is grounded when the tide is 'at its lowest ebb'. Both sayings suggest one has reached a nadir.

True Colours: Whilst it was common practice for warships to disguise themselves and sail under a flag of a neutral state or even fly the enemy's colours it is a rule of warfare that you show your true colours before opening fire. So, to 'show your true colours' is to make clear your real allegiance.

Two-six, heave: a term commonly used to prepare to heave, or pull something heavy so the work is done in unison. The exclamation derives from the team required to heave a cannon into pace; technically however the numbering may be wrong, each man was given a number but two and six were not opposite so a pull by these two would have been imbalanced.

Waister: Here the meanings of waist and waste have been confused. A waister was a novice seaman who was too inexperienced to work up in the rigging so he worked on deck in the waist, the middle of the ship, not unexpectedly they were often the men pressed into service (see press-gang). Such a sailor might be regarded as useless; it now implies someone who is a waste of time.

Wait until the coast is clear: a self-explanatory sea-faring term.

Weather, 'to be under the weather' is to be unwell; another nautical term. Sailors who were sick were sent below deck and were therefore literally below the weather (out of the wind and rain). It also refers to the fact they were being sent below the 'weather deck', the deck open to the weather.

Whipping; as well as the obvious meaning of striking someone with a whip a whipping is also the seizing on the end of a rope.

Whistle; 'to whistle in the wind'. Its nautical origins are complex; some sailors thought whistling would help bring a good wind whilst others thought whistling brought bad luck. The rather negative connotation of this, and the similar phrase 'go whistle for it', suggest sailors by and large thought whistling a bad thing.

Women: like cats, women received a mixed reception on board ships. Some thought them lucky others thought it very unlucky to have women, or a cat, in the ship.

Wrack and ruin: from the original term for a ship that is wrecked, it was in fact 'wracked'.

Yard arm: is a cross tree fixed to a mast and is used to hold sails in position. In square-rigged sailing ships the yard arm was self-evidently at 90° to the mast. This made a convenient point from which to hang sailors condemned to death by Court Martial. Hence being 'hung from the nearest yard arm'. The last such official execution in this manner was on 13th July in 1860 when Royal Marine, Private John Dalinger was hanged for the attempted murder of the Captain of HMS Leven whilst stationed in Talienwan Bay, China [12]. A more welcome reference to yard is the saying 'when the sun is over the yard arm'; it has the literal meaning and indicates a suitable time (about midday) to start drinking (alcohol) - for which the blue and yellow stripped 'Gin Flag' might be flown.

You scratch my back and I'll scratch yours: its origins reflect the brutal punishments meted out by stern discipline at sea. Rather cruelly sailors often had to punish their comrades — including flogging them and even to the extent of assisting in the hanging of those to be executed. If one sailor was to flog another he might come to an arrangement; 'you scratch my back and I'll scratch yours' in the hopes that the flogging would be moderated by this reciprocal arrangement. [13].

A number of the explanations in the glossary were drawn from the following books:-

'A Few Naval Customs...', by Captain WNT Beckett.
'Jackspeak' by Dr. Rick Jolly.
'Just An Old Navy Custom' by A C Hampshire.
'Red Herrings & White Elephants' by Albert Jack and
'Port Out, Starboard Home', by Michael Quinnion.

Their contribution is acknowledged.

Bibliography

Admiralty, Manual of Seamanship, U.K., H.M.S.O., 1964.
Admiralty, Naval Ratings Handbook, U.K., H.M.S.O., 1954.
Allen, Oliver, Pacific Navigators, London, Time Life, 1985
Armstrong, W., Battle of the Oceans, London, Jarrolds.
Arthur, M., Forgotten Voices, UK, IWM, 2004.
Bacon, R.H., Earl Jellicoe, London, Cassell, 1936.
Bacon, R.H.S. (ed.), Britain's Glorious Navy, London, Odhams.
Barrow, Sir J. Mutiny of HMS Bounty, London, Folio Soc.1976
Beckett, Captn WNT, A few Naval Expressions. Gieves, UK circa 1925.
Bernard, Carmen, The Incas, Thames & Hudson, Black, J., British Seaborne Empire, Yale, London, 2004.
Botting, D., The Pirates, London, Time-Life, 1987.
Botting, D., The U-Boats, London, Time-Life, 1984.
Brayley, M., WW2, Allied Women's Services, UK, Osprey, 2001.
Brett, B., Modern Sea Power, Middlesex (UK), Hamlyn PG Ltd., 1986.
Brooks, R., Long Arm of Empire, London, Constable, 1999.
Brown, D.K., Rebuilding the Royal Navy, London, Chatham, 2003.
Brown, R., Phantoms and Legends...Sea, London, P Stevens, 1972.
Buderi, R., The Invention that changed the World, UK Abacus 1998.
Bulfinch, Thomas, Myths of Greece & Rome, UK, Penguin, 1981.
Burns, K.V., Badges & Battle Honours, (UK), Maritime Books, 1986.
Callender, G., The Story of H.M.S. 'Victory', London, P Allan, 1929.
Cawthorne, N., Strange Laws of Old England, London, Piatkus, 2004
Chalmers, W.S., Earl Beatty, London, Hodder & Stoughton, 1951.
Chapman, A., England's Leonardo, London, IoP, 2005.
Clark, G., History of Britain, London, Octopus, 1982.
Crampton, W., Flags, London, Kingfisher, 1989.
Critchley, M., British Warships & Auxiliaries (Series), UK, Annual.
Critchley, M., British Warships Since 1945, Cornwall (UK).
Cunliffe, B.(ed.), British & Irish History, London, Penguin, 2002.
Dampier, W, A Pirate of Exquisite Mind, London, Doubleday, 2004.
Deary, T., The Barmy British Empire, London, Scholastic Ltd., 2002.
Dixon, T.B., The Enemy Fought Splendidly, UK, Blandford, 1983.
Douglas, J., HMS Ganges, Warwickshire (UK), Roundwood, 1997.
Earle, Peter, Pirate Wars, GB, Methuen, 2004.
Fisher, J., Memories, London, Hodder & Stoughton, UK. 1919.
Fry, Plantagenet Somerset, Kings & Queens, London, D-K, 1998.
George, J.L., History of Warships, London, Constable, 1999.
Goodwin, Peter, Men-o'-War, Carlton/NMM, London 2003.
Goss, J., Portsmouth Built Warships 1497-1967, K Mason, 1984.
Haines, G., (ed.) Battleship Cruiser Destroyer, UK, PRC Ltd., 1994.
Hamilton, J., War at Sea, Dorset (UK), Blandford, 1986.
Hampshire, A., Just an Old Naval Custom, W.Kimber, London, 1979.
Hardy, A.C., History Sea War, London, Nicholson & Watson, 1948.

Herman, A., To Rule the Waves, UK, Hodder & Stoughton, 2005.
Heyman, Charles, Armed Forces of the UK, UK, Pens & Sword, 2003.
Hodges, P., The Big Gun, London, Conway, 1981.
Hore, Capt P.,The Habit of Victory, London, Pan 2005.
Howard, M., Oxford History of the 20th Century, UK, O.U.P.,2000.
Howarth, David, Sovereign of the Seas, Glasgow, Collins, 1974.
Howarth, David, The Dreadnoughts, London, Time-Life, 1985.
Humble, Richard, Naval Warfare, London, Orbis, 2002.
Inwood, S., The Man Who Knew Too Much, London, Pan, 2002.
Ireland, B., War at Sea, London, Cassell, 2002.
Ireland, B., War in the Mediterranean, UK, Pen & Sword, 2004.
Jack, A., Red Herrings..., London, Metro Publishing Ltd., 2004.
James, L., Rise and Fall of the British Empire, London, Abacus, 1998.
James, W.,The Naval History of Great Britain, London, Collins, 2002.
Jane's, Fighting Ships of World War II, London, Random, 2001.
Jellicoe, Jack, The Grand Fleet, London, Cassell, 1919.
Jenkins, H.D., English Channel (Charts) 7th Ed., UK, Potter, 1918.
Jolly, R., Jackspeak, G.B., Palamanando, 1999.
Kaplan, P., Battleship, London, Aurum, 2004.
Kennedy, Paul, ...British Naval Mastery, London, Penguin, 2004.
Keegan, J., The Price of Admiralty, UK, Century Hutchinson, 1988.
Kemp, P., (ed.), History of the Royal Navy, London, A. Barker, 1969.
Kemp, P., (ed.), Oxford Companion to Ships..., London, OUP, 1976.
Kenyon, J.P., Dictionary of British History, UK, Wordsworth, 1981.
King, C., Rule Britannia, London, Studio Publications, 1941.
Kinsey, T., Songs of the Sea, London R Hale, 1989.
Larn, R., Cornish Shipwrecks, UK, David & Charles, 1971.
Lavery, B., Ship, London, NMM, 2004.
Lawrence, Richard (ed.) Naval Battles, London, Constable, 2003.
Lehane, Brendan, Northwest Passage, London, Time Life, 1985.
Lewis, M., The Navy of Britain, London, Allen & Unwin, 1948.
Lewis, Val, Ships' Cats, Shepperton, England, Nauticalia, 2001.
Llewellyn, S., Who Was Admiral Nelson, UK , Short, 2004.
Macintyre, D., The Battle of the Atlantic, London, Pan, 1969.
Maddocks, Melvin, The Great Liners, London, Time-Life, 1982.
Marshall, HE., Our Island Story, UK, Galore Park, 2005.
Massie, R.K., Castles of Steel, London, Jonathan Cape, 2004.
McFee, W., The Law of the Sea, London, Faber, 1951.
Mehl, Hans, Naval Guns, Rochester (UK), Chatham Press, 2002.
Miller, D. & C., Modern Naval Combat, London, Salamander, 1986.
Milton, G., White Gold, Hoder& Stoughton, UK 2004.
Ministry of Defence, The Royal Navy Handbook, UK, Conway, 2003.
Mordal, Jacques, London, Abbey Library, 1959.
Morley, S., 99 Years of Navy, London, Quiller, 1995.
O'Brian, P., Master & Commander, London, HarperCollins, 1996.
Oman, C., Nelson, U.K., Reprint Soc. Ltd. Hodder & Stoughton, 1947.

Powell, F., Sea War, London, Robert Hale, 1990.
Philips, Science & Technology Enc', London, G. Philip Ltd., 1998.
Phillipson, D., Band of Brothers, Gloucester (UK), Sutton, 1998.
Plevy, Harry, Battleship Sailors, London, Chatham Press, 2001.
Pollen, A., The Navy in Battle, London, Chatto & Windus, 1918.
Preston, Antony, Battleships, London, Bison, 1981.
Preston, D. & M.,Pirate of Exquisite Mind, UK Transworld Pub. 2004.
Puleston, W.D., Sea Power in World War 2, London, Yale, 1947.
Quinnion, M., P.O.S.H., London, Penguin Books, 2004
Regan, G., Naval Blunders, London, Guinness, 1993.
Raven, Battleships of WW2, (Greenwich Library).
Riley,R.,Portsmouth;Ship, Dockyard & Town, UK, Tempus, 2002.
Roberts, John, The Battleship Dreadnought, London, Conway, 2001.
Rodger, N.A.M., The Safeguard of the Sea, UK Harper Collins, 1997.
Rodger, N.A.M., The Command of the Ocean, UK Penguin, 2004.
Rohwer, J., War at Sea, G.B., Chatham/Caxton, 1996.
Roskill, S., Naval Policy Between the Wars, London, Collins, 1976.
Roskill, S., The War at Sea, London, H.M.S.O., 1954.
Sadden, J., Portsmouth In Defence of Realm, UK, Phillimore, 2001.
Sebag-Montefiore, H., Enigma, London, Pheonix, 2001.
Speed, K., Sea Change, Avon (UK), Ashgrove, 1982.
Spink, Coins of England, London, Spink & Son Ltd., 2001.
Stark, S., Female Tars, London, Constable , 1996.
Thomas, D., Battle & Battle Honours, (UK), Pen & Sword 1998.
Thompson, Julian (ed.) Modern Warfare, UK, Pan, 2003.
Time-Life (ed), The Seafarers (series), USA, Time Incorporated, 1985.
Tomalin, C., Samuel Pepys, London, Penguin, 2002.
Triggs, A., Portsmouth a Shattered City, (UK), Halsgrove, 2003.
Triggs, A., Portsmouth Between the Wars, (UK), Halsgrove, 2000.
Triggs, A., Portsmouth First, Devon (UK), Halsgrove, 1999.
Triggs, A., Portsmouth from the Air, Sussex (UK), Phillimore, 1995.
Turner, J.F., V.C.'s of the Royal Navy, London, White Lion, 1956.
Tute, Warren, The True Glory, London, Macdonald, 1984.
Verity, L., Animals at Sea, National Maritime Museum, UK, 2004.
Warlow, B., Shore Establishments of the RN, UK, Maritime, 2000.
Warlow, B., R.N. in Focaus (series), (UK), Maritime Books.
Warner, O., Nelson's Battles, (UK), Pen & Sword, 1965/2003.
Wells, J., The Royal Navy an Illustrated Social History, UK 1994.
Wells, J.G., Whaley, U.K. H.M.S.O., 1980.
Wheatley, K, Maritime Britain, London, Webb & Bower, 1990.
White, C. (ed.), The Nelson Companion, U.K., Bramley, 1995.
Willmott, H.P., Battleship, London, Cassell, 2002.
Willmott, H.P., Sea Warfare, Chichester (UK), Antony Bird, 1981.
Wilson, T., Flags at Sea, U.K. H.M.S.O., 1986.
Winton, J., Naval Heritage of Portsmouth, UK, Ensign, 1994.
Wragg, D., Snatching Defeat... Victory, UK, Sutton, 2000.

In addition to those published works the following E-Mail and World
Wide Web sites (WWW....) have also been most helpful and instructive:-
Royal-navy.mod.uk
Figureheads.co.uk
RDHmedals@aol.com...
Bermuda-triangle.org....
Newscientist.com...
Occultpedia.com...
Memorials.inportsmouth.co.uk.

And of course Shakespeare, always good for a quote or two; see
The Oxford Shakespeare, the complete works,
Wells & Taylor, Oxford University Press, 1988; see also
'Surprising Shakespeare' Pickpocket Book, UK 2003.

Footnotes

Chapter 1 Origins

1   History of Britain, Sir George Clark, p11 (Caesar et al) and Phantom & Legends of the Sea, R.L. Brown p.136 (Britannia helping Caesar).

2   British and Irish History, Barry Cunliffe et al p 38 (Roman Conquest) and The Naval Heritage of Portsmouth, J Winton p 9.

3   History of warships, James George, p 24. (Boarding Corvus)

4   Brit and Irish History p 62 (Vickings)

5   True Glory, Warren Tute, p 12/15 and Naval Heritage p11 (Vikings)

6   op cit   and The Naval Heritage of Portsmouth p 10. (King Alfred's sea battles)

7   op cit p 12/13   and The Naval Heritage of Portsmouth p 10 (Kings Alfred and Athelstan sea battles)

8   True Glory p 17 and Navy of Britain p 34. (Cinque Ports)

9   25 Centuries of Warfare by J Mordal; p. 44 (Sluys)

10   Navy of Britain, M Lewis page 35 (Sluys)

11   Kings and Queens Plantagenet Somerset Fry page 61 (Sluys)

12   Coins of England, Spink p160 (Coin, Noble)

13   True Glory p 21   (Sluys as First sea battle)

14   Naval Warfare, Richard Humble page 18 (bi, tri, quadremes)

15   True Glory p 21 (first guns at sea)

16   25 Centuries of Warfare p 43 (Salamis)

17   Navy of Britain page 35 (Salamis)

18   Safeguard of the Seas p 99 (Sluys/Salamis)

19   True Glory p 14 and 26 (Admirals and control of the seas)

20   Kings & Queens p 77 (Henry V)

21   Safeguard of the Sea p 68/71/335; True Glory p32 and Naval Heritage p14 (Docks)

22   History of Warships, J l George, p 89 (two power standard)

23   History of the Royal Navy, Peter Kemp, p 13 (Serpentine guns)

24   History of Warships, George, p 45 (first ship sunk by gun fire)

25   Safeguard of the Sea N.A.M. Rodger p 172

26   Naval Blunders G Regan p.118 (Mary Rose sinks)

27   Rebuilding the Royal Navy, D K Brown. (shipbuilding)

28   Portsmouth Historic Dockyard, Portsmouth Trust, p.5

29   True Glory p 29 and Oxford Companion p 889 (Trinity House).

30   History of Britain, p73 (peasants/land use and tithes).

31   Rise & Fall of the British Empire p 52 and Naval heritage p 17 (hiring ships and raising capital/taxes)

32   True Glory p44 (Spanish Armada)

33   Sea Change, K Sped p 117

34   Dict Brit Hist p 321 (Ship Money)

35   Safeguard of the Sea, p 342 (ship money)

36   Dict Brit Hist p 285 (poll tax)

37   True Glory p.34 (Heavy Cannon)

38   Sovereign of the Sea p 206 (gun ports)

39   The Men-of-War, p 21 (Regent)

40   The Men-of-War, p 23 (Great Harry)

41   Safeguard of the Sea p199/200 (Letters)

42   The Law of The Sea p 292 (Law of Oleron)

43   The Law of The Sea p 285 (Law of Oleron)

44   Pilot's Guide for the English Channel 1918.
45   Dict of Brit Hist p296 (W. Raleigh's execution)
46   Safeguard of the Sea, p 342 (Naval Forces for protection)
47   dict of brit hist p 136
48   True Glory p 52/53 League of Augsburg.
49   Safeguard of Seas p 365 (money)
50   Safeguard p. 386 (money)

Chapter 2 1650 - 1805
1   Kings & Queens p 138/9 (Cromwell)
2   Navy of Britain, Lewis p 51/53 (Cromwell's Navy)
3   True Glory p 62 and History of Britain, Lewis p 53 (strength of fleet)
4   Law of the Sea McFee p 130/1 (Navigation Acts)
5   Safeguard p 150; Law of the Sea p 130/2 and 25 Centuries of Sea Warfare. P 68 (Navigation Acts and control of the seas)
6   25 Centuries, p 73 note (brooms at the masthead).
7   Pepys, Tomalin (the diary re sex, money and the Navy).
8   Navy of Britain, passim (improvements to Navy in Pepys time)
9   Portsmouth Ships, Dockyard and Town, Rily p 9 (Portsmouth)
10   Men of War p 78 (Physician of the Fleet)
11   History of the RN, Kemp p30 (examination entry to RN)
12   True Glory p 59 and Men of War p 59 (Naval Discipline Acts)
13   Navy of Britain p 238 and 277 (pay and half-pay)
14   Navy of Britain p 359 (Articles of War)
15   Navy of Britain p 505 (Byng's error)
16   History of RN, Kemp p 31 (Penn/Venables in the Tower)
17   Men of War Chapter 3 (Blake/Mediterranean, Pirates)
18   Oxford Comp Ship and Sea p 58 (Barbary Pirates)
19   Men of war p 84 (Blake/Pirates)
20   Oxford Companion Ship and Seas p 155 (Charts)
21   Flags at Sea p 77 (flag signals)
22   Navy of Britain Part VI page 425 (cannon)
23   Oxford Comp p499 (Lord High Admiral)
24   True Glory, Tute p 78/80 (Rating Ships, Anson)
25   The Navy of Britain p 54 (The Merry Monarch and the Navy)
26   True Glory, Tute p 51 (wars against Dutch & French)
27   Battles and Honours Thomas, p 188 (Seven Years War)
28   Battles and Honours Thomas, p 225 (Battle of The Saints).

Chapter 3 RN & Empire
1.   True Glory p 94 (Maps and Charts)
2.   Rise & Fall of the British Empire, p 143 (terra nullis)
3.   Sea Change, Keith, Chapter 8, p 118 (HMS Endurance)
4.   Rise & Fall ps 59, 177 & True Glory p151 (gunboat diplomacy)
5.   Navy News, passim, eg (2004, Caribbean hurricanes)
6.   History of Britain, Clark, Chapter 1, (Roman settlement)
7.   History of Britain, Chapter 2 (Vikings rule)
8.   History of Britain p 40 (Murdrum)
9.   Naval Warfare, Humble p 36 (Sluys)
10.   Information supplied by the Commonwealth Institute in 2004

11.   Pacific Navigators, Allen, passim and A Pirate of Exquisite Mind, p3 (Pacific exploration)
12.   Northwest Passage, Lehane, passim, (Arctic exploration)
13.   25 Centuries of Sea Warfare p 131, (Chesapeake Bay)
14.   Battles and Honours p 66 (Chesapeake)
15.   The Incas, Bernard, passim
16.   Rise & fall p 96 (fair play - Quebec Act)
17.   Britain's Glorious Navy (Bacon) p284
18.   True Glory p129 and History of Warships, George, p 62
19.   History of Warships p62 (steam ships)
20.   Britain's Glorious Navy p285 (Australian Cruiser)
21.   Rise and Fall... p 235 (Far East/ Opium)
22.   Shore Establishments and Oxford Companion, p 393
23.   World Wide Web 'Yantse'.

Chapter 4 Pirates & Press Gangs
1   Pirate Wars, Earle, p XI and Oxford Companion,
2   Safeguard of the Sea p199 (Letters of Marque and Reprisal)
3   Law of the Sea, Chapter 9 (Letters of Marque and Reprisal)
4   Pirates, Douglas Botting, p 58 (the Plank)
5   Pirate Wars, p222 (the Plank)
6   Pirates, Douglas Botting, p150 (Rackham)
7   Pirate Wars, p 199 (Bonny).
8   A Pirate of Exquisite Mind, p250.
9   Pirates, Botting, p170 (HMS Swallow v Skyrme)
10   Pirate Wars p 145 (HMS Drake v Bannister)
11   Pirate Wars p203 (HMS Greyhound v Harris and Lowe)
12   Navy of Britain, Part IV Ch 2, p 307 onwards, (Manning the ships)
13   Web Site; Gibbons Burke, io.com/gibbonsb/... (Artcles of War)
14   Web Site; cfcforums.com/archive/index//...(Mutinies)

Chapter 5 Steam & Steel
1   History of the Warships, George p 69 (first iron clad)
2   History of Warships p 64 (paddle v screw)
3   History of Warships p 72 (battleships without sails)
4   Naval Blunders page 53 (round ships)
5   History of Warships p 77 (la jeune école)
6   Naval Blunders p 48 (HMS Trinidad's torpedo)

Chapter 6 Dreadnoughts
1   History of Warships, George, chapter 6 (Cuniberti)
2   Naval Warfare p 137 (obsolete battleships)
3   Battleship, Willmott p35 (Tsushima)
4   Rebuilding the Royal Navy (boat design)
5   History of Warships p91 (design of Dreadnought)
6   History of warships p92 (launch of Dreadnought)
7   Battleship (Willmott) appendix 3 / p244 (statistics of Dreadnought) and The Battleship Dreadnought, Roberts, chapter 1 (ditto).
8   The Grand Fleet Jellicoe page 310 (table of ships Torpedoes)
9   Encyc of Science (turbines) A turbine is unit with multiple propellers (within) the engine, this makes better use of the motive power, steam or water, and produces more energy/speed.

10   Battleship by Willmott chapter 2, p38-40 (on the dreadnought race).
11   Battleship by Willmott chapter 2, p40 (on losing the battleship race).
12   Shakespeare the Oxford Complete works, Julius Caesar Act 3 Sc 2 line 75. (Anthony on fallen heroes)
13   The Dreadnoughts D Howarth p51 (Abyssinia hoax)
14   Battleship Willmott p 44 and 246 (table of ship numbers).
15   Jellicoe Grand Fleet Page 8 (4th Battle Squadron)
16   Grand Fleet Jellicoe p 208 (ramming U 29)
17   Safeguard of the Sea p 270 (day to load a cannon)
18   For discussion see: Philip's Science Encyclopaedia p 431; History of Warships p76 and Mike Critchley's 2004 book of British Warships
19   R N Handbook 2003, p 34

Chapter 7 HMS Malaya
1   Jane's Fighting Ships p 25 (Malaya's basic details)
2   Jane's (WW2 warships) p25 and Battleship…, (Kemp) p 37 (Refit 1920/30s)
3   Public Records Office (Kew); Ref: ADM53/47974 (launch details)
4   Oxford Com Ships passim (Jellicoe and Scheer)
5   Battleship…, Kemp, p 37 (5th BS and BC Squadron May 1916)
6   Battleship…, Kemp, p 37 (beginning of Jutland, Coward)
7   Battleship,.., Kemp, p39 (a quote from the battle scene)
8   Bacon on Jellicoe Fate p266 (fate of nation in his hands)
9   Jellicoe/Bacon p 294 (Malaya sees Germans)
10   Jane's p 25 (Planes)

Chapter 8 Malaya's Log
1   Battle & Honours D Thomas (table of honours)
2   Battleship Cruiser Destroyer, p94 (Operation Neptune)
3   Jellicoe by Bacon p 237 (Malaya joins the fleet)
4   Grand Fleet, Jellicoe 272 (joins fleet Scapa Flow)
5   Jellicoe by Bacon p293/4 (spot enemy and say nothing)
6   The Dreadnoughts, Howarth, (Malaya at Jutland)
7   PRO Archive Reference ADM 178/131 (collision)
8   Great Liners, Melvin Maddocks, p 118 (fog)
9   War at Sea, Roskill,   p 270 and 89.
10   PRO ADM 53/113274 (for Suffolk incident)
11   Record of Service; CPO Powell RN; supplied by M.O.D. Directorate of Personnel Support (Navy).
12   War at Sea, Roskill p 294 (Malaya in Mediterranean with HMS Eagle)
13   History of Sea War, Chapters 16 and 17.
14   War At Sea, Roskill, p 295
15   War at Sea, Roskill 298 (Mediterranean fleet too slow)
16   War at Sea, Roskill (Mediterranean action)
17   War at Sea, Roskill p 421 (Op' Excess underway)
18   War at Sea, Roskill at p 425 and Everyman p202 (Genoa bombardment)
19   History of Sea War, C.in C. (awarded Knight Grand Cross)

20   War at Sea, Roskill p 375 and Pan Grand Strategy p 71. Convoy SL67
21   War at Sea, Roskill 375/76 (enemy b/cruisers spotted)
22   History of Sea War, p 21 (Battle of Matapan)
23   War at Sea, Roskill p 427 (Matapan)
24   The U-Boats p 17 (U Boats in North Atlantic)
25   History of RN
26   War at Sea, Roskill p 375/369 (Malaya sights Scharnhorst and Gneisenau).
27   PRO ADM53/112650. (New York refit)
28   War at Roskill, p 455 (damage and refit Malaya and Resolution).
29   History of Sea War, (Scharnhorst and Gneisenau bombed)
30   History of Sea War, (bombardment of Bardia and Fort Capuzzo)
31   History of Sea War p197 (Malaya moves West)
32   War at Sea, Roskill p494]
33   Battleships of WW2 (Raven) (Chap, "Modernisation") Greenwich Library.
34   Shore Establishments p148 and Battleships of WW2 p.217 to 225

Chapter 9 Guns and Ships
1   True Glory p21 (gun powder)
2   Navy of Britain (breech loading)
3   Navy of Britain p 577 (rifling and elongated bullet)
4   N of B p 579/582 (Armstrong guns)
5   Sovereign of the Seas Chapter 16 (about Sovereign of Seas)
6   Naval Warfare p 27 (gun ports)
7   Navy of Britain p 421 Mary Rose (sinking and stone shot)
8   Man of War page 33 see also "Rebuilding the RN" Brown/Moore
9   Naval Warfare Page 138/9 (gun-raft)
10   History of Warships page 50/51
11   The Big Gun, Peter Hodges, Chapter 3, (ballistics)
12   Naval Warfare p142/3 (on range finding and fire control)

Chapter 10 Sailors
1   Nelson, Oman, p 129 (loss of eye)
2   Nelson's Battles, passim (but note Trevenen's comments page 17)
3   Oxford Companion p88; Sovereign of Seas p189 and History of Britain p26 (on Blake)
4   Oxford Comp and The Pacific Navigators (Cook)
5   Oxford Comp p 88 and p100 (Cook)
6   Oxford Companion. (Lord Fisher)
7   Naval Blunders, Regan, p 19.
8   Castles of Steel, Massie Chapter 31-34, (Jutland)
9   Castles of Steel, Massie, p 585 (Beatty's at Jutland)
10   War at Sea Roskill passim
11   Oxford Companion, (on Cunningahm)
12   Web sites, various; (on Woodward)

Chapter 11 The Sailor

1   Portsmouth First (Triggs) p 1 (Corsets)
2   Great Liners p128 (Titanic)
3   Biographical Encyclopaedia (Scott)
4   Ganges Association.
5   Myths of Greece & Rome, p 293. (Sisyphus)
6   Naval Policy Between the Wars, Stephen Roskill (Treaties)
7   The Oxford Shakespeare (Wells & Taylor) p978 (Tiger)
8   Whaley, Wells, eg p 112 (Zoo)
9   Jackspeak, uniforms, below/above rank Petty Officer. p422
10   Battleship, Cruiser Destroyer, (sailors in a battleship)
11   Naval Warfare, p142 (Dreyer and Dumaresq gunnery control)
12   The Navy of Britain, p 356 (rum)
13   Jackspeak, (rum)
14   Science & Technology Encyclopaedia, p415 (tin cans)
15   Public Record Office, Document ADM/53/114600. (ref Malaya
sights enemy)
16   War at Sea (Roskill) Vol p. 376 (Malaya Sights enemy)
17   Imperial War Museum web site (the man who never was).
18   Raymond D Holdich, Medals & Militaria.

Chapter 12 Women and the Royal Navy
1   Spinks, coins of England p 58 (Sestertius Britannia)
2   Web site; britannia.com (history of Britannia)
3   Samuel Pepys (Tomalin) p156 (Frances Stuart).
4   Sovereign of the Seas (Howarth) p 142 (Armada)
5   The Pirates (Botting) p 150 (women pirates).
6   The Royal navy an illustrated History p117 (wrens)
7   WW2 Allied Women's Services, p 10 (wrens).
8   Web site royal-navy.mod.uk/ (QARNNS)
9   Web site rsr.org.uk (Agnes Weston).

Chapter 13 Ghosts and the Royal Navy.
1   Brown, R.L. Phantoms... passim. (Ghosts etc.)
2   Brown, p. 21 (Flying Dutchman and HMS Bacchante)
3   Quasar Web site Bermuda-triangle.org passim.
4   Web site; memeorials.inportsmouth.co.uk.
5   Brown, p 99 (the limping sailor)
6   Brown, p 130 (Scharnhorst) and p 25 (U65).
7   Web site occultpedia.com (mermaids).

Chapter 14 Rats, cats and weevils.
1   Men-o'-War, Goodwin, (Weevils)
2   AA countryside page 496 (a Weevil)
3   Flags at sea p 84 (Q flag)
4   Web Site www.petsmiles.com.... (animals for food)
5   Navy News September 2004 p 15 (Dog)
6   Navy News September 2004 p 27 (Budgie)
7   Web Site 'Dickin Medal'
8   Web Site, www.army.mod.uk/...(pigeon 2709)
9   Web Site, www.navynews.co.uk...(Devonport Loft)
10   Ships' Cats p 7 (Mascot Club)
11   Navy News November 2002, (dog, Just Nuisance)

12   Navy News September 2003 (bear cub)

Chapter 15 Finally, the Battle and Blunders.
1   25 Centuries of Sea Warfare, Mordal, p400, (list of battles)
2   Battles & Honours, Thomas, passim, (sea battles)
3   True Gllory, Tute p260 (RN actions since WW2)
4   Naval Warfare p 58, (Armada)
5   25 Centuries of Sea Warfare, P 68 (3 Dutch Wars)
6   Nelson's battles, Warner, p 148 onwards (blockade & combat)
7   Oxford Companion, p89 (blockade rules)
8   Naval Warfare, Humble, p 253 (channel dash)
9   Naval Blunders, Regan, p79 (Operation Menace)
10   The War in the Mediterranean, Ireland, P46 (Op Menace).
11   War in Med'. p51 (Taranto and Pearl Harbour)
12   True Glory, Tute, p 248, (Overlord)
13   History of the RN , Kemp p266 (Operations inc. Overlord)
14   History of RN, p233 (Dynamo)
15   War in the Mediterranean, Ireland, p82 (Crete evacuation)
16   Royal Navy Web site (SBS)
17   Navy News, October 2003, (Iraq)
18   The Armed Forces, Heyman, p 6 (Mission of armed forces)
19   The Armed Forces, Heyman, p 172 (defence industry)
20   British Naval Mastery, Kennedy, Chapter 12 (defence costs)

Footnotes to glossary:
1   The Law of the Sea, McFee, chapoter 15 (Bottomry)
2   Jackspeak, Rick Jolly (brass monkeys)
3   P.O.S.H., Quinion, (brass monkeys)
4   Red Herrings..., Albert Jack p 12 (brass monkeys)
5   Red Herrings..., Albert Jack p 6 (Dead Horse)
6   Navy of Britain, (Impressment)
7   Dictionary of British History, p 185 (Impressment).
8   Battleship/Kaplan p186 (Longest Shot)
9   P.O.S.H , Michael Quinnion, p 236 (square meals).
10   Red Herrings..., Albert Jack, p 87 (cats)
11   Safeguard of the Seas, p xxi (tons and tuns)
12   Strange Laws of Old England p 166 (last yard-arm hanging)
13   Red Herrings, Albert Jack p 15 (flogging)

Δ

Appendix 1: Service Record:

RECORD OF SERVICE: P.J. POWELL:

Ship	Rating	From	To	Time
Ganges	Boy 2nd	10.9.25	8.5.26	8 months
"	Boy 1st	9.5.26	25.6.26	1 month
Iron Duke	"	26.6.26	13.1.27	7 months
"	"	14.1.26	16.1.27	2 days
Victory	"	17.1.27	4.2.27	8 days
Tiger	Able s'man	5.2.27	16.5.29	7 months
Victory	"	17.5.29	30.5.29	8 days
Excellent	"	31.5.29	5.11.29	6 months
Excellent	"	6.11.29	10.1.30	2 months
Vernon (Skate)	"	11.1.30	1.9.30	8 months
Suffolk	"	2.9.30	30.6.33	3 years
Victory	"	1.7.33	11.8.33	1 month
Dryad	"	12.8.33	30.6.34	10 months
Victory	"	1.7.34	25.7.34	24 days
Revenge	"	26.7.34	17.1.36	1½ years
Victory	"	18.1.36	27.2.36	1 month
Winchester	"	28.2.36	30.3.36	1 month
"	A' L' Sea	31.3.36	29.5.36	2 month
Excellent	"	30.5.36	28.8.36	3 months
Victory	"	29.8.36	30.3.37	7 months
"	Ldg Sea'	31.3.37	28.5.37	2 months
Iron Duke	Ptty Officer	29.5.37	25.10.39	6 months
Victory	"	26.10.39	10.11.39	15 days
Excellent	"	11.11.39	20.4.40	5 months
Malaya	"	21.4.40	17.9.41	1½ years
Victory	"	18.9.41	27.9.41	9 days
Excellent	"	28.9.41	14.10.42	16 days
Shrapnel	"	15.10.42	16.10.42	1 day
Osborne	"	16.10.42	11.11.42	1 month
Victory iii	"	12.11.42	31.1.43	19 days
Nile (Easton)	"	1.2.43	31.1.43 ?	?
Victory	"	1.2.43	29.4.43	3 months
Excellent	"	30.4.43	16.6.43	2 months
Cormorant	"	17.6.43	16.6.43 ?	?
Hannibal	"	17.6.43	10.8.43	1 month
Chatham	"	11.8.43	8.3.45	11 mnths
Victory	"	9.3.45	20.3.45	11 days
Excellent	"	21.3.45	5.3.47	2 years
Le Macha	"	6.3.47	7.10.48	1½ years
Excellent	"	8.10.48	28.9.49	1 year
Victory	"	29.9.49	26.10.49	Shore

Appendix 2: table of measurements:

term		meaning
Barrel		Various sizes according to contents; beer was 36 gallons.
Cable		100 fathom or 200 yards
Calibre		Bore of gun or length of barrel as ratio of bore.
Chain cable		Chain of 8 shackles each 12½ 100 fathoms in length.
Degree		1 degree is 60 nautical miles.
Fathom	Fm	Six feet
Foot	1'	Twelve inches or .3048 metres.
Gallon		8 pints or 4 quarts or 4.546 litres.
Gill		¼ of a pint.
Horse Power	Hp	550 foot/pounds per square inch
Inch	1"	2.54 centimetres.
Knot	Kt	(speed) 1 nautical mile per hour.
League		Roughly 3 nautical miles.
Mile	Ml	1760 yards or 8 furlongs or 1.61. Kilometres.
Nautical mile	nm.	1.15 statute miles or 6080 yards or 1852 metres.
Ounce	oz.	One sixteenth of pound.
Pint		.568 litre or 20 fluid ounces and weighs 1¼ pounds.
Pound		.454 kilograms, or 16 ounces.
Pound	lb.	16 ounces, often reduced it to 14 or 15 by the Purser (contrast this with a 'baker's dozen' gives an extra loaf - 13).
Quart		2 pints or one quarter of a gallon.
Sea Mile		1000 fathoms or 6000 feet.
Sextant		measures 60 degrees (a quadrant 90.)
Shackle		12½ fathoms, a measurement of a section of chain.
Ton		1.016 Tonnes or metric ton = 1000 kilograms
Yard		36 inches

Appendix 3: Articles of War 1749:-
These Articles of War were originally established in the 1650s, amended in 1749 (by an act of Parliament) and again in 1757. It is an amazing document to ponder, especially the number and degree of offences which were punishable by death.

1.   All commanders, captains, and officers, in or belonging to any of His Majesty's ships or vessels of war, shall cause the public worship of Almighty God, according to the liturgy of the Church of England established by law, to be solemnly, orderly and reverently performed in their respective ships; and shall take care that prayers and preaching, by the chaplains in holy orders of the respective ships, be performed diligently; and that the Lord's day be observed according to law.

2.   All flag officers, and all persons in or belonging to His Majesty's ships or vessels of war, being guilty of profane oaths, cursings, execrations, drunkenness, uncleanness, or other scandalous actions, in derogation of God's honour, and corruption of good manners, shall incur such punishment as a court martial shall think fit to impose, and as the nature and degree of their offence shall deserve.

3.   If any officer, mariner, soldier, or other person of the fleet, shall give, hold, or entertain intelligence to or with any enemy or rebel, without leave from the king's majesty, or the lord high admiral, ... every such person so offending, and being thereof convicted by the sentence of a court martial, shall be punished with death.

4.   If any letter of message from any enemy or rebel, be conveyed to any officer, mariner, or soldier or other in the fleet, and the said officer, mariner, or soldier, or other as aforesaid, shall not, within twelve hours, having opportunity so to do, acquaint his superior .... by the sentence of the court martial, shall be punished with death, or such other punishment as the nature and degree of the offence shall deserve, and the court martial shall impose. And so on for thirty more laws many punished with death penalty. With acknowledgements to Gibbons Burke; web site .io.com/gibbonsb/......

Appendix 4:
Ships built in Portsmouth:
1497 to 1967

Names are decided by the Admiralty's 'Ship Name & Badge Committee'. By tradition names can repeated, for example 'Portsmouth' was used at least six times. But there should only be one ship in commission with the name. Alternate names are given in brackets. This is a list of Portsmouth built ships from 1497 to 1967 but others were built before and after these dates but these dates define its time as a Royal Dockyard. The first *Sweepstake* was the first ship built in Portsmouth and HMS *Andromeda* the last ship built in HM Dockyard.

Actaeon	1831
Actaeon (Dido)	1869
Admiralty	1831
Ajax	1767
Albatross	1842
Alexandria	1806
Amphion	1934
Andromeda	1967
Archangelesk (Royal Sovereign)	1915
Argus	1894
Arrogant	1848
Arrow	1823
Asia	1764
Association	1697
Aurora	1936
Avon	1867
Bacchante	1859

Bacchante	1876
Banterer (Plucky)	1870
Barfleur (Britannia)	1762
Barham	1889
Barrosa	1889
Beagle	1889
Bellerphon (Waterloo)	1818
Bellerphon	1907
Beelzebub (Firebrand)	1842
Berwick	1775
Bittern	1840
Blazer	1870
Blonde (Shah)	1873
Boadicea	1875
Bolton	1709
Boyne	1810
Brazen	1808
Bristol	1653
Britannia	1762
Britannia (Prince of Wales)	1860
Britannia	1904
Britomart	1820
Bruizer	1867
Bulwark	1807
Buzzard	1834
C3 (favourite)	1829
C28 (Orestes)	1824
C77 (Favourite)	1829
C470 (Shah)	1873
Caesar	1896
Calliope	1884
Camperdown	1885
Canada	1881
Canopus	1897
Carnatic	1823
Centaur	1845
Centaur (Royal Arthur)	1891
Centurion	1732

Centurion	1892	Ecureuil (Squirrel)	1704
Challenger	1826	Effingham	1921
Champion	1824	Electra	1837
Chanticleer	1861	Elizabeth	1769
Charybdis	1831	Elk	1868
Chatham	1758	Enchantress (Helicon)	1865
Cherub	1865	Eurydice	1781
Chestnut	1656	Eurydice	1843
Chichester	1753	Excellent (Boyne)	1810
Childers	1812	Exeter	1697
Cleveland	1671	Exmouth	1934
Colossus	1882	Expedition	1679
Columbine	1826	Express	1695
Comet	1870	Falcon	1771
Comet	1931	Fanny	1831
Cordelia	1881	Favourite	1829
Coronation	1685	Ferret	1821
Cracker	1867	Firebrand (Beelzebub)	1842
Crescent	1892	Fly	1694
Crocodile	1781	Fly	1696
Cromer	1867	Fly	1752
Crusader	1931	Forester	1693
Cutter	1673	Formidable	1898
Cygnet	1776	Fowey	1709
Cygnet	1819	Fox	1829
Danae	1867	Fox	1893
Daring	1844	Frederick Williams (Royal Frederick)	1860
Dartmouth	1655	Frolic	1842
Dauntless	1847	Furious	1850
Defiance 111 (Vulcan)	1889	Fury	1790
Delight	1819	Gannet (Nymphe)	1888
Devastation	1871	Gibraltar	1754
Dido	1869	Gladiator	1896
Dorsetshire	1757	Glasgow	1861
Dorsetshire	1929	Goree (Hayling)	1729
Drake	1834	Grafton	1750
Dreadnought	1801	Grampus	1802
Dreadnought	1906	Grasshopper	1813
Driver	1840	Greyhound	1672
Duke (Vanguard)	1678	Guillaume (Pallas)	1816
Duncan	1859	Hastings	1707
Duncan	1932	Hayling	1729
Eagle	1679	Hazard	1749
Eclipse	1894		

Helicon	1865	Melpomene	1888
Helicon (Calliope)	1884	Mercury	1694
Hermes	1811	Minerva	1820
Hermes	1835	Minstrel	1865
Hunter	1673	Monck	1659
Icarus	1814	Montagu	1654
Imperieuse	1883	Musquito	1825
Inconstant	1836	Myrtle	1825
Indus	1839	Nassau	1699
Inflexible	1876	Navy	1673
Invention	1673	Neptune	1757
Iron Duke	1912	Neptune	1832
Isle of Wight	1673	Neptune	1909
J1	1915	Neptune	1933
J2	1915	Netley	1866
Jasper	1820	New Zealand	1904
Jennet	1539	Newcastle	1750
K1	1916	Newport	1694
K2	1916	Nightingale	1931
K5	1916	Nonsuch	1668
Kent	1901	Nonsuch	1686
King George V	1911	Norwich	1691
Lacedaemonian	1812	Nubian	1960
Launceston	1711	Nymphe	1888
Laurel	1651	Old Truelove (True-love)	1707
Leander	1848		
Leopard	1955	Orestes	1824
Leveret	1825	Orion	1910
Lichfield	1694	Orwell	1866
Lion	1770	Osprey	1844
London	1899	Ossory	1682
London	1927	Ottawa (Crusader)	1931
Looe	1697	Pallas	1816
Lyme	1654	Pandora	1900
Lynx	1833	Pembroke (Duncan)	1859
MV1 (Drake)	1834	Pembroke (Nymphe)	1888
Madagascar	1812	Perth (Amphion)	1934
Magpie	1868	Peter Pomegranate	1510
Majestic	1895	Philomel	1823
Marigold	1653	Pheonix	1671
Marlborough (St Michael)	1669	Pitt	1816
		Plover	1821
Martin	1652	Plucky	1870
Mary Rose	1509	Plumper	1848

Podargus	1808	*field)*	
Portsmouth	1650	Rifleman	1846
Portsmouth	1665	Rinaldo	1860
Portsmouth	1667	Ringdove	1867
Portsmouth	1690	Roebuck	1704
Portsmouth	1703	Rose	1821
Portsmouth	1742	Royal Alfred	1864
Postboy	1695	Royal Anne (Royal Charles)	1673
President	1829		
Prevention	1672	Royal Arthur	1891
Primrose	1810	Royal Charles	1673
Prince Albert (Princess Royal)	1853	Royal Frederick (Queen)	1839
Prince Frederick (Expedition)	1697	Royal Frederick	1860
		Royal George (Royal James)	1675
Price George	1895		
Prince of Wales	1794	Royal George (Royal Charles)	1673
Prince of Wales	1860		
Prince Regent	1820	Royal George (King George V)	1991
Princess (Ossory)	1682		
Princess Charlotte	1825	Royal James	1671
Princess Louisa (Launceston)	1711	Royal James	1675
		Royal Oak	1664
Princess Royal	1773	Royal Sovereign	1857
Princess Royal	1853	Royal Sovereign	1891
Princess Royal (Britannia)	1762	Royal Sovereign	1915
		Royalist	1823
Pyramus	1810	Russell	1692
Queen (Royal Charles)	1673	St George	1785
		St George (Britannia)	1762
Queen (Royal Frederick)	1839	St Michael	1669
		St Vincent	1908
Queen Charlotte (Boyne)	1810	Sapphire	1708
		Sapphire	1827
Queen Elizabeth	1913	Sapphire II (Imperieuse)	1883
Queenborough (Fowey)	1709		
		Saudadoes	1669
Racer	1833	Scipio (Bulwark)	1806
Ranger	1820	Scourge	1844
Rapid	1829	Scout	1694
Rapid	1840	Seaflower	1830
Recruit	1829	Seaford	1697
Rhyl	1959	Seahorse	1711
Richmond (Wake-	1655	Sealark	1843

Serpent	1789	Trafalgar	1887
Shah	1873	Truelove	1707
Shannon	1855	Tweed	1823
Shark	1732	Vanguard	1678
Sheppey (Drake)	1834	Vernon II (Marlborough)	1855
Shrewsbury	1695		
Sirius	1868	Vernon 9 (Skylark)	1932
Sirius	1940	Vesuvius (skylark)	1932
Sirius	1964	Victoria	1859
Skylark	1932	Victorious II (Prince George)	1895
Solebay	1711		
Sphinx	1775	Victory (Royal James)	1675
Spy	1721		
Squirrel	1703	Victory	1737
Squirrel	1704	Vindictive	1813
Stromboli	1839	Volage	1889
Success	1712	Volcano	1836
Suffolk	1903	Vulcan	1889
Suffolk	1926	Wakefield	1655
Sussex	1652	Warrior	1781
Swallow	1868	Warwick	1767
Sweepstake	1497	Wasp	1749
Swift	1699	Waterloo	1818
Swift	1777	Weymouth	1693
Swift	1793	Wildfire (Nymphe)	1888
Sylvia	1827	Wolf	1826
Talavera (Waterloo)	1818	Woolf	1699
Tenedos II (Duncan)	1859	Worcester	1732
Termagant	1838	Worcester	1769
Thor	1944	Worcester (Royal Frederick)	1860
Thunderbolt	1842		
Tiara	1944	YC 1 (Drake)	1834
Tiger (Grampus)	1802	Zealand (New Zealand)	1904
Tilbury	1745		
Tilbury (Chatham)	1758	Zephyr	1809
Tireless	1943		
Token	1943		

The following works are acknowledged in the compilation of this list: The Naval Heritage of Portsmouth by J Winton and Portsmouth Built Warships 1497-1967 by J Goss.

Appendix 5: Parts of a ship
From the Admiralty Manual of Seamanship 1964

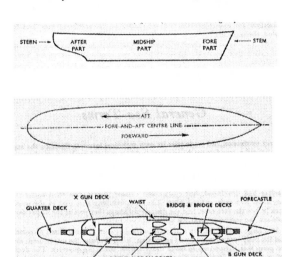

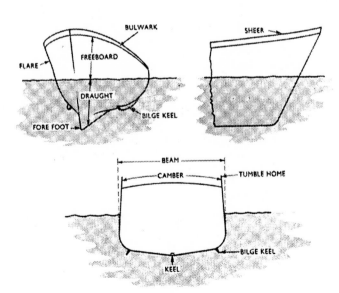

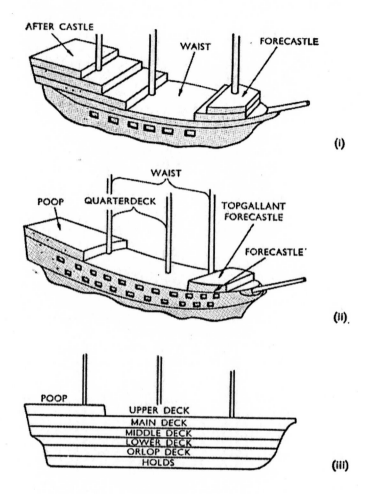

Index:

Biography

Michael Williams was born and educated in Portsmouth. He was an Indentured Sailmaker in H.M Dockyard Portsmouth when it was still a Royal Dockyard. As an Apprentice Michael Williams assisted in the completion of the last two ships to be built by HM Dockyard, they were the Leander class frigates HMS Sirius and Andromeda. He now works as a Government Inspector of Care Homes but keeps in touch with the Royal Navy through his family connections.

The London Press:- www.thelondonpress.co.uk..

Cover Notes

A 'Brief History of the Royal Navy' is just that; a layman's guide to the Royal Navy, the Senior Service; tracing its early development, its contribution to the British Empire and the protection of trading routes and innumerable sea battles. A Brief History of the Royal Navy was timed to coincide with the bicentenary celebrations of Nelson's Battle of Trafalgar in 2005 and explains why Nelson was regarded as one of Britain's greatest heroes. This brief history is factual and deals succinctly but sensitively with matters such as the British Empire, slavery and piracy. It also includes a section on the menagerie of animals, cats, dogs, bears, parrots and pigeons, which were kept on board Her Majesty's ships. Women's role in the development of the Navy is also recognised including female pirates and early forms of nursing, or least ministering to the needs of sailors, which were not always medical in nature. It ends with an entertaining and illuminating glossary, explaining many common phrases and sayings, like feeling 'under the weather', which have their origins in the days of men-o'-war.
A Brief History of The Royal Navy is a succinct and useful resource book for any school or library.

Printed in the United Kingdom
by Lightning Source UK Ltd.
117538UKS00001B/223-240